Afraid
OF THE
Dark

*What Whites
and Blacks
Need to Know
About Each
Other*

JIM MYERS

Lawrence Hill Books

Library of Congress Cataloging-in-Publication Data

Myers, Jim, 1941–

Afraid of the dark: what whites and Blacks need to know about each other / Jim Myers.

    p. cm.

    ISBN 1-55652-342-4

    1. United States—Race relations. 2. Racism—United States. 3. Afro-Americans—Attitudes. 4. Whites—United States—Attitudes. I. Title.

E185.615 .M94 2000

305.8'00973—dc21   99–047760

                                                          CIP

Foreword © 2000 by Rev. Jesse L. Jackson, Sr.
First edition
Published by Lawrence Hill Books
An imprint of Chicago Review Press, Incorporated
814 North Franklin Street
Chicago, Illinois 60610
ISBN 1-55652-342-4
Printed in the United States of America
5 4 3 2 1

To Deborah,
Who was not afraid

CONTENTS

PART III   CROSSING THE DIVIDE

FOREWORD

R ace, more than any other single dynamic, has shaped the
American landscape and way of life.
Race was at the core of the slave trade and was the underlying issue of the Civil War, the deadliest conflict on American soil.
It prevented my father, who fought with white soldiers to defeat the
Germans during World War II, from riding in the same railway pas-
senger car with white soldiers once they returned home. But the law
did not prevent the Germans, the enemies, from sitting side-by-side
with white Americans.

This deeply hurt my father and left an impression on me. Racism
was also the reason why I could not use the Greensboro Public
Library (during my youth), which was better equipped than the
blacks-only library, why I could not dine where whites dined, and
why I transferred from the University of Illinois, where I received an
athletic scholarship, to North Carolina A&T University.

The system of slavery is illegal. Jim Crow is dead. But America
the beautiful remains mostly segregated. Equal protection under the
law, affirmative action, diversity in the workplace, multicultural education, and the attempts for a race dialogue have simply sparked a
backlash. Racism has reared its ugly head once again. And there
remains this gap between the races.

In this book, Jim Myers explores the race issue by taking us on a journey to places no author has taken us before. It is more than a history lesson about race. It unravels the mystery that has kept the races separated.

He exposes the subtle racism. He reveals the fears and misconceptions whites and blacks have about each other. He explores the taboos—about the browning of America and interracial marriage. And he forces us to see the results of the ways we still think about race.

It is my belief that the race debate is an east/west argument that needs a north/south solution. When we simply discuss race and offer no solutions, America makes no progress. *Afraid of the Dark* helps us get to the root of the problem, so that we can find solutions.

In my efforts to build bridges to the movers and shakers on Wall Street, LaSalle Street, and the Silicon Valley, most of whom are white, I have discovered that the class gap is a result of the cultural gap. These powerful and influential leaders simply do not tap into the underserved markets where there are underutilized resources and capital, because black and brown people do not exist in their social circles. These corporate leaders simply have no contact with minorities. They do not know them, and they refuse to do business with people they do not know and trust.

This practice does not expand but rather hampers America's growth. When the playing field is level and the rules are clear, we all excel. Baseball and basketball are better sports since Jackie Robinson and Michael Jordan than before blacks were allowed to play on the same field as whites. Now the challenge for African Americans is to equalize the playing field in the business arena so that we can share in this nation's unprecedented wealth and prosperity.

It takes a sophisticated and clever writer like Jim to explore this controversial topic. The subject of race is complex and serious, but he presents it in a lighthearted way to help us digest it. We leave full of knowledge, but hungry to get America on the right course.

His account is powerful and honest. You step away from this book with the belief that for Jim, integration is a way of life. You capture his understanding and his sincerity, a wealth of knowledge that can only be derived from someone who has crossed the color line and believes that only through acceptance and understanding will America truly be beautiful.

As we head into a new millennium, we must bring light to dark places. *Afraid of the Dark* does that. Jim's book is a testament that this is a new day. We can move forward by our hopes and not backward by our fears. And most of all, we can keep hope alive.

REV. JESSE L. JACKSON, SR.
November 1999

INTRODUCTION

WHAT WE DON'T KNOW

And Why Me?

Blacks can jump higher and run faster because of their big-
ger thighs. I'm telling you that the black is the better athlete
and he practices to be the better athlete and he's bred to be a
better athlete, because this goes all the way to the Civil War
when, during the slave trading, the owner, the slave owner,
would breed his big black with his big woman so that he
would have a big, black kid, you see. . . . They've got every-
thing. If they take over coaching, like everyone wants them to,
there's not going to be anything left for white people. . . .
There's 10 people on a basketball court. If you find 2 whites,
you're lucky.

—Jimmy "the Greek" Snyder

Jimmy "the Greek" Snyder, an oddsmaker and loquacious football "analyst" for CBS TV, embarked on this discourse about black athletes during an impromptu TV interview in a Washington, D.C., restaurant on January 15, 1988, the occasion of Martin Luther King, Jr.'s birthday. What Snyder said that day about the selective breeding of slaves and other matters, including the suggestion that whites would soon be without a role to play in their own country, quickly turned into a notorious "incident" along the American color line. His words were played and replayed, quoted and requoted as news—and, it seemed, as a way to censure Snyder's thinking—until many Americans knew his theories by heart.

CBS fired Snyder the next day, sending him into an exile inhabited by those who misspeak about race. Snyder, however, also had his defenders. Well-known black athletes insisted their friend was not a man of unseemly prejudice. Still, Snyder remained in exile, shunned for apparently fundamental transgressions against the rules that govern race. But what exactly were these transgressions? What specifically had Snyder done or said that was wrong? When I first heard about Snyder's discourse, I was struck, among other things, by my own ignorance. Was there a measure of truth in what he said? Did slave owners really scheme in this way, or were Snyder's pronouncements total nonsense? And here I was considered a journalist sufficiently experienced in race matters that my colleagues at *USA Today* sometimes sought my opinion on the subject. "Is it OK to say this?" "Will someone get upset if we print it this way?" "Can you believe they want to print this?" I got all kinds of questions.

Snyder's words revealed that most of us are so ignorant about race as to be helpless when ideas like these come along. I wondered whether the higher-ups at CBS were themselves so expert on the history of slavery as to detect errors in what Snyder said or so well versed in genetics as to spot scientific flaws in his discourse. In fact, how many Americans are well enough educated to address Snyder's words or other such claims, rumors, or myths about race? Snyder's views—however inelegant—left many more questions than answers.

Consider that the executives who fired Snyder were probably no more knowledgeable about race than Snyder; that the journalists who reported the incident, quoting and requoting Snyder, were no more expert than the executives; or that many Americans ended up thinking Snyder was fired for remarks that were actually true.

In this view, Snyder's sin would not have been spreading false information. His real blunder—and the one many Americans are still fearful about—was speaking about a subject that was supposed to be off-limits. We were not supposed to talk about race in 1988, the heyday of political correctness, and millions of Americans still see race as a dangerous topic.

The reaction of journalists in the Snyder case—*USA Today* included—seemed odd. Most did not enquire into the history of the antebellum South, genetics, or evolution. Snyder's allegedly offending remarks were quoted endlessly, but little effort was made to signal what was right or wrong in them. *Time* magazine, the notable exception, pointed out that Snyder's ideas touched on notions about selective breeding from a steamy novel, *Mandingo*, which was made into a movie in 1975. Hence, such ideas had been floating around for a while. *Time* also noted that the author of *Mandingo*, Kyle Onstott, was an expert on the breeding of dogs, which seemed to have fired his imagination on breeding in general. To its further credit, *Time* also noted that Lee Evans, an Olympic gold medalist who is black, was quoted—without challenge—in a 1971 *Sports Illustrated* article as saying, "On the plantations, a strong black man was mated with a strong black woman. [Blacks] were simply bred for physical qualities."

So maybe *Sports Illustrated*, *Time*'s sister magazine, was where Snyder got his ideas. Evans, some may recall, was one of two U.S. athletes who wore black berets and gave the Black Power salute on the medal stand at the 1968 Olympic Games.

The Snyder case, however, also showed that journalists could grant a special immortality to foolish ideas, launching them around the world at the speed of light, while truth takes a slower route. Following my own urges, I eventually called historian Eugene Genovese, author of several books on slavery; he found Snyder's remarks amusing, because there is no evidence slave owners tried to breed slaves to be bigger and stronger. "It's utter nonsense," Genovese proclaimed. "The slaveholders' biggest headache was that slaves ran away. The last thing they'd want to breed for was running away faster."

Experts on genetics suggested I research the 18th-century efforts of King Frederick William I of Prussia, who had hoped to breed a super regiment of grenadiers by mating the biggest and strongest women in the land with the biggest and strongest men. To the king's dismay, many children of these pairings turned out smaller than their parents. So this same genetic reality would likely have foiled any slave owners trying to produce bigger, stronger slaves. Therefore, Snyder was wrong in that assumption, too. But few in America knew this.

From what I could see, the journalists around me were confused about what to do when the subject of race came up—caught between saying nothing, which political correctness encouraged, or speaking and risking the ill fate of people like Snyder. More significantly, political correctness, which surely began as a well-meaning intention to stop calling each other nasty names, seemed to suggest that if we all said nothing about race, or only very nice things, race might vanish as a problem.

But blacks and whites still had plenty of peculiar ideas and suspicions about each other, which they kept to themselves. This reticence was clear; it even showed up in such allegedly enlightened places as newspaper offices. While *USA Today* prided itself on hiring more black employees than most newspapers, it seemed to have achieved the worst possible result: nobody was happy along the *USA Today* color line. Both blacks and whites believed the deck was being stacked against them. And one seemingly trivial matter involving hair illustrated the degree to which whites live in one world, blacks in another—even in the communications industry.

Several black women confessed to me that they couldn't help being irritated by the habit some white women have of "tossing" or "flipping" their hair—ostensibly to keep it from falling in their face or eyes. In fact, this tossing or flipping of hair is roughly what models in shampoo ads do.

The black women felt the white women were deliberately flipping and tossing their hair to call attention to themselves, in effect saying, "Look at me and my beautiful hair." And some white women *did* seem to act with airs of self-satisfied superiority, just like shampoo models. The black women took it personally, almost as if the white women were announcing, "Our hair is better than yours. Therefore, we are better people than you are."

Sound far-fetched? This suspicion about white women and their hair is genuine, one of the many quiet details that contribute to alienation between blacks and whites. Yet the white women are usually oblivious to it. The white women who toss their hair—it seems an almost unconscious act—have no inkling about black women's reactions. Nor were white women likely to see an April 1994 essay in the black newsmagazine *Emerge* entitled, "Don't Be Thrown by Casual Appearance of 'the Toss,'" because our reading matter in America is often racially segregated.

The black women at *USA Today* were thrilled; the article described their feelings exactly: "The toss is the ultimate symbol of the White Girl," wrote Monica De Leon. "For her admirers, it symbolizes her position in society: the priceless possession of any man who may claim her. She is put on a pedestal and there she sits contentedly, as the world struggles along. The WG [White Girl] is an object of jealousy for some coarser-haired sisters who perm, press and even weave in other people's hair in an attempt to achieve her status; alas, to no avail. . . . Different types of tossing serve as communication for the White Girl in various situations. There is the 'I-know-you-can't-help-but-look-at-me-I'm-beautiful' toss . . . the 'don't-you-wish-you-had-hair-this-long-and-straight' toss."

What a contretemps for the office of a newspaper dedicated to reporting on the great issues of the day! Yet no subject produced more fretting, hemming and hawing, or caution at *USA Today* than stories involving race. It was considered best to avoid them. White editors studied such stories with a grim expression, which seemed to indicate one slip on matters of race could be your downfall. And then all hell will break loose. There were plenty of examples: disasters even befell college presidents. Take the 1995 case of Rutgers University President Francis Lawrence who—he claimed it was a "slip" of the tongue—said: "The average SAT for African Americans is 750. Do we set standards in the future so we don't admit anybody with the national test? Or do we deal with a disadvantaged population that doesn't have the genetic hereditary background to have a higher average?" Those were his exact words. And all hell broke loose at Rutgers—student protests, sit-ins, and angry rhetoric. Just as in the case of Jimmy "the Greek," a presumably learned professional tumbled into the abyss filled with claims that race is a factor in determining our abilities. Specifically, Lawrence "slipped" into the old claim that blacks are less intelligent than whites. And the reaction of black students was hardly mysterious: who wants to be labeled the product of a disadvantaged genetic hereditary background?

Scientists now broadly dispute many such claims about race. While racial anomalies in SAT or IQ test scores get widespread note, geneticists have increasingly discredited the concept of race—and especially broad categories like black or white—as a meaningful classification of human beings. Great differences may exist between any two individuals of the same or different races, but far less difference is found between the broad racial groupings. Or, put another way, once the genes for surface traits like skin color—a simple adaptation to climate—are discounted, all human beings are very much alike.

Furthermore, how do we classify those whose ancestries involve members of two or more races, and, for that matter, what race is the child of one black parent and one white parent? Nevertheless, while anthropologists and geneticists tend to discount old thinking about racial difference, the rest of us must fight our inclinations to assume that intelligence, athletic ability, or character traits can be foretold by unrelated characteristics such as skin color. They cannot, and it is ridiculous—and unscientific—to believe they can.

Yet the idea of human homogeneity is also a relatively simple one, and we are accustomed to thinking of race as a complex matter, full of mystery. For journalists, especially, one quiet hope that accompanied the efforts to hire blacks and other minorities as reporters and editors, beginning in the 1960s, was that they could bring a new "sensitivity" to news operations—or, specifically, that they might help lift the veils that made race such uncertain territory for white journalists. The hope was that they would warn well-meaning whites about situations that might create offense, especially the ones whites feared themselves so ill equipped to anticipate. They would be an early warning system that could say, "Watch out here—if you say that, blacks will picket the building."

But these hopes also ignored the psychological dynamics of being a minority in a white-majority world. The exchange of ideas across the color line at USA Today, for example, was seldom as free-flowing as management dreamed, primarily because many black employees sensed great risk in being too open about their thoughts. Many of my black colleagues believed that to question what white editors were doing, especially what they were enthusiastic about, was to be seen as having "an attitude." And white bosses, it seemed, didn't always react warmly to warnings about their pet ideas and beliefs.

Black writers and editors instead found—or feared—that whites would consider them "angry blacks" if they raised questions relating to race. And my black colleagues believed the reputation of being "angry" or having "an attitude" could kill your career; therefore, it was infinitely wiser to keep silent.

At USA Today, black employees assiduously avoided dress or hairdos or other symbols of black "consciousness." Black reporters cautiously pressed issues such as crime or poverty that would be identified as "black." And some black employees guarded details in their personal lives that might be seen as too personal or "too black." For example, when two women in the office both lost nephews—both gunned down in other cities in the same week, a shocking coincidence, to say the least—few whites at USA Today even knew about it. There was a black grapevine in the office and a white grapevine, and the two were seldom connected. There were also two social worlds outside the office: sometimes social gatherings involving dozens of *USA Today* workers and their families would be entirely white or entirely black, which is the way much of America works and plays—racially segregated.

At the same time, black employees were frequently upset about stories *USA Today* ran on racial issues or about negative stereotypes that crept into stories about black celebrities and newsmakers. But they were afraid to say so. They spoke among themselves and rarely shared their views with white colleagues. Often, the rationale for silence was that it is "no use saying anything" because "white folks are going to do what they're going to do." Or they say, "You have to tell white folks what white folks want to hear."

Meanwhile, most whites in the office didn't know that theirs was being seen as such a closed world or that their behavior was being pigeonholed as "white." The absence of more openness across the color line occasionally worked out embarrassingly for *USA Today*, as in the case of a 1993 front-page story that reported black gang members in Los Angeles were itching to riot again and would target police, Asians, and whites next time.

The cover story was also accompanied by a photo of five young black men, two holding handguns, with a rifle and telescopic sight displayed on a table in the foreground. The men looked stern-faced, and, if anything, the photo appeared to say that these were some of the black gang members who wanted to kill police, Asians, and white people.

Several black reporters or editors may have viewed this material as it was being prepared for publication but said nothing to alarm white editors. White editors, from the top down, were convinced they had a "great story"—that phrase was repeatedly used—about blacks itching to kill cops and whites. Here is how the story began:

> John Wilder is 21, slightly drunk, explosively bitter. Fresh out of prison, he has angry eyes and an expression as hard as the streets on which he grew up. He hates Asians, whites and all police. He thinks last year's riots were the best thing since Martin Luther King. . . .
>
> Some black gangs, which now have a cause, are a scattered army readying for war, an army with plenty of training. They're not scared to pull a trigger. They understand violence because they've been shooting—and being shot at—since junior high. . . . They're not afraid of police or punish-

ment. One in three have done time. Terrence Townsend, who runs with the PJ Crips, calls jail a "reunion party. All my friends are there."

"There will be more shooting," says John Kazee, 21, affiliated with a gang since 1988. "They're targeting people. The police . . . bad police. And judges, prosecutors, anyone responsible for injustice, although it doesn't really matter which ones. If they can find white people, that's fine and dandy, too."

So what's wrong with this? Many whites believe that a world like this awaits in black sections of U.S. cities. Many whites believe that blacks are angry and potentially violent, especially when high on liquor or drugs. Meanwhile, most of the black reporters and editors at *USA Today* reacted with shock when they saw the front page the next day. They immediately wanted to know: why would *USA Today* want to promote the fear that black people want to kill whites? What good does it do? In fact, my black colleagues believed that presentations like this, full of scary images, only inflame whites—and make life for black people all the more difficult.

However, whites at *USA Today* didn't have much sympathy for this reaction. Most assumed that the story, written by a white reporter, was accurate. They believed that the angry black gang members did want to kill whites. They were scared of black gangs, just as my black colleagues were scared about what white editors and reporters had just done.

This was no amusing misunderstanding about hair. Here in the civil confines of a corporate office, whites on one side of the room suspected that black people—in Los Angeles or wherever—wanted to kill whites. And blacks on the other side of the room suspected white people were overeager to portray blacks as killers. (And this was 16 months before the O. J. Simpson case came along.)

Then, to *USA Today*'s chagrin, the five tough-looking gang members pictured on the front page complained—and threatened a lawsuit—because they had believed they were being photographed for a story about a new program that offered jobs to gang members who turned in guns. That's what they thought they were doing.

Oops!

USA Today blamed the error on a "communications" mix-up; the photo was supposed to be for another story, but the screwup became a news story of its own. Black critics charged that *USA*

Today—or "the white media"—was so eager to portray blacks negatively that it would pose a phony photograph if need be.

USA Today editors were embarrassed and mystified, insisting their intentions were honorable. After all, it seemed crucial to them to say blacks wanted to kill whites, if blacks, indeed, wanted to kill whites. The editors were sure they weren't racists, because they hired black people. And they believed, too, that race in its mysterious and unfathomable ways had risen to smite them. And privately, they still insisted that the tale about the gang members was true and—I heard this several times—"a great story."

You be the judge. That original cover story *also* contained clues suggesting there was something bogus about it. *USA Today*'s editors missed that. Much of the evidence for the inflammatory premise that blacks wanted to kill whites was atmospherics and adjectives loaded with common assumptions—stereotypes, really. "John Wilder is 21, slightly drunk, *explosively bitter*. Fresh out of prison, he has *angry eyes* and an expression *as hard as the streets on which he grew up*. He hates Asians, whites and all police."

Most of the supposed evidence that black gang members were intent on violence came in phrases like "explosively bitter" or "angry eyes." And, after all, what are *angry eyes*? How do you know they are angry? How, for example, do reporters distinguish between angry eyes and eyes that are just ticked off? It is possible that nervous whites might sense themselves surrounded by angry eyes in any black neighborhood. But what does this impression mean? Seeing angry eyes may actually say more about the eyes of the beholder—what the beholder *expects* to see—than about the eyes being beheld. And that may have been true in this case: maybe, this story about gang members was more about what white reporters and editors believed to be true than what was actually going on.

But were the misunderstandings and suspicions at *USA Today* exceptional events in corporate America? Probably not. *USA Today*'s woes on race issues are more a norm in the American workplace than an exception, and *USA Today* was doing better than companies like Denny's or Texaco, where misunderstandings escalated into multimillion-dollar lawsuits.

Other news organizations had similar problems. The June 27, 1994, cover of *Time* magazine raised a furor over a police mug shot of O. J. Simpson that had been retouched and darkened. *Time* editors later admitted the shadows had been added to suggest there might be a "darker" side to Simpson's persona. Black critics quickly asserted this represented a sinister truth about white thinking: whites equate darkness with danger and evil.

The Simpson case quickly became evidence of a seeming disconnection between whites and blacks—a prime example of "racial polarization," as journalists called it. Yet on one level, the disconnection over the Simpson case involved the same themes surrounding the *USA Today* story about gang members. Whites believe blacks can be dangerous. Blacks believe whites are far too willing to believe that blacks can be dangerous.

It is, in fact, almost a norm in race relations that the same themes recur. And events like the Simpson case seem to resonate with ideas we already have—especially bad ideas we have about each other. Whatever the truth actually was behind the murders, the Simpson case followed a simple formula that is common in white thinking: blacks are criminals; whites are victims. But it also followed a simple formula that is common in black thinking: whites will see blacks as guilty until they are proven innocent beyond a shadow of doubt. The Simpson case also advanced the idea that whites and blacks are incomprehensible to each other. Show them the same facts, and they will draw opposite conclusions.

Journalists promoted this idea, but I knew it wasn't so. Blacks and whites can be very comprehensible to each other, if they don't let assumptions like racial polarization get in the way. The assumption that a vast racial divide exists is true for millions of Americans, but it is not true for all Americans. The lives of many Americans, black and white, are so removed from the color line as to make the other side seem alien. But not everybody sees the world this way.

Some see the color line as less daunting, less mysterious, less fraught with danger—and I consider myself one of them. We see the good in relations with those of other races as so greatly outweighing any bad that the bad rarely comes to mind. It is no contest. We see a potential for joy, laughter, and discovery in race relations—much more than fear. And in exercising this attitude, I have often had the privilege of hearing what is said on both sides of the color line.

I do not believe it takes unusual qualities other than the ability to find the lives of others interesting. And, oh yes, you need to believe that if you give a little, it's likely you'll get a little in return. Many people have difficulty believing this proposition will work.

It is likely that readers of this book will have questions: Who are you? How can you claim to know what blacks and whites are thinking? Where do you get your information? And—most important—what color are you? The last question looms most important, because in America we assume that color shapes what we say. And because I am white, some readers will assume I must have a "white" perspective; I can't escape that. Then, too, readers will find out that I am married to a black woman and conclude—oh, that explains it—she's won me over to the other side. But it doesn't always work like that. All blacks don't think "black," and all whites don't think "white." In fact, most people who are sensible on the subject of race have a mixture of ideas, because they've learned to give a little and get a little, which makes race relations like marriage.

My wife and I have a house in a black-majority neighborhood near Capitol Hill in Washington, D.C., a city that is two-thirds black and widely identified across white America as full of "black" problems. Things happen in D.C. that many whites claim just don't make sense. For example, D.C. voters reelected Marion Barry as mayor in 1994 after he was convicted of drug use and after his offense and arrest were taped and repeatedly shown on TV. That seemed crazy to many whites (and a few blacks, too). Several times in the 1990s, the city became the statistical murder capital of the United States. It was briefly termed "Dodge City" until it was pointed out that the legendary town in the Old West was hardly as violent.

Or when it snowed 28 inches in February 1996, many assumed that D.C. with its large population of black people would be ill equipped to deal with so much snow. Many white Americans thought the whole idea—a black-run city faced with mountains of snow—was amusing. The same year, Congress took over the city government to keep it from going belly-up. For many white Americans, D.C. became a stereotype of what happens when you leave black people in charge. But I don't think that way—and not just because I know black people who run successful businesses and live in million-dollar homes, or because I've gone to a black doctor.

Readers who think only in stereotypes may conclude that I must have taken leave of all sense—I even went to the Million Man March and enjoyed it. But I've also enjoyed the Indianapolis 500 and Daytona 500 auto races, events as "white" as the Million Man March is "black." My life provides me with a practical vantage point on

black-and-white interaction or the lack thereof: I live on the color
line. I crisscross it daily. I need not travel far to see what's happening on either side.

Yet I see the color line as a major canyon traversed with fear
and uneasiness, a massive barrier that divides our culture and our
landscape. As a journalist, I have been warned against visiting
places others consider unsafe. Earlier in my career, while at the
Democrat and Chronicle in Rochester, New York, I wrote a series
of articles called "Walking Rochester." The premise was that I would
walk the streets, neighborhood by neighborhood, and talk to people I met along the way.

This also proved a scary notion to some readers. "Blacks and
whites often appear to be living in two different worlds," I wrote.
"Few whites in the city claim to know anything about black neighborhoods and various whites expressed surprise that I [a white
reporter] would even consider walking down West Main Street or
Jefferson Avenue. Blacks, meanwhile, said they prefer their neighborhoods. Some said they also prefer not to venture elsewhere."

Anticipating where I was going, readers called with tips. About
Jefferson Avenue, white readers called to say, "Hey, Myers, you're
not planning to walk down Jefferson Avenue, are you? You've gotta
be crazy." Yet while walking on Bartlett Street, just off Jefferson, precisely where these readers presumed no good could come to a white
person, I was introduced to a community activist named Deborah
Stith. She is now my wife, and our family extends on both sides of
the color line. I have two sons; she has two sons and a daughter as
well as 10 grandchildren. In our family, we get to see the ups and
downs of life on both sides of the great divide. At times, I feel like
I am rushing back and forth, hearing the ideas on one side, then
hearing the ideas on the other, and wondering about how paradox-
ically connected and disconnected these two views of the world can
be. Yet I always argue that both make sense—but you have to give
a little and get a little to understand that.

Sometimes, when I talked from this perspective, friends and journalist colleagues suggested I write a book. Who, me, I thought, a
white guy? And after a 1993 interview with Jesse Jackson about racial
issues in sports, he took me aside and asked, "Have you ever thought
of writing a book?" But what book? An idea took shape—perhaps not
the book Jackson intended—that would view the massive nonrela-
tions along the color line as the key factor in understanding race in

America. Whites and blacks are living in their own worlds, often miles apart, and developing strange and often mistaken ideas about each other.

I initially thought, on the suggestion of a colleague, that the book should be called *Them*—referring to the misshapen images blacks and whites have of each other across this vast divide. And many of my black friends loved that title; they found the idea of referring to whites as "them" appropriate. But some of my white friends were puzzled. They sensed that *Them* sounded angry or suggested that whites and blacks thought of each other as science fiction creatures. They wanted a more reassuring title for a book they hoped would help them get over their uneasiness about black people or tell them the "right" things to say. My black friends, meanwhile, liked the possibility that I might point out the ways that whites act strangely when black people are around.

Yet this was another racial divide: blacks and whites thought they wanted a different book; and this divide could also help define what an effective book about race should be about. Blacks want whites to know what it's like to be black and to know what still bothers them about America. And whites are interested in finding a convenient way out of a predicament that still makes them uneasy.

These two aims are not necessarily mutually exclusive. A good book about race would need to answer basic questions:

- Why do whites expect that blacks will be angry?
- Why are blacks so sure that whites will be prejudiced?
- Why do whites fear that something they say will set black people off?
- Why do blacks believe they should not reveal what they think to whites?

Such a book would also have to explain why little things we do, like the white women who flip their hair, have such disproportionate impact on what we think about each other. Why do blacks and whites see fresh evidence every day that reaffirms the negative ideas they already have? What leads black people to conclude that whites are cold and uncaring? What leads whites to conclude that blacks are hostile and angry?

All this suspicion and misunderstanding takes place along the color line—a discernable separation that crosses our landscape and our minds. The line is evident in our offices, workplaces, schools, and neighborhoods. It can be near us or far away; still it shapes our behavior and attitudes; and like the big bad wolf, the American color line comes in varied guises, some silly and some serious. The Big Bad Color Line is not without its ironies. To many Americans on either side, it can seem far bigger and more threatening than it should, almost an insurmountable barrier. Many fears on both sides are clearly exaggerated, yet the color line is truly dangerous terrain at times. We all know that. Both whites and blacks are afraid; blacks and whites share common ground in this one predicament.

Many Americans on both sides of the color line, journalists included, appear infatuated with their own preconceptions and unwilling to abandon them. On the other hand, some blacks and whites seem to imagine there is more interaction between the two groups than there really is. Some black women, for example, believe white women are stealing all the good black men. Many whites are sure blacks are taking over sports and entertainment—or the country. And both these premises are demonstrably untrue.

Nor do many Americans readily admit the extent of their own isolation. Maybe it sounds bad to say you don't have black friends or white friends. Yet to a surprising degree, I find that many whites living in black-majority neighborhoods (or blacks living in white-majority neighborhoods) have limited social contact across the color line. Blacks and whites can live on the same block yet in their own worlds. And the common ground of American experience got even smaller in the 1990s. Blacks and whites now don't even watch the same TV shows.

To overcome the isolating effects of such trends, we need to work at it—and care about what happens along the color line rather than ignore the subject. And this effort could produce practical results, especially when blacks and whites are increasingly thrown together in the American workplace, where an odd standoff often continues, with both eyeing each other suspiciously even when nothing bad is happening.

How do I know? My friends keep telling me about the stupid things that people say and do along the color line. One friend, the only black salesperson in a suburban car dealership, found himself working under a white boss who—in my friend's interpretation—treated him like a hapless child. The boss rebuffed all attempts to discuss the matter with comments like, "I've got nothing against black people. I think everybody should own one."

My friend eventually filed a discrimination complaint, and the boss was edged into an early retirement. "It was a joke," he protested. "Can't these people take a joke?"

Meanwhile, a white neighbor complained, "I'm so sick of hearing these blacks complain about being mistreated." But where was she hearing these complaints? Not from black friends—she didn't have any. Were black people calling or coming to the door to complain? Of course not. Her impression came mainly from hearing other whites complain about hearing blacks complain. In fact, golfer Fuzzy Zoeller stirred a rush of complaints—*they're* always complaining; *they* can't take a joke—when asked what advice he had for Tiger Woods, who had just won the 1997 Masters with a record-setting score.

"That little boy is driving well and he's putting well," Zoeller replied. "He's doing everything it takes to win. So, you know what you guys do when he gets in here? You pat him on the back and say congratulations and enjoy it and tell him not to serve fried chicken [at the banquet] next year. Got it?" Zoeller turned and walked away, but he wasn't satisfied with his attempt at wit, so he added, "Or collard greens or whatever the hell they serve."

And all hell broke loose for Zoeller. His use of the word *boy*, an old and deep insult to black men, was faulted, as was his linking of blacks to fried chicken and greens. K-mart immediately dropped his sponsorship, even as whites across America dialed radio talk shows to grumble that black people should "lighten up and learn to take a joke." Yet did Woods start this? Can black people take a joke? Will Zoeller apologize? Will Woods accept Zoeller's apology? Woods didn't start it at all, but black people were soon being accused of being thin-skinned and getting worked up about nothing. Why was that?

That's another matter a book on race would have to explain— why white points of view inevitably percolate to the surface, even when they are odd. Some readers, however, may also wonder why I have focused so exclusively on blacks and whites when we have a wider diversity in our midst, a fact that Woods, whose mother is Asian, represents. Indeed, it is likely our attention will shift to other groups—Hispanic, Asian, and others—without our ever having resolved the issue that has dogged us for centuries: American society is still clearly divided along a black-white color line.

Now I suspect that some white Americans will welcome the "problem" of Asians and Hispanics as relief from the black "problem," which seems more intractable. It is also likely that black

Americans will soon sense that their cause is being passed over as Hispanics edge closer to surpassing black Americans as the nation's largest minority. Whites may also find that resolving whatever misunderstanding they have with Asian Americans is easier than altering attitudes about people of African descent. After all, it must be noted that stereotypes about people of Asian descent often involve suspicions that Asians are *too* intelligent and *too* capable, while blacks are viewed much more negatively. Which stereotypes would you rather have?

The continuing divide between blacks and whites also represents a great historical challenge to American ideals. Can there be brotherhood and sisterhood between the descendants of enslaved Africans and the descendants of European immigrants? Even today, blacks and whites see each other as polar opposites on traditional lines of thought. Yet it is also surprising the extent to which blacks and whites will define themselves in terms of each other—saying "we" are not like "them." How perversely we need each other to claim qualities those on the other side of the color line are supposed to lack. But this idea of interdependence of opposites also invites us to consider that the union between black and white—and other groups, too—could add up to so much more than we are by ourselves. Here's hoping it soon does.

I
WORLDS APART

1
WHAT'S THE PROBLEM?

If We Could Just Be Friends

October 16, 1995, was a signal day for race in America. The cover of *U.S. News & World Report* featured O. J. Simpson, the giant letters *O.J.*, and the message: "What Now? The Great Racial Divide." The cover of *Newsweek* said, "The Verdict: Whites vs. Blacks. Inside the Jury. O.J. and His Kids," and the magazine's lead article was headlined:

Whites
v.
Blacks

That was the day's principal message to the world. Also that morning, President Clinton left D.C. to deliver an address about race relations in Austin, Texas. The *Washington Post* printed his full text the following day; Clinton described the nation as "two worlds," one black and one white, divided along a "rift . . . that is tearing at the heart of America."

But even as the president spoke, the heralded Million Man March was massing on the National Mall west of the Capitol and near the White House, which Clinton had left that morning. These two events, Clinton's speech and the march, showed how crazy relations can get between blacks and whites: a million black men assemble in D.C., the largest gathering of African Americans in U.S. history, yet the president flies 1,200 miles to Texas to give a major speech about race.

But the president wasn't the only white person who skipped town. The Million Man March was seen by many, whites in particular, as part of the tearing apart of America that the president mentioned. Elsewhere in downtown D.C., the streets on October 16 were curiously—*strangely*—deserted. Estimates were that at least 40 percent of federal workers in D.C. stayed home, but only 9 percent were black men who might have gone to the march. Most of the absentees were white. The *Washington Post* reported that commuter traffic from D.C. suburbs was down 70 percent—70 percent! Suffice it to say that many whites in the D.C. area were uneasy about the Million Man March, some believing it would unleash violence and destruction in the city, because many whites still believe that is what large gatherings of black people are likely to do. Black people get stirred up, the theory goes, and rampage though the streets, smashing windows and looting stores. And woe to the white person who might get caught up in their midst.

Meanwhile, the mood was quite different in the D.C. neighborhood where my wife and I live on a tree-lined street of Victorian row houses near Capitol Hill. On October 16, our neighborhood, about 75 percent black, was filled with excitement that an event of such magnitude was taking shape nearby. Many men, young and old alike, were going to the march, and in that sense, the Million Man March was a very mainstream event in a black neighborhood, hardly a radical enterprise. Friends from other cities began to arrive at our house before dawn: guests including two carloads from Rochester, New York, my wife's hometown, and a van full of schoolteachers from Chicago. My wife's son, Sherod, came with her father, a retired factory worker, who, at 72, was in failing health but buoyed by the moment. "I never thought I'd live to see such a day," he said more than once.

Some explanation of what he meant is in order. The man we called Daddy was no angry radical, but he did like to listen to Minister Louis Farrakhan, who had called and organized the Million Man March. Sometimes, when Daddy watched Farrakhan on a cable access TV channel in Rochester, he would quietly say, "Get 'em, Farrakhan," because he liked the way Farrakhan stands his ground against white criticism. Maybe it is nothing more than that—here is one black man who refuses to back down. So when Daddy said he never expected to see such a day, we must remember that Daddy, who grew up in seg-regated Georgia in the 1920s and 1930s, believed that without a firm figure like Farrakhan, white people would never have allowed the march to happen. A million black men in one place? Hell, no. Whites would do whatever they could to stop that.

Understand, too, that Daddy was not alone in imagining that white people would be against the Million Man March. Prior to October 16, the subject of the march rarely came up among the black residents of my neighborhood without someone wondering aloud if it was a plot to bring black men together to kill them or cart them away. Some peo-ple said it with a laugh; some said it more ominously. And the same idea later popped up in Spike Lee's movie about the march, *Get on the Bus*. So it was part of the general consciousness of the day. It is a detail in a mind-set about white people that you will find in black America.

For those readers who believe that the concept of whites killing blacks or putting them in concentration camps is totally outrageous in the 1990s, I should insist that at least some black Americans believe whites are capable of such actions. And this is a measure of the extremes in our racial division. A less extreme view of the events of October 16 might be that one America, white America, was represented by the pres-ident's view that a rift along the color line was threatening to tear the nation apart. And another America, black America, was represented by the marchers who came to D.C. hoping that black Americans could come together to realize their full potential.

One day. Same event. Two totally different views of what was going on.

But race can also precipitate strange doings: the president flew to Texas, and when he got there, he spoke of the marchers in D.C., which he had just left, almost as if he were speaking to them personally. He praised their dedication to renewing personal responsibility in their lives. Then, in reference to Farrakhan, a figure most whites are extremely wary of, he noted, "One million men do not make right one man's mes-sage of malice and division."

Then, later that same day in his speech at the Capitol, Farrakhan spoke almost personally to the president, who was half a continent away: "Sir, with all due respect, that was a great speech you made today. And you praised the marchers, and they are worthy of praise. . . . But, of course, you spoke ill, indirectly, of me as a purveyor of malice and hatred."

So much for dialogue across the color line that day. Perhaps more than we like to realize, it is a long-distance affair.

All this unfolded in the edgy time in American race relations just six days after a black-majority jury in Los Angeles acquitted O. J. Simpson of charges involving two murders that most Americans—most white Americans—thought he had committed. The racial divide and "playing the race card," a phrase that popped up to describe the maneuverings many whites believed to have produced Simpson's acquittal, were now troubling the nation—and many whites in particular.

Basically, it had come to pass that in months of watching the Simpson case, whites looked at blacks and blacks looked at whites as they had not done for a while. And they seemed to fix on certain notions about each other. Millions of white Americans were suddenly concerned that black Americans had strange thought processes, a topsy-turvy way of seeing in respect to the ways whites think and see things. And whites were suddenly much perturbed about this. How can we disagree—see things so differently—over an act so clearly wrong as murder?

The Simpson case shocked many whites, who awoke to a new or forgotten dimension in their understanding of race. Blacks and whites could seemingly view the same events and the same evidence on a matter involving right and wrong, yet draw such differing conclusions as to be incomprehensible to each other. Or so the media was repeatedly telling us. "Were we watching the same trial?" the October 16 *Newsweek* asked. "After the verdict, the two communities talked past each other, with passionate misunderstanding."

Journalists invested energy and resources in their "discovery" that whites and blacks saw the case so differently. Whites, journalists seemed to be saying, looked at the facts of the case—the evidence. Blacks, however, are suspicious of the police, and their attention turned to race when they heard that Mark Fuhrman, one of the detectives in the case, had repeatedly made derogatory statements about black people. As the case progressed, America was divided, so we were repeatedly told by journalists and pollsters, into black and white camps: whites thought Simpson guilty; blacks thought him innocent. (So, incidentally, Simpson was now rejected in the world where he had been most popular, and many black Americans noted whites can be fickle friends.)

Polls showed that this black-white split on the Simpson case started in July 1994, just after the murders. And it continued, largely unchanged, to October 1995, after the verdict in the criminal trial, when *USA Today* found 73 percent of whites said Simpson was "definitely" or "probably" guilty, and 62 percent of blacks said Simpson was "definitely" or "probably" innocent. That was it—in black and white.

This "racial polarization" was treated as news, even though such black-white splits in perspective were, in fact, nothing new. For decades, any poll about justice, the police, or prejudice in American society was likely to produce a similar split. Whites would say the justice system or the police are fair; blacks would say they're not. But no matter. In the rush to focus on the black-white split in the Simpson case, other aspects of demographic reality were overlooked.

For one thing, the racial polarization over the Simpson case, the "Whites v. Blacks" of the *Newsweek* headline, did not involve opposing groups of equal size. The "white" side was much larger—almost nine times larger in actual numbers than the "black" side—with the equivalent of 121 million white adults saying Simpson was guilty versus only 14 million black adults saying he was innocent.

So in simple numbers, "Whites v. Blacks" was a mismatch.

For another thing, black Americans who believed Simpson was innocent were also outnumbered *more than two to one* by the 33 million whites who also believed Simpson did not commit the murders. Get that? Black people, then, were only 30 percent of the Americans who believed in Simpson's innocence. But white America was never described as "divided" over the case. Nor did anyone fret about all those white people who thought Simpson was innocent. It was black people's views that were considered irrational, race-fixated, and upsetting to white Americans. So the *Newsweek* headline could have justifiably read:

Whites

v.

Whites

But it didn't.

This demographic irony might indicate that we have trained ourselves to focus on situations in which blacks and whites are at odds. If race is involved in a conflict, it is assumed to be much worse than when the same ideas are at issue in an argument between whites alone. As a result, journalists will find a conflict between 121 million whites and 14 million blacks much more alarming than a dispute between 121 million whites and 33 million whites who dissent from the majority view. Does that make sense?

But on the other side of the color line, black Americans are also likely to forget about the 33 million white allies who agreed with them and focus on the 121 million whites who opposed them—that is also in the nature of our thinking about race.

Still, the Simpson case provided a delightful trivia question that usually stumps any audience: "Who, demographically speaking, was the largest population group of Americans who thought O.J. was innocent?"

Everyone answers, "Black people."

No, it was white people.

And why those 33 million white people thought Simpson was innocent was never really explained or explored. Was there something wrong with their minds? Were they social outcasts and misfits? What was their problem? Yet most whites looked at black people strangely after the Simpson case, as if something had to be wrong with their heads or their eyes. They see race in everything. And they can't see beyond race.

Once such an idea gets planted in our collective thoughts, it is hard to uproot it. After the Simpson case, many seemed ready to assume there would always be differences between whites and blacks that preclude understanding or agreement across the color line. Scenes of black people cheering the nonguilty Simpson criminal verdict then further angered whites, who regarded the behavior on the part of black people as singularly tasteless and unseemly. Even if it was only a few blacks who cheered, what kind of people would cheer at a moment like that?

Meanwhile, journalists did a dreadful job of exploring what black Americans actually thought about the case. For the most part, they failed to recognize the fears a minority group might have in a situation like this. Many black Americans, my wife included, found the innocent verdict more a relief than anything else. Many black people had sensed themselves under heavy scrutiny from whites in the previous months, because the Simpson case raised the specter of a very common stereotype about black people: they're all criminals and murderers.

More than believing Simpson hadn't committed the crimes, many black Americans deeply *hoped* he hadn't done it, so white people wouldn't conclude from the Simpson example that all black people harbor desires to harm white people. Think of it: if the affable Simpson, who was so at home among whites, was believed to suffer from a hidden urge to kill white people, then all black people might be suspected of having the same such urges.

Yet Simpson's acquittal in the criminal trial did not work out well for black Americans either, because they were forced immediately to watch warily as whites fumed over the verdict. My black colleagues at *USA Today* used the word *icy* to describe the mood in the office—their white colleagues seemed suddenly distant and uncommunicative. Some white colleagues seemed icier than others. This, too, was noted—and who were the iciest ones and who were the ones who were a little less cold? Meanwhile, at least among themselves, many black Americans concluded from this iciness that whites are so used to getting their way that they get very upset when they don't. Eventually, however, the second Simpson trial—the civil trial—seemed to prove that whites, indeed, will sooner or later get their way. And it also showed that whites, too, will cheer the verdict in a murder case. Because shout and cheer they did in various instances shown on TV.

White Americans may not have realized the degree to which black Americans saw the Simpson case as a case study on *white* behavior. Few whites were even aware they were being watched—just as they were watching and drawing conclusions about black people. In one extreme case, a black man called the black D.C. radio station WOL to claim that the very brutality of the murders proved Simpson innocent; the killer had to be white. "We just don't kill that way," he said.

Whites might wonder: what was this guy thinking? Most whites don't realize that they go through life accompanied by stereotypes, and, in some eyes, they have a reputation for extreme or bizarre forms of mayhem—just think of Jeffrey Dahmer, who *ate* some of his victims. His name comes up in black circles surprisingly often as an example of scary white behavior. It was also possible for black people to conclude the following from the Simpson case:

- Whites will always be suspicious of black people.
- No good comes from getting too involved with white people.
- Whites can easily turn against black people, even those they claim as their friends.

Such ideas are still to be found along the color line. Similarly, whites could just as easily see from the Simpson case that old stereotypes and fears are valid:

- Black men are inherently violent and lust for white women.
- It's dangerous to associate with black people, even those who seem charming and friendly.
- Black people will always stick together, even in support of blacks who commit murder.

Much of this theme is nonsense, but there are those who believe at least some of it is true all the same. Still, as it affects long-term relations between whites and blacks, the most destructive impression arising from the Simpson trials was that racial differences produced two verdicts—a "black" verdict in the criminal trial and a "white" verdict in the civil one. As viewed by many whites, the verdict by the black-majority criminal jury was irrational or, at best, swayed by emotional appeals about race. And the verdict produced by the white-majority civil jury involved a more reasoned approach to the evidence, not emotional appeals. Therefore, in simplest terms, the Simpson case produced—or reaffirmed—an unfortunate portrait of race that haunts everyday relations between blacks and whites, and these ideas are as old as the hills: blacks are irrational and get carried away with emotion; whites are rational and can control their emotions. The fault line between these two assumptions crosses innumerable misunderstandings between blacks and whites—and here it was underscored in one of the most highly publicized murder dramas in the 20th century.

Meanwhile, at the time of the Simpson case, many black Americans believed they saw other evidence that white Americans were in an ugly, threatening mood. When Republicans took over Congress in 1994, journalists described the pivotal voting bloc as "angry white males," an unfortunate echo for blacks with the image of whites running around in hoods and sheets. Even upscale black Americans, who might be assumed to be doing well in the American mainstream, with nice homes in the suburbs and corporate jobs, were muttering, "Maybe it's time to move to Canada." Angry *white* terrorists blew up the federal building in Oklahoma City, with black women and children among the victims. In black neighborhoods, Oklahoma City was cited as another example of a white predisposition toward violence. White people in combat gear were also shown on TV running about rural America, shooting assault weapons and claiming alien forces had taken over the country. For black people, these scenes represented more warning about white anger.

At the same time, many white Americans had come to believe that the evils of white prejudice were withering away as a factor in American life, that the only people who kept such fears alive were those who wanted to "play the race card." Many white Americans believed, too, that if only we could forget about race for a while—put it out of our minds—race relations might just take care of themselves.

One white friend with whom I discussed these matters was *USA Today*'s polling editor, who insisted that race relations were improving—and he had polls to prove it. Among his most compelling arguments were polls indicating that most black and white Americans were now saying they had good friends on the other side of the color line.

Here is the specific evidence he cited: in a 1989 *USA Today* poll, 62 percent of whites said they had "a close personal friend" who is black and 83 percent of blacks said they had "a close personal friend" who is white. Convinced? Then, five years later, in a similar poll, 73 percent of whites said they had "a good friend" who is black, and 78 percent of blacks said they had "a good friend" who is white.

So what was going on? How can the president claim the nation's heart is torn by race or *Newsweek* say it's "Whites v. Blacks" if so many of us are supposed to be involved in these close friendships?

Good question.

How can whites and blacks be so at odds in the Simpson case—or anything else—and be close friends at the same time? How can whites worry about "the race card" or blacks worry about "angry white males"? According to these polls, almost 80 percent of all Americans say they have friends from the other side of the color line. And that sounds impressive. Beyond that, the polls do not say who these friends are or where the friendships occur—at work or where?—just that there is this massive fellowship that seems to contradict suggestions that America is disastrously divided. Furthermore, at least before the Simpson case, many white Americans seemed eager to believe that the friendship model of race relations was prevailing and that the angry voices along the color line were out of touch. And the less said about race, the better.

Yet there was *something* in these polls on interracial friendships that seemed unclear. How come all this friendship involving 80 percent of the U.S. population isn't more visible? How come when you walk down a city street, you see both blacks and whites, yes, but usually not together? How come the farther one gets from the office or workplace, the more segregated life seems to be? How come we needed a poll to tell us that we are all friends?

In a search for friendships between blacks and whites, it is necessary to recognize that white attitudes about race have changed significantly since World War II. The odds on the eventual triumph of interracial friendships should be going up. And it would seem that white people deserve some credit for the ways they have changed. Largely gone are weird ideas about toilets, drinking fountains, and lunch counter seats. Since the 1940s, polls indicate that whites show an increasing willingness to interact with black people, and this must also be one reason why many white Americans assume that race relations are getting better. They know that they have *personally* abandoned bad attitudes toward black people.

- In 1942, only 30 percent of whites believed black and white children should attend the same schools. By 1985, 92 percent of whites believed they should.
- In 1963, 32 percent of whites said they would be "concerned" if a black person tried on clothing before them in a store. By 1978, the number was 14 percent.
- In 1963, 24 percent of whites said they would be "concerned" about using the same public rest room as black people. By 1978, the number was 7 percent.
- In 1963, 20 percent of whites said they would be "concerned" about sitting next to a black person on a bus or at a lunch counter. By 1978, it was 6 percent.
- In 1963, three in five white Americans (60 percent) believed marriages between blacks and whites should be illegal. By 1988, this had dropped to 25 percent. But in a 1997 Gallup poll, 39 percent of whites say they "disapprove" of intermarriage.

Clearly, most of these developments represent increasingly open-minded attitudes about contact with blacks. Pollsters became so satisfied that some of these issues were sufficiently settled that they stopped asking many of the questions. So why aren't black people happy?

An important detail about the mathematics of American life often gets ignored—a seemingly small percentage of white Americans can add up to millions of people. Therefore, a mere 10 percent of 224 million whites is 22.4 million people, and a mere 16 percent is 35.8 million, which outnumbers the entire black population of the United States.

Hence, even if 6 percent of white Americans, 13.4 million people, remain "concerned" about sitting next to a black person on a bus, it seems probable that black Americans could easily end up next to one of these "concerned" white persons from time to time. And that fact can shape their expectations about the white people they see on buses. It can put black people on guard, make them wonder, "Is *this* one of those white people who don't want to sit next to a black person?" They might even consider not sitting next to white people on buses to make sure they don't encounter one of those "concerned" ones.

But consider, too, that the 39 percent of whites who disapprove of intermarriage could add up to 87 million people who are out there on buses, trains, or wherever. Mathematically, they would form a much larger presence on the American scene than all of black Americans—men, women, and children together.

Another problem with polls about race is that some are so hypothetical as to have no bearing on events in the real world. For example, 77 percent of white people said in 1985 they would not object to having a black dinner guest in their home, but *only 28 percent of whites had actually had a black dinner guest in their home.* This meant that 60 million white Americans had had a black dinner guest—an impressive figure—but 155 million whites, the vast majority, had not.

So what does this say about the poll findings on black-white friendships? Do they represent a believable portrait of improving race relations in America? Or is there something fishy about them? Here are my calculations, based on the U.S. population of adults over age 18: the 73 percent of whites with a "good" black friend adds up to 115 million white adults. The 78 percent of blacks with a "good" white friend is 16.3 million black adults.

It also seems likely that the 16.3 million black Americans with good white friends are probably the same black people referred to by the 115 million white Americans who say they have good black friends. You follow? And if all these numbers are accurate, it represents a ratio of about seven white people who say they have a good friend who is black for each black person who claims a good white friend.

Also, this ratio of 7 to 1 is not just some incidental quirk in these polls. It corresponds roughly to the ratio of whites and blacks in the U.S. population: 224 million white Americans and 35 million black Americans are also just short of 7 to 1 (6.4 to 1). So this ratio of 6 or 7 to 1 appears to be significant, because it describes race relations in ways that are too seldom considered. In effect, a 6- or 7-to-1 rule is operating in many issues involving race. In this case, for each white person who claims to have one black friend, each black person involved in these friendships must, on the average, have seven white friends. Or the deal won't work.

I must pause here to discuss the exact nature of these important ratios of whites to blacks. The ratio of friendships, as extrapolated from polls, is more than 7 to 1; the ratio in overall census projections for the year 2000 comes out to 6.4 to 1—or, when rounded off, 6 to 1. Either ratio, 6 to 1 or 7 to 1, points out that there are many more whites than blacks in America, and this difference is important.

Adult Black-White Friendships		
	Percent of White or Black Population	Actual Numbers (in millions)
whites with a black friend	73	115
blacks with a white friend	78	16.3

It is also helpful to visualize what a 6- or 7-to-1 ratio looks like for an understanding of the reality of race in America. For some, when shown a simple diagram of the relationship, the number of blacks seems way too small and the number of whites surprisingly large. But this ratio is the reality of race relations, and for all white Americans to have at least one black friend apiece, all black Americans must get busy befriending white people. And that's the rub in the polls on friendship; it is easy to find black people who say they have one or two white friends but not seven. "*Good* friends?" they ask. "No, not seven good friends."

Some black Americans represent even worse news: by choice or by chance, they have no white friends. Theoretically, this means that some white Americans must be going without black friends—and maybe going without black friends through no fault of theirs—unless other black Americans in our calculations have *more* than seven friends.

A 7-to-1 Ratio of Whites to Blacks

So do all those white people really have good friends who are black? And vice versa? We can't possibly tell, but it doesn't *look* like it is so. People could be describing casual acquaintances or people with whom they exchange pleasantries as "good" or "close personal" friends. Surely, they've never been so close to most of these "good" friends as to invite them over for dinner.

We might also note that there are too few black people in America for an optimum level of interracial friendships—that there is actually a serious shortage of black people for these purposes—or too many whites. It is also apparent from the 6- or 7-to-1 ratios that there are not enough black people in America to take all the jobs white Americans have, to move next door to every American family, or to marry the sister of every white male in the land.

The basic 6- or 7-to-1 scenario also indicates there is likely to be a serious disparity in the number of contacts blacks and whites have across the color line. Black and white experience will be different in this regard. On the average, blacks will always have more contacts across the color line and whites fewer contacts. Black Americans will get more experience dealing with whites than white Americans get dealing with blacks. This imbalance in experience in dealing with interracial situations will likely haunt race relations wherever they occur.

Polls—bless them in this instance—do indicate that blacks have more contact with whites than vice versa. *USA Today* asked in 1995: "How often would you say you have conversations or other personal contact with people whose race is black/white?" Among white Americans, 39 percent said they had contact with a black person "every day"; 18 percent said "pretty often"; 22 percent said "occasionally"; 20 percent said "rarely"; and 1 percent volunteered "never."

In simple terms, this means that 3 of 5 white Americans—or 96 million white adults—do not deal with black people every day. But in the same poll, 61 percent of black Americans—3 in 5—said they had contact with whites "every day." So there is a clear disparity here. Three in 5 black Americans *do* deal with whites every day, while 3 of 5 whites *don't* have daily contact with blacks.

Given such figures, it is enticing to imagine what an "average" encounter between black and white Americans would be like. The black individual will, on the average, have about seven times more experience along the color line than the white individual. So black Americans might even be more assured in dealings across the color line, while white Americans might find themselves less comfortable about what to say.

Readers can judge for themselves whether this plays out in their own reality. I have raised this issue with many whites and find that a surprising number admit to the uneasiness described here. To be sure, it is not a terrible or paralyzing affliction in most cases, but it is there all the same. Whites are so often unsure of themselves that blacks recognize they must approach the situation in ways that will put whites more at ease. In fact, there is a large body of conventional wisdom in black America about how to deal with white people in ways that will not stir white fears. For example, it is said that you always have to tell white people what they want to hear; that it's not wise to let them know you have strong opinions or are knowledgeable about anything; or you must never let white people suspect they're not smart or in total control of the situation.

Also, it becomes likely, given the race-relations experience gap, that certain patterns will be repeated. Thus, in an "average" encounter, blacks will often find it necessary to explain themselves or explain about black life and culture. They will be asked to explain "what black people think." Why? Whites just don't know that much about black people, black culture, or the black world. Meanwhile, whites will not need to explain themselves or what whites think, because blacks are already likely to have formed very strong ideas on these subjects.

Whites will repeatedly ask, "What do blacks want?" And even this has become a notorious question because it seems that whites assume that all black people are alike and have the same desires. But it keeps getting asked because so many whites, especially those who have few relationships with black people, really think they don't know the answer.

Blacks, however, are likely to wonder how, after all these years, can whites know so little about black people? The answer: there is an almost endless supply of white Americans who live in circumstances— in the suburbs or elsewhere—where they have little contact with black people. So it is easy for whites, especially those who live in over-whelmingly white circumstances, to imagine they don't know what black people want.

Blacks who tire of answering questions from whites—or of remaining silent while whites make statements that are wrong—often wonder among themselves, "When will whites get it?" One expression of this annoyance was a popular T-shirt appearing in several variants around 1993. The shirts, rhetorically addressed at white people, proclaimed: "It's a black thing—you wouldn't understand."

And many whites took these T-shirts as a sign that black people *prefer* to remain mysterious, not realizing that many black Americans are fed up with having to deal with white naïveté. Whites may consider themselves to be a race of smart people, the inventors of airplanes, computers, and much that is wonderful. But they can also look very dumb—almost learning disabled—on the subject of black people. And that group often includes whites who are trying very hard to be decent and fair-minded.

Unfortunately, an endless repetition of these situations—blacks being comfortable, whites being slightly uncomfortable—will seem to prove that mere interaction across the color line does not automatically produce positive results. It is even possible that the more interaction there is across the color line, the more negative impressions blacks and whites will get of each other until whites emerge from their racial isolation and gain more experience in race relations. Mistaken impressions will abound.

Blacks will interpret white uneasiness as evidence that whites are not being open or honest—that whites are hiding some of those old "concerns." And such suspicions will be bad news for anyone who expects that poor race relations will simply evaporate if we just get to know each other better.

Such a turn won't happen, and here's why. In the same poll in which 78 percent of blacks said they had a good friend who is white, an overwhelming majority of the black respondents also asserted a number of negative impressions about whites in general: 76 percent said whites are "insensitive to others" or "don't want to share control of power and wealth with nonwhites," and 79 percent said whites "believe they are superior." And remember, these are the blacks who say they have white friends!

This cannot be good news. Apparently, friendships with individual whites do not shake the negative impressions these black Americans have about whites as a group. Perhaps these "friendships" with whites only reinforce the negative impressions black people already have. Social scientists cite similar findings. Lee Sigelman and Susan Welch, who have analyzed black attitudes in a book, *Black Americans' Views of Racial Inequality*, note that they cannot "advance interracial friendship as an important influence on blacks' perceptions. . . . For blacks and whites, interracial friendship appears to have only a minimal perceptual impact."

So the friendship the *USA Today* polling editor cited as evidence that relations are improving between blacks and whites may not be working all the magic that many Americans assume. In fact, these "close friendships" may even augment the bad impressions blacks and whites already have of each other.

If friendship—or what suffices for friendship in polls—isn't enough to close our racial divide, what is? Will any solution to this dilemma require something more than friendship? Pray tell, then, what would that be? We don't seem to know. And that, as much as anything, is part of the problem.

2
TROUBLE WITH NUMBERS
Why Can't We Count Straight?

A stubborn misunderstanding about race involves the simple matter of how many of us there are. How many whites? And how many blacks? These might seem to be straightforward questions, but persuasive evidence shows that Americans are deeply confused about demographic reality. This in turn leads them to false ideas about who "we" are.

We often hear the phrase "what America looks like," but most Americans don't know. And we're even more confused about what America will look like when the 21st century unfolds.

Many Americans on both sides of the color line believe a day is coming when black people, or "people of color," will rule America. When that day arrives, it is assumed America will look darker and be culturally different, too. Not surprisingly, this vision of our future has made America become a promised land for many black Americans, a time when "people of color" will be the majority. Many blacks I know have such faith in a coming of majority of color that they look askance at anyone who questions the mathematics of the proposition. "Where are you getting your numbers?" they ask.

Curiously, confirmation for their faith in the impending majority of color comes from an unexpected source: white people. Whites also appear convinced a darker America is coming; they write books and articles about changing demographics in cities like Los Angeles and San Francisco, places that can exemplify the idea that whites are being edged toward minority status. And, naturally, many whites are less enthusiastic. Some grumble that blacks or foreigners are "taking over everything." Meanwhile, black people have a common stereotype of white people that they study everything and count and measure everything. So, blacks figure, if whites are worrying about the darkening of America, it must be a real prospect.

One problem with these visions is basic. The demographic numbers don't add up to an emerging majority of color. The darkening of America is real enough, that is, if *darkening* is the right word. The growing Hispanic and Asian populations, added to the fact that whites are having fewer children, are producing a nation that is proportionately more Hispanic, Asian, and black. But this is not the same thing as having these groups take over.

Still, the idea that *someone* is taking over is an old one. Some readers might have first been introduced to the idea of a darkening threat in this impressive passage from F. Scott Fitzgerald's *Great Gatsby*, published in 1925; such fears were fashionable in the 1920s.

> "You make me feel uncivilized, Daisy," I confessed on my second glass of corky but rather impressive claret. "Can't you talk about crops or something?"
>
> . . . "Civilization's going to pieces," broke out Tom violently. "I've gotten to be a terrible pessimist about things. Have you read 'The Rise of the Colored Empires' by this man Goddard?"
>
> "Why no," I answered rather surprised in his tone.
>
> "Well, it's a fine book and everybody ought to read it. The idea is if we don't look out the white race will be—will be utterly submerged. It's all scientific stuff; it's been proved."
>
> "Tom's getting very profound," said Daisy, with an expression of unthoughtful sadness. "He reads deep books with long words in them. What was that word we—"
>
> "Well, these books are all scientific," insisted Tom, glancing at her impatiently. "This fellow has worked out the whole thing. It's up to us, who are the dominant race, to watch out or these other races will have control of things."
>
> "We've got to beat them down," whispered Daisy, winking ferociously toward the fervent sun.

Actually, the book in question was *The Rising Tide of Color Against White World-Supremacy*, published in 1922, by Lothrop Stoddard, a Harvard Ph.D. And it is still around. The text is available on the Internet, where it is popular among worried white supremacists. However, reference to a coming majority of color can be found in more recent sources as well. In his 1993 book *Loose Canons: Notes on the Culture Wars*, Henry Louis Gates, Jr.—now a Harvard professor—wrote, "A majority of our citizens will be people of color by the year 2020."

Here Gates is mistaken—it appears whites will still be the majority in 2020—but our confusion about this matter is complex and not of Gates's doing. Apparently, most Americans subscribe to a skewed interpretation of the U.S. population. What they see turns out to be an illusion, as a 1995 *Washington Post* poll showed. On the average, both blacks and whites estimated the black population at double the actual figures. Whites said blacks comprise 23.8 percent of the U.S. population, while blacks claimed 25.9 percent. The correct figure, according to U.S. census figures for 1999, is 12.8 percent.

Whites then estimated that they make up 49.9 percent of the population; blacks estimated 45.5 percent. The correct figure for white people, according to the U.S. census: 82.1 percent.

It would appear from the *Post* poll that both blacks and whites believe we are a country where the ratio of whites to blacks is about 2 to 1 and—get this—*whites are already a minority.* Yet all this, quite simply, is delusion. Still, similar results showed up in a 1996 ABC *Nightline* poll: whites estimated blacks were 33 percent of the population; blacks said blacks were 37 percent. And both groups placed the white population at 61 percent.

What Do Americans Think the United States Looks Like?						
Estimates	***Washington Post***		***ABC Nightline***		**U.S. Census**	
	whites	blacks	whites	blacks	whites	blacks
by blacks	45.5%	25.9%	61%	33%	82.1%	12.9%
by whites	49.9%	23.8%	61%	37%		

So what is going on? Are these polls a reflection of wild and uninformed guesses? Are Americans unable to translate what they see into mathematical percentages? And why, then, do blacks and whites see the racial composition of the U.S. population so similarly? Here both blacks and whites are in agreement. And both are wrong. But they may come to their conclusions in different ways. It is suggested, for example, that black Americans, who often live in crowded urban neighborhoods, conclude that what they see around them applies to the whole country. And initially this explanation sounds reasonable.

But why, then, do white Americans, especially those who live in overwhelmingly white neighborhoods, *underestimate* the number of whites so precipitously? In short, blacks overestimate their own presence and whites underestimate theirs. Blacks see themselves as a larger group than they really are and whites as a smaller group. And whites see themselves as a smaller group than they really are and blacks as a larger group.

The cause of these illusions may not initially be as important as the results. Skewed notions about our population must surely affect many attitudes about race or about issues such as affirmative action. Imagine, for example, that whites are in fact about to become a minority. The idea of giving an affirmative-action advantage to members of the new majority could seem menacing. So the larger the black population appears to be, the more threatening and unjust affirmative action seems to whites. Some whites might also find suggestions of an ominous future in simple words like *diversity* or *multiculturalism*. It is even possible that the mere sighting of a black person reminds some whites of fears about a darkening land, instilling a sense that "They're coming! They're coming!"

And whites do have a noticeable habit of overestimating the presence of darker people as "waves," "tides," and "perils." But black people sometimes recognize this can happen on a street corner, too. Suppose four or five black men are standing on the corner. Whites will see eight or ten. Suppose it is a slightly larger group of black people. Whites will see a "big crowd" or a "mob," cause to be frightened or call the police. In fact, it seems that any number of black people will loom larger and more threatening to white people than the same group would appear to black people.

Worries about a darkening America and this habit of seeing more dark people than there are can operate in tandem. The warnings journalists have sounded about a changing America form an ominous credo for whites: *America is getting darker*. Even if you live in Iowa or Montana, TV images from the streets in New York City can say, "They're coming! They're coming!" And many whites are convinced that the presence of more black people on TV—in sports, entertainment, and news—is added evidence the country is changing.

Meanwhile, black Americans who also believe America is darkening might be wondering when the positive effects will appear. Where are they? When will life in America stop seeming so *white*? Are whites acting to forestall the coming changes? That would be just like whites.

Hold on, everybody! What are the facts?

Producing satisfying figures on the exact nature of the darkening or nondarkening of America is not easy. The most complete set of numbers comes from the U.S. Census Bureau. And, unfortunately, individuals on both sides of the color line don't trust the government. Some believe the government might manipulate population figures to serve all kinds of purposes—to deny blacks their fair representation, or to keep whites in control. And the government even admits that the census misses people.

But who has better figures on U.S. population?

Here, then, is what the census says about the U.S. population. This, as best we can determine, is reality—what America looks like:

The U.S. Population in 2000 (Bureau of Census Projections)		
Total U.S. population	**274.6 million**	100%
whites	225.5 million	82.1%
blacks	35.4 million	12.9%
Hispanics (includes some listed as blacks and whites)	31.4 million	11.4%
Asians	11.2 million	4.1%

Note: Because Hispanics are an ethnic group, defined by language and cultural heritage and not by race, they are also listed separately as blacks and whites—counted twice, as it were, so the total of all these groups adds up to more than 100 percent. But these figures are the basic data on race in America—information so simple it is too seldom taken seriously enough.

Whites currently outnumber blacks by 6.4 to 1, a demographic picture that is slightly darkening, which has been often said. But how dark is America going to be? Even in the most extreme census projections for the year 2050, black people will *not* outnumber white people, so don't make that mistake. In 2050, according to middle-of-the-road census projections, white people, including white Hispanics, are expected to be 74.8 percent of the population. And black people, including Hispanics, will be 15.4 percent of the population, a figure slightly higher than now but still only a ratio of five whites for every black person.

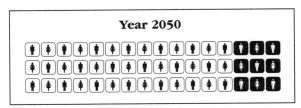

Year 2000

A huge difference? Who thinks so?

But should we believe these census projections? What other estimates do we have? According to the middle-of-the-road projections, the U.S. population in 2050 will be about 394 million, including 295 million whites and 61 million blacks.

Therefore, for black people to become the majority in 2050, an additional 234 million black people would have to be added. Or 234 million whites would have to disappear, die, or go somewhere else. Or a combination of whites disappearing and blacks arriving would have to add up the 234 million. And that would be some combination of events.

Year 2050

So why, then, do we have such confusion about the future? One answer is that we've been sufficiently bombarded with this idea of a darkening America that it is hard to shake. Still, most of the confusion seems to center on Hispanics and whatever color they are. Currently, the nation's 31.4 million Hispanics are the second largest U.S. minority, but they are also projected to become the largest minority group, passing black Americans, in about 20 years.

But what race will all these Hispanics be? In current parlance, Hispanics often seem to be thought of as "people of color." And the common thinking is that as the Hispanic population grows, America will get darker. But really, what color are Hispanics? That is the question generating confusion. Those who believe Hispanics—a cultural and linguistic designation, not a racial one—are black might well tune in on the Univision Spanish-language cable channel and see how many black people are in view. Usually not many. In fact, some Hispanic people in the United States are white, some are black, some are Native Americans, and many are a mixture of these origins. Currently, 60 percent of Hispanics are of Mexican origin, and only 6 percent of Hispanics identify themselves as black according to census figures.

In the future, it is likely many Hispanics will consider themselves white and "disappear" into the white population, as have the descendants of so many immigrant groups who were once considered swarthy. Will these white Hispanics *also* consider themselves "people of color" or ally themselves with black people? Who knows? Will the perspectives of black Hispanics closely coincide with those of black Americans? Again, who knows?

One thing is clear, however: the "darkening" that Hispanics bring to America will be subtle. In the long run, we may hardly notice the difference. The country will still look much the same. It also is clear that whites will still be the largest population group and an overall majority in the nation. So we will have to live with that.

Basic fairness demands recognition that 35 million black Americans is no small group, even if outnumbered by whites. Their numbers equal the population of Argentina and are greater than the populations of Canada, Iraq, or Greece and almost twice that of the continent of Australia. Black Americans also have an estimated annual income of $500 billion, which almost equals the gross national product of Canada, exceeds that of Spain, and is almost twice that of India. For comparison's sake, it is also interesting—and maybe surprising—to note that the number of black Americans exceeds the 32.6 million Americans who listed their ancestry as English in the 1990 census. But English Americans are only the third largest white ethnic group in America, behind those who identify themselves as German Americans (58 million) and Irish Americans (38 million).

A worldwide perspective also influences our thinking about race. Black Americans can think of themselves as part of a worldwide majority of "people of color," but white Americans are likely to think of themselves as part of a group, including white Europeans, that is outnumbered by the darker peoples of the world. In real figures, however, the world's four biggest population groups are:

- Chinese
- South Asians (from India, Pakistan, Bangladesh, Nepal, and Sri Lanka)
- Africans
- Europeans, including whites in the Americas

And these four groups are actually surprisingly similar in size. No one group is a majority and no two or three groups have the necessary affinities to ally them irrevocably against the other groups. Roughly speaking, one billion Chinese are balanced against one billion South Asians, one billion white Europeans, and 850 million blacks of African origin. Blacks are the most cosmopolitan of the racial groups, having the largest segment of their population living outside their continent of origin. Whites are in second place.

The slave trade changed the complexion of the United States. So, given all the talk about a darkening future, it is instructive for us to recognize that America was darker in 1790, the year of the first census, than it is today. It was even darker in the days of Washington and Jefferson than it will be in 2050. Black people were almost 20 percent of the population in 1790, and the 1790 figures included 694,280 slaves and 59,557 "free Negroes."

In 1860, on the eve of the Civil War and the end of slavery, 4.4 million black people, including nearly 4 million slaves, represented 12.4 percent of the population, closer to today's figure. But a proportional decline in the black population began after the Civil War and continued during the decades of the massive white immigration through Ellis Island. In 1930, black Americans were only 9.7 percent of the U.S. population. The proportion of blacks has been slowly rising ever since.

One important reason for this rise is the lifestyle choices white Americans made. Whites are active players in the trends they sometimes see as ominous. Since World War II, more white women have entered the workplace, focusing on careers and postponing childbearing. One result: white families are having fewer children. The black birthrate in 1992 was 42 percent higher than for whites. In 1993, it was 39 percent higher, in 1994, 35 percent higher, and in 1995, 28 percent.

The higher birthrate for black Americans has been accompanied by another demographic trend that deserves more scrutiny: black Americans have a shorter life expectancy—seven years shorter than whites.

Naturally, this imbalance alone could stir black Americans to wonder about the fairness in American life, but it also produces a little-noted demographic divide between blacks and whites. Blacks are lower than whites in income and other economic indicators, but they are also younger. The color line is also a mini-generation gap, with the average white American six years older than the average black American. The average age of whites is 34.3; the average age of blacks is 28.2. Also, the white population has proportionally more elderly people, while the black population has proportionally more children. As a result, more than half of the black population is under 30 years of age, while 58 percent of the white population is now over 30.

And what does this age difference mean, and how might it play out? Certainly, when it's noted that blacks and whites have different perspectives, a generation gap might logically be a factor. The concerns of black Americans might focus more on children or the problems of teens and young parents, while the concerns of white Americans are likely to focus on middle age or the problems of aging. And this sometimes seems to be the case, with blacks concerned about jobs, schools, and daycare and white Americans concerned about social security, retirement, and medical care for the aging.

Similarly, the culture of black America might naturally have an energetic, youthful focus—and it seems to—while the culture of white America might reflect the tastes of individuals who are starting to slow down or who have nostalgic recollections of past decades. And that sometimes seems to be the case among aging baby boomers. At times, white Americans might even seem to be looking at black Americans in the terms that older people have traditionally viewed younger people or vice versa. Older generations see younger ones as undisciplined, out of control, or forsaking traditional values; younger generations often see older ones as too controlling or stuck on old-fashioned ways.

Beyond that, a younger population might be more liberal and open-minded, while an older population becomes more conservative and resistant to change. Doesn't that ring true? And this variation raises some inevitable questions, especially when it is suggested that blacks and whites will inevitably see things differently. Is it race that makes this difference? Or is it something else like age or economic status? In the long run, these are important questions to ponder.

Other demographic indicators also get largely ignored in discussions about race. If blacks and whites are supposed to see things differently, can we ignore the degree to which they live in their own separate worlds? Separation increases the likelihood that blacks and whites will have limited contact with each other and fewer shared experiences.

Most black Americans—55 percent—live in cities. They are city people. Most white Americans—51 percent—live in the suburbs. They are suburbanites. And city people and suburbanites are different. If race were not an issue, we would recognize a difference in tastes, lifestyles, and experiences between these two groups. We should similarly recognize the differences when race is involved.

This issue of separation—and its impact on our thinking about race—is a critical point. Some readers may find it controversial. Don't we have integration? Isn't integration the law of the land? Are not black Americans entering the nation's mainstream?

Yes, but half of U.S. counties are still at least 99 percent white, a fact that is ignored in accounts of the darkening of America. In extreme cases, as in the states of Vermont, Idaho, and Montana, the ratio of whites to blacks approaches or tops 300 to 1. How often are black people seen there?

States	percent black	percent white	white-black ratio
States of Extreme Isolation (1990 Census figures)			
Vermont	0.3	98.6	285:1
Idaho	0.3	94.4	282:1
Montana	0.3	92.7	311:1
Maine	0.4	98.4	201:1
South Dakota	0.5	91.6	196:1
North Dakota	0.5	94.6	171:1
New Hampshire	0.6	98.0	151:1
Utah	0.7	93.8	140:1
Wyoming	0.8	94.1	118:1
Oregon	1.6	92.8	57:1

The extreme segregation of blacks and whites also operates in and around major cities, with heavy concentrations of black people in cities. Detroit, for example, is 75 percent black, the highest figure for any U.S. city, but the overall metropolitan area that includes Detroit is only 21 percent black. Many whites in metropolitan Detroit live in overwhelmingly white surroundings: Livonia, Michigan, 15 miles from downtown Detroit, has a population of 101,000, of which only 0.3 percent are black. Warren, Michigan, six miles from downtown Detroit, has a population of 145,000, of which 0.7 percent are black.

Is America darkening? Not in these suburban enclaves. Consequently, the most accurate image of America may not be of a darkening nation but of blacks and whites segregated in their own separate worlds. For example, I live across the street from a Washington, D.C., elementary school that is 100 percent black. It was a "colored" school before desegregation in the 1950s; it is a black school today. These students have no interaction with white kids—zero. They are not darkening anyone else's America. Their version of American experience involves almost total racial segregation. And their experience is not unique.

In 1993, Harvard researchers reported that 63 percent of black youngsters in America—almost two thirds—attend schools that were more than 50 percent black. And according to the Harvard researchers, that represented segregation. Then, in 1996, *Time* magazine, noting that one third of black students in America attend schools that were more than 90 percent black, declared, "After four decades of struggle, America has now given up on school integration."

Consider, too, that the most significant aspect of American segregation is ignored in these calculations: we're only examining the segregation of *black* students. By these same standards, white students are also segregated and isolated, even if the primary cause is demographic reality, the 6.4-to-1 ratio of whites to blacks. Most white youngsters in America attend schools that are more than 90 percent white, which means that many white youngsters have little contact at all with black children.

According to the mathematics of race—225 million whites and 35 million blacks—even *perfect* integration would not solve the problem of white isolation: all white children would attend schools that are about 82 percent white, and all whites would live in neighborhoods that are about 82 percent white. Strangely enough then—pay attention here—the most isolated and segregated group in America is white people. And it is likely to remain so. But when did you hear that said? Whites are likely to have the least contact with people of other races and the least opportunity for contact, a problem inherent in the mathematics of race.

Whites will be segregated and isolated in a host of circumstances, big and small. Indeed, how or where can whites escape the pervasive isolation of their experience? Not in school. Not at our colleges and universities. On our most prestigious campuses, white students will inevitably encounter a shortage of black students with whom to interact: Harvard, Yale, Stanford, and other top schools have student bodies that are only 5 or 6 percent black, producing ratios of whites to blacks of 20 or more to 1.

Yet the presence of black students on campus, even in disproportionately small numbers, often stirs another curious claim about race—that black students, or black people in general, are separating and isolating themselves. In fact, this is one of the most common ideas that whites have about race—that blacks seem to prefer to be by themselves. White students say that black students sit by themselves in dining halls or choose dorms where they will be surrounded by other black students. A similar idea is common in the American workplace—that blacks separate themselves at lunchtime or repeatedly gather to talk in black-only groups.

This charge that blacks separate themselves haunts opinions on race, even if college dining halls and workplace eateries are often filled with even greater numbers of whites eating together or campus dorms are filled with white students sharing living quarters. Why do we forget about that? Why does the focus fall on what black people are doing? But a more important question is whether these perceptions that blacks are segregating themselves are actually true?

University of Michigan researchers say no. They studied campus habits and found that black and other minority students are much more likely than whites to eat with, study with, or date students of another race or ethnic background. In fact, the study found that white students had the least interaction with students of other races and ethnic backgrounds. And this included campuses where there was no shortage of minority students with whom the whites could interact. The study found that whites cluster together more than any other group. "The current concern about whether minority students are promoting and practicing self-segregation is misplaced," researcher Sylvia Hurtado reported. "In fact, students of color are crossing ethnic-racial lines the most, while white students seem to be segregating themselves."

Do these contentions about segregation apply elsewhere in society? Yes, they do. Please name the setting where they don't apply—where whites and blacks are likely to come together. It does not happen in our churches. The adage that "America is most segregated at 11:00 A.M. on Sunday" is borne out in polls. A 1997 Gallup survey found that 70 percent of Americans worship in congregations that are essentially segregated.

Only in the American workplace do we see more consistent interaction across the color line, but blacks are often underrepresented there, too. The workplace is not darkening as much as it might seem.

Though they are 12.9 percent of the total population, blacks hold only 10.1 percent of U.S. jobs and are dramatically underrepresented in many professions. For example, only 3.2 percent of lawyers, 3 percent of doctors, and less than 1 percent of architects are black, which again underscores the isolation of white Americans. Black lawyers, doctors, and architects will have lots of interaction with white peers. But their white counterparts will likely have very little professional interaction with black peers because there are so few of them with whom to interact.

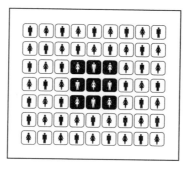

With so many factors contributing to American segregation, how can it be surprising that blacks and whites do on occasion see things differently? Some common differences in perspectives can be illustrated graphically by arranging groups of blacks and whites according to a 6-to-1 ratio and placing them as they so often are on the American landscape—black people clustered in black neighborhoods, whites clustered in white neighborhoods. Does anyone argue this doesn't happen in the real world?

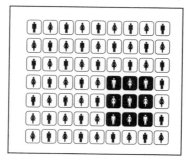

Readers should examine the examples on this page as illustrations of the circumstances in which many whites and blacks live. Note, for example, that many whites are farther away from potential contact with black people than any of the black people are removed from

potential contact with white people. And if all the black people are living in one neighborhood, this significantly diminishes the opportunities whites have for contact with black people. Note, too, what the black
or white individuals in these illustrations might see when they look
across the color line.

First, it is likely that black Americans might sense themselves surrounded by whites, certainly more so than whites should sense themselves surrounded by blacks. Can black people take over America? It sure
doesn't look like it. Hence, the very predicament some whites seem to
fear—darker people will take over—is closer to the reality blacks already
face: white people are everywhere and seem to control everything.

Next, black people might peer out into the white and see little
else but white people interacting with other whites. This surrounding
white presence might create an impression—and it might not necessarily be accurate—that white people prefer white surroundings. Hence,
just as whites sometimes accuse black people of segregating themselves and preferring their own company, so might it seem that whites
are doing the same thing.

Some readers, however, may protest that the world in these illustrations is too starkly segregated. Don't we see daily evidence of integration in our neighborhoods, our workplaces, or on TV? I respond:
the separation of blacks and whites—the self-segregation of American
life—sufficiently predominates that these pictures are more accurate
representations of most American *experience* than we like to admit.

Still, some readers may correctly insist that their lives are truly integrated, a true mix of black and white. They are rare individuals; they
are to be congratulated. Many other Americans may live in an integrated
neighborhood, while their actual lives are more segregated. Even
whites who live in black-majority neighborhoods—or blacks who live
in white-majority neighborhoods—often end up with little meaningful contact across the color line (even if they wish they had more).
Blacks and whites can live on the same block—and still be in separate worlds. In D.C. and elsewhere, I find many whites who live in
black-majority neighborhoods but still have no close black friends.

Simple—or simplistic—as they may be, the illustrations offer insight into
relations between blacks and whites. They show how the basic mathematics of race influences common impressions blacks and whites

have about each other. For example, the predicament inherent in being a minority, being forever outnumbered, is an essential ingredient in a black perspective. How could it not be? Black Americans inevitably see things this way—and whites don't—because blacks repeatedly have this experience of being in the minority, and whites do not. Most white Americans rarely encounter situations in which they are surrounded by black people. For the most part, whites avoid such situations. Black people have no such choice.

The numbers involved in race can have a psychological impact. If, for example, whites prefer vanilla ice cream and blacks prefer choco-late, vanilla will always be tops in sales, because the market for vanil-la will be so much larger. On occasion blacks might sense themselves as outsiders in a vanilla world, where the wishes and wants of a vanil-la-loving majority consistently prevail. Where are the chocolate lovers? They are described as different and out of step, almost as if there is something wrong with them. Everyone, from entertainers to politi-cians, seems to talk effusively about the love of vanilla. It's always vanilla, vanilla, vanilla.

So it passes that majority tastes or concerns seem normal, sane, and sensible, while minority tastes can seem abnormal, irrational, or oddball. Similarly, whatever engages majority attention will be considered impor-tant. Inevitably, white concerns will show up on covers of *Time* or *Newsweek*; black concerns will be less likely to do so. Indeed, this phe-nomenon of focusing on seemingly white interests happens so often in American life that black Americans often claim, echoing the theme of Ralph Waldo Ellison's classic novel, *Invisible Man*, that whites treat black people as if they don't count for anything—like they don't exist.

Some white readers might be surprised how often black Americans express this sense of being ignored. Whites don't listen. Whites don't care. Whites only hear what pleases them. Whites think they are the be-all and end-all. Whites are uninterested in anyone else. This, too, can create expectations about what interaction along the color line will be like. And these expectations may not always be correct. Many black Americans fully anticipate that white store clerks or other white functionaries will ignore them. And the expectation often ends up fulfilled by the slight-est suggestion of inattentiveness by whites or by the slightest intimation that whites have their thoughts elsewhere or on themselves.

Since white Americans rarely find themselves in the minority, the thought of being outnumbered makes most of them uncomfortable. Many whites are frightened by the prospect of being alone in a crowd of black people, even a small crowd. And they are unlikely to appreciate the pleasures black people can find in their own company, which can be likened to the joy of discovering you are in the majority for a change.

Whites tend to be wary when they see crowds of black people enjoying themselves. At times—and this seems a bit strange to me—whites feel left out of the fun blacks appear to be having. Some whites wonder what special thoughts black people share at such moments, while others imagine that blacks might be conspiring against white people: Are they talking about us? What are they saying? Is someone stirring them up?

Suspicions about "troublemakers" obviously arose in the segregated South, and it involved the nutty notion that someone would arouse black people to the inequities of their circumstances, as if blacks didn't already know. Similar suspicions arose in 1995 over the Million Man March. Whites were left out, and many feared that Minister Louis Farrakhan would stir up black people against whites. And it was extremely difficult for many whites to warm to the thought of a million black men enjoying each other's company or discovering a sense of power that might be inherent in their gathering.

Meanwhile, for many black Americans the Million Man March had to look like evidence of a coming majority of color—that promised land, with black people as far as the eye could see. However, on the day following the march, the National Park Service, which up until then made an "official" estimate of Washington crowds, announced there was no such million. By the "official" reckoning, only 400,000 people were on hand.

This downgrading seemed to please many whites. Some of my white colleagues at *USA Today* grinned, as if black people had been caught in a falsehood, but in effect their pleasure revealed they had been rooting for the march to fall short of its goal, as if its failure would be in white interest. Many whites seemed relieved that another common stereotype about black people had triumphed—that blacks are prone to exaggerate. Blacks promise things they can't produce.

March organizers, however, cried foul and threatened a lawsuit, claiming a deliberate government undercount. And those disposed to suspect that the government will lie about numbers where black people are involved found further confirmation—and new evidence white people will treat black people as invisible, if they think they can get away with it.

And once again, there was trouble with numbers along the color line. The "white" side in the dispute had counted and measured 400,000 people, and the "black" side said it was, maybe, *two* million. It must also be noted that across black America it was suspected that a U.S. government that can read license plates from outer space could surely count a million black people in one place, if that's what the government wanted to do.

Enter a group called the Center for Remote Sensing at Boston University. They had previously used computers and satellite photos to count the sand dunes in Egypt and trees in California forests. They now studied aerial photos of the Million Man March and produced a new, and presumably more accurate, estimate: the center said between 870,000 and 1.1 million people attended the Million Man March, a triumph for march organizers. Unfortunately, however, this only rearoused old suspicions that you can't trust the government to count black people accurately. And it helped ensure that our trouble with numbers—and all the suspicions and misconceptions that go with it—will endure.

3

THE COLOR LINE

The Partitioning of Our Minds

If blacks and whites remain so profoundly segregated from each other, powerful forces must be at work to produce this result. Racial integration may have been a stated national goal for over half a century, but millions of blacks and whites remain isolated on opposite sides of the color line, as W. E. B. DuBois, in his classic *Souls of Black Folk*, published in 1903, foresaw. "The problem of the 20th century is the problem of the color-line—the relation of the darker to the lighter races of men in Asia and Africa, in America and the islands of the sea."

It seems he was right; his prediction may even cross into the 21st century as well.

According to our nation's laws since the 1960s, blacks and whites have equal access to both sides, yet a fundamental commandment of the color line still holds powerfully: thou shalt not cross. As a result, whites rarely venture into the territory of blacks, and blacks are not convinced they are welcome—or even safe—in white territory. And we know this is so even if we prefer not to describe our nation in these terms.

The forces that keep us so efficiently divided along the color line must also be at work deeply within us to work so well. From the way race relations—or *non*relations—unfold, it would seem there is a compass in our souls that is set on "white" or "black" as polar opposites. And this compass must be hooked up to our visceral responses in such a way that whenever we near the line that divides blacks and whites, we sense a warning signal of unease. Even when blacks and whites meet in otherwise cordial circumstances, faint alarms may still go off as these inner mechanisms keep doing their work.

We might pretend that the color line is well hidden, deep in our subconscious, if it affects us at all. If it runs down certain streets, along expressways, railroad tracks, or other landmarks, this is nowhere marked on maps, though the results are remarkably similar to what DuBois had in mind. For example, near my house in Washington, D.C., an observable demographic change occurs at 13th Street—that is, if you are looking for it. Otherwise, it is an unremarkable frontier; the houses on one side are indistinguishable from the houses on the other side. Yet to the west, most of the residents and people on the streets are white, and to the east, most are black. Many black residents in my neighborhood rarely venture west of 13th Street, while some whites on Capitol Hill act as if unseen dangers await east of 13th Street, and they hesitate to go there.

Meanwhile, if we pore through census data, we will find other phenomena linked to the color line at 13th Street. The farther east you go, the poorer the neighborhood becomes. Unemployment rises, too, becoming visible on corners. The one elementary school east of 13th Street—it is across from my house—is 100 percent black, while schools west of 13th Street are mixed.

A seemingly invisible barrier—it serves as a color line, too—often seemed to surround my black colleagues at *USA Today*. Whenever black people are talking or sitting together, whites tend to shy away as if they must not intrude. A strange, unstated etiquette makes it rude to cross the color line at such moments.

White Americans stay away from black America so consistently that it increases their fear when they actually *must* cross the color line. They snap the doorlocks on their cars or clutch their purses with extra care believing they're now in dangerous territory. But whites can avoid the color line most of the time; they generally have no need to enter black America. Most jobs—or whatever else whites want—are found in white America. Meanwhile, whites might not grasp the apprehension blacks can feel upon crossing into white America, because whites find the white side of the color line a comfortable place to be.

Yet on occasion, stark examples of the dangers blacks face in white surroundings occur, as happened one July night in 1989 in the Howard Beach section of Queens in New York City. Three black men who had car trouble set out on foot across a white, working-class enclave to find a phone or a mechanic, when a gang of whites, who must have imagined that they were protecting Howard Beach from black intruders, accosted the men. In the ensuing fight, one black man was beaten, another escaped, and the third—Michael Griffith, who tried to flee across a busy highway—was hit by a car and killed.

Griffith's death quickly turned Howard Beach into a symbol for black Americans, proof that crossing into white America can be a fatal mistake. There have been other examples since then. The near-fatal beating of 14-year-old Lenard Clark, Jr., by white youths in Chicago in April 1997 was cited by President Clinton on several occasions. And most Americans were stunned by a June 9, 1998, atrocity in Jasper, Texas: three white men offered a black man a ride, then chained James Byrd, Jr., to the back of their pickup truck and dragged him down a country road until his head came off. Prosecutors said the white men committed this mind-boggling act for no other reason than that Byrd was black.

However, even when there are other examples, white Americans can convince themselves that terrible events like these are relatively isolated incidents. Yet when a *USA Today* poll, taken a month after the Howard Beach incident, asked if such an attack could happen in "your" town, an arresting truth emerged. Virtually half of white Americans polled—49 percent—and 79 percent of black Americans said yes.

This was a shocking statistic for an allegedly civil nation. A majority of Americans acknowledged they thought that crossing the color line into white America could be a deadly mistake for black people—just think about that. In the midst of considering issues and attitudes about race—or the question of whether we are making "progress" in race relations—we should dwell for a moment on this chilling idea. No matter what else is true about our attitudes, the admission that the color line is a life-and-death matter must be recognized as a cornerstone in our thinking about race. Warning: Americans have found that disobeying the commandment of the color line can be dangerous to your health.

Meanwhile, the incidents at Howard Beach and elsewhere run contrary to conventional wisdom about which side of the color line is the dangerous one. Most whites, which means most Americans, believe that the *black* side of the color line is where the danger lies.

In my immediate neighborhood, which is 75 percent black, white residents say that white friends and relatives are afraid to visit, because the black side of the color line is considered such a dangerous place. Many whites outside Washington avoid much of the District of Columbia, which is 64 percent black, because they're afraid. Whites in other cities—it often happened to me in Miami, for example—warn out-of-town guests not to enter certain black neighborhoods. And because so many whites are fearful of black neighborhoods, you rarely see a white face in large sectors of black America, just as you will rarely see a black face in large sectors of white America.

At this point, we should immediately ask how true it is that black America is unsafe for white people. Millions of white Americans assume they will be robbed, assaulted, or killed—or the odds rise of this happening—if they go near the black sections of big cities. But is this so? In fact, their specific fear of being robbed by a black person seems to have foundation, because in some years, the largest single category of robberies in the United States, slightly more than a third of all robberies, involves black robbers and white victims. Next come robberies in which robber and victim are white.

The statistics suggest that black robbers either choose white victims because white victims are plentiful, whites being 82-plus percent of the population, or because whites are also assumed to carry more that is worth robbing. In the latter instance, white skin merely is an economic indicator; we need not ask economists who is doing well in America. We can ask street muggers.

But on which side of the color line do all these robberies of white people take place? Not in black America, because white America doesn't go there. In the world around my neighborhood, for example, the number of thefts, robberies, and burglaries—basic property crimes—is much higher west of 13th Street, where more white people live, and lower east of 13th Street, where more black people live. So speaking of robberies and burglaries, the black side of the color line is actually safer than the white side. However, if more whites dared cross 13th Street into black America, this argument might collapse; whites would get robbed there, too. So it is likely this particular crime pattern follows white people—and their perceived affluence—wherever they go.

Meanwhile, more serious crimes like murder and rape have their own stark pattern of racial segregation. Whites are seven times more likely to be killed by a white murderer than by a black one. Murders in which a black person kills a white person are only 6 percent of all homicides. White women are seven times more likely to be raped by a white rapist. Rapes in which the assailant is black and the victim white account for only 9 percent of all rapes.

In fact, the most serious criminal threats to white people come from other white people—and whites should, perhaps, be warned about this. Robberies, however, appear to be skewing white attitudes. Enough robberies—and carjackings, assaults, rapes, and murders, too— occur in which the perpetrators are black and the victims white to fuel white fears about black people. Indeed, this fear of being victimized by black criminals might be considered a national white obsession were it not considered indelicate to mention it.

However, fear of crime, exaggerated and misdirected or otherwise, is not the only reason whites won't cross the color line. Whites are also convinced they are unwelcome in black America, a conviction that must arise from a belief it might just be reasonable for black people to dislike whites, given the sorry history of race relations.

For whatever reason, 46 percent of whites said in a 1995 *USA Today* poll that "many" black people dislike whites, and another 11 percent said "almost all" black people dislike whites. Together, this adds up to 57 percent of all whites—about 125 million people—who believe that "many" or "almost all" black people do not like them. That's a lot of dislike that whites are picturing. At the same time, in the same poll, 31 percent of black Americans said that "many" blacks dislike whites and 4 percent said "almost all" dislike whites. So more than a third of black Americans agree that whites have reason to be wary.

Of course, these perceptions are a major disaster for the cause of good will along the color line. If 125 million white Americans suspect that the next black person they meet will dislike them, their wariness could easily affect their behavior around black people. And is it possible black people will not notice? Of course, they will notice. Suspicions on this scale are hard to hide.

It also means that that black-white relationships start under a cloud of suspicion, with more than half the whites believing that blacks are concealing hatred or negative feelings.

Meanwhile, blacks notice white wariness, particularly whites' fears about crime. Black people sense themselves being watched in white surroundings. Black men, in particular, are likely to be stopped by police, enough so that being stopped—or the expectation thereof—

becomes a relatively constant reminder that whites are suspicious of them. On occasion, police may tell black men that they "fit the description" of someone for whom police are looking, but in fact—there is no subtle way to put this—black men *exactly* fit the description of what many whites most fear: black men.

There is no corresponding experience for white men—not really; they don't get stopped by police often enough to think much about it. But being stopped by police happens frequently enough to black men that the "offense" is called DWB—driving while black—by those who can still joke about it. More recent statistical studies indicate police are aware of the pattern—and are trying to avoid the appearance of outright prejudice. But in 1995, for example, 71 percent of those stopped and searched along one stretch of I-95 on the East Coast were black.

And the anecdotal evidence is plentiful, too: Cornel West, a diminutive philosophy professor, now at Harvard, tells of being stopped for "driving too slowly on a residential street." Simpson prosecutor Christopher Darden says he is pulled over in his Mercedes about five times a year. I could go on about black journalist colleagues, friends, and members of my family. And even if the reality is changing, the expectation that this will happen in any moment remains.

This, of course, is another disaster along the color line; the various disasters start to add up. And the results are very logical, too. If black Americans suspect that they will be greeted in white America as potential criminals—or as angry people who hate whites—it is understandable that many black people might choose to stay away from white territory whenever possible.

And this avoidance occurs more often than whites might think. Each day, in millions of instances great and small, black Americans choose *not* to cross the color line, if only to avoid dealing with what might happen on the other side. The overall effect of these attitudes and fears on the patterns in American life is also quite obvious. Blacks hesitate to enter white America because they don't want to be beaten, killed, or suspected of criminal intent. And whites hesitate to enter black America because they don't want to be robbed, beaten, or killed either—or treated like they've entered a world where they're not wanted. And in its way, the law of the color line gets the better of many instincts we might have to do better by each other. It also definitely reduces the possibility that blacks and whites will soon become truly close friends.

Having explored all these disasters and fears along the color line, it is necessary to examine the corresponding territories inside our heads. Our thoughts, too, seem to be crossed by a color line that divides the way we think about ourselves from the way we think about others.

Sports clearly demonstrate this divide in our thinking, because sports are an interracial drama that is widely watched, and the role race plays seems easy to see, hidden in plain view. Race is so often assumed to govern sports performance that we hardly question premises involved. Black or white athletes end up clustered in the activities or positions in team play at which blacks or whites are presumed to excel.

Racial segregation by task is overwhelming in some professional sports. Specific positions in football and baseball and in specific Olympic sports have become almost totally black or white in ways that also just happen to parallel age-old stereotypes about race. The stereotypes follow a simple pattern: blacks are supposed to be physically "gifted," but whites are smarter.

Black athletes end up clustered in activities that require speed and quick reflexes, and white athletes often end up clustered in activities that are believed to require intelligence and leadership. Hence, in the National Football League, the running backs, wide receivers, and defensive backs have tended to be black, while the quarterbacks and offensive linemen have tended to be white.

These trends are still evolving, with black quarterbacks and offensive linemen becoming less rare. However, in 1991, we devised a *USA Today* poll for a series of articles on race and sports that produced intriguing suggestions that we see sports as evidence that whites and blacks have different abilities. In the poll, which involved rating black and white athletes and their attributes on a scale of 1 to 10, both black and white respondents tended to identify black athletes with physical attributes, "speed" and "strength," and white athletes with mental abilities, "thinking" and "leadership."

How We Look at Blacks and Whites				
	Black athletes		**White athletes**	
As rated by	**blacks**	**whites**	**blacks**	**whites**
speed	8.1	7.6	5.9	6.0
strength	7.5	7.0	6.4	6.3
thinking	7.3	6.1	7.2	7.1
leadership	7.0	6.1	7.5	7.2

Here, then, is evidence of a color line that divides how black and whites view the abilities of athletes. Blacks have *these* abilities and whites have *those* abilities.

The results of our poll also clearly echoed those old stereotypes about brains and brawn. Again, the claim was that whites have intelligence; blacks have physical skills. Note, too, that blacks and whites generally agreed on most ratings, which is the case with many stereotypes. Blacks and whites don't necessarily see things all that differently.

In this case, blacks and whites disagreed most noticeably on the "thinking" and "leadership" abilities of black athletes. Blacks rated black athletes higher on "thinking" and "leadership," while whites rated black athletes lower. This suggests that while whites may still believe that blacks are less intelligent or unqualified to lead, black people see blacks as more intelligent and better leaders than whites think.

Yet all these conclusions represent a headfirst dive into a vast pool of foolishness and confusion about race, wherein we draw unwarranted conclusions about intelligence or athletic ability based on visible differences such as skin color. According to the poll, Americans must believe that people with dark skin can run faster and people with white skin are smarter. But most of us also know that this does not play out in reality. Not everyone with black skin is fast, nor is everyone with white skin smart. So that's one problem.

Scientists now recognize that the variation among individuals within each race is far greater than the differences between racial groups. An American Anthropological Association "Statement on 'Race'" notes: "Evidence from the analysis of genetics (e.g., DNA) indicates that most physical variation, about 94 percent, lies within so-called racial groups. Conventional geographic "racial" groups differ from one another in only about 6 percent of their genes." So that's another problem: race is a very shaky predictor of ability; conclusions about ability based on race are likely to be wrong.

Also, the clearest differences that we identify with race are little more than skin-deep. Yet we allow variations in skin color to foster an illusion that similarly dramatic differences must also operate beneath the surface of what we see. And this is foolishness. Skin color, a simple adaptation to climate, is one isolated characteristic among thousands. But it is the one we have fixated on, and we sometimes insist on seeing skin color as an explanation for intelligence or athletic ability, when neither has much to do with skin. We might similarly imagine connections between sports ability or intelligence and hair and eye color or the shape of one's ears and buttocks, but mercifully, our thoughts do not generally run in these veins.

And finally, any seemingly clear link between race and ability has to be further challenged by the absence of a definitive biological line between racial groups. There is no such color line. We cannot tell where one race ends or another begins. Most "black" Americans have white ancestry, too, and many have native American ancestors. Some "white" Americans have black ancestry. Meanwhile, newfound genetic indicators also suggest that skin color is even more illusory as a biological classification. For example, scientists have found more genetic similarity between white Europeans and black sub-Saharan Africans than between Africans and Melanesians. Yet Melanesians, who inhabit islands north of Australia, also have dark skin and similar hair texture and facial features to Africans.

Still, we should also wonder why the evidence of color prejudice shows up so clearly in a poll on sports. Some might still argue that the respondents in the poll were reacting to the results of real biological differences between blacks and whites—that blacks are faster and stronger, or whites are more intelligent and better equipped to be leaders. Others might argue that the pervasive segregation by position in sports is based more in the way we think about race than biological reality. The logic is this: if coaches merely think blacks are better running backs and whites are better quarterbacks, eventually that's where blacks and whites are likely to end up playing.

Suffice it to say that whatever the cause, a color line operates in sports, even if its exact placement is very unclear. Are all blacks faster than whites? Are all whites smarter than blacks? Or are proportionately more blacks faster? And proportionately more whites smarter? Or are only some blacks faster? And only some whites smarter? Or are the few fastest blacks faster than the few fastest whites? And the few smartest whites smarter than the few smartest blacks?

We must also recognize that the color line in sports produces encouragement for those pursuing the "right" activities and discouragement for those pursuing the "wrong" ones. Whites or blacks who do not fit into the prevailing pattern will face inevitable doubts, including their own, when they attempt activities for which others are supposed to be more favorably endowed. Speedy whites or blacks who exude leadership skills might have to prove these abilities against a tide of conventional wisdom, maybe even far surpass the competition to prove their point.

In particular, stereotypes about intelligence have long functioned as a barrier for black Americans—and not just in sports. The contention that black people are less intelligent is a social malignancy that does not go away, surely costing our nation billions of dollars in wasted lives and lost productivity. But we still keep hearing about racial disparities in IQ or SAT scores that keep this idea operating in our daily affairs.

Even among my fellow journalists, I've seen whites who roll their eyes over misunderstandings with black colleagues, as if to invoke the intelligence stereotype as an explanation for their differences. It also surfaces, perhaps unwittingly, in comments whites make about black people they wish to praise by saying how "articulate," "educated," or "intelligent" a black person is, as if it might be more reasonable to expect the opposite.

The contention that black people are less intelligent commandeered the covers of news magazines in 1994 with the publication of *The Bell Curve: Intelligence and Class Structure in American Life.* Authors Richard J. Herrnstein and Charles Murray argued that social problems such as poverty are related to innate differences in intelligence, as indicated on "standard" IQ tests on which, on the average, blacks score 15 points lower than whites. Or so it is claimed.

It was difficult to be alive in America in 1994–95 and miss this claim. For months, journalists stirred a debate over *The Bell Curve* on TV news shows, in newspapers and in magazines, and—just as an example— the cover of the October 24, 1994, *Newsweek* showed a black man and white man in profile behind the words: "IQ. Is It Destiny?"

This question clearly suggested that the truth about intelligence has yet to be established, so if blacks tend to be poorer than whites— an economic color line—this result could be rooted in our genes that govern our brains. As the debate continued, many Americans were left to conclude that the argument had two legitimate sides, a pro and a con, and, maybe—just maybe—blacks aren't as smart as whites. It seemed you couldn't have done more harm to black Americans if it was your intention to do so.

Of course, the premises of *The Bell Curve* were widely and honorably challenged, but surely the greatest impact it had came in the endlessly repeated references to the 15-point IQ gap. If black or white Americans hadn't heard about this gap before *The Bell Curve*, they knew about it afterward. In fact, the orgy of discussion about the 15 IQ points went on at such length that the stigma of low IQ scores seemed to follow black people down the street. Let's be honest: how many whites did *not* look at black people without the specter of the intelligence issue intervening? How many black people did *not* sense they were being watched for evidence they are less intelligent? Surely, this was no crowning moment in race relations.

Since its publication in 1994, critics have quietly feasted on the theories of *The Bell Curve*. Entire books have been dedicated to *Bell Curve* fallacies and criticism, yet I'll venture that what most Americans still remember is the contention about the 15-point IQ gap. Not many know that claims in *The Bell Curve* have been widely challenged in scientific and academic circles. The media has long since rushed off to other matters.

Critics attacked *The Bell Curve* on various fronts. Can intelligence or human worth be depicted in a single number? Can we rank people's ability in linear fashion, with this individual being a point or two better than that one? Is IQ fixed in our genes and never subject to change? Critics say these are all shaky premises. Some cite a particularly telling phenomenon that shows up around the globe: minorities who have been victims of discrimination frequently score lower on IQ tests. One study found that the minority Catholics in Northern Ireland scored 15 points lower than majority Protestants. Other IQ gaps were found between the majority French and minority Flemish in Belgium, between Slovaks and Gypsies in Slovakia, and between Jews and Arabs in Israel. In the United States, students of Korean and Japanese descent score above average in IQ tests, and scientists say the two nationalities are genetically close. But in Japan, the Korean minority scores lower on IQ tests.

The argument, then, is that environment plays a greater role in IQ development than the authors of *The Bell Curve* suggest. Environment can affect IQ development just as nutrition can influence height. No matter what their genetic heritage may be, well-nourished children grow closer to their potential height than do those suffering nutritional deficiencies. Furthermore, even if a 15-point gap shows up between blacks and whites, other variables in black and white experience cast grave doubt on conclusions about the genetic differences. Such an IQ gap could be shaped by differences in childhood nutrition, prenatal health care, early learning experiences, or much more. Meanwhile, a disproportionate number of black Americans have clearly lived in poverty, with poorer nutrition, health care, child care, and educational opportunities—and this is still true.

Critics of *The Bell Curve* say all these environmental factors can suppress IQ development. Yet Herrnstein and Murray posit that IQ is 60 percent heritable among whites, therefore it must be 60 percent heritable among blacks, even though the conditions under which blacks and whites have lived are substantially different. The possibility remains—it has not been proved otherwise—that if their economic and social conditions were the same, blacks might score as high or higher than whites on IQ tests. The only real test of this premise would be under conditions of true equality.

Also, our estimates of the intelligence of minority groups often change over time. Polish Jews arriving in the early 1900s, for example, were commonly viewed as stupid, and their children got low grades and test scores. Today, the offspring of these immigrants are considered one of our brightest ethnic groups.

When have allegations of an embarrassing deficiency involving white people ever gotten such attention? Curiously, too, in all the fuss over *The Bell Curve*, why was the problem of low intelligence among white Americans not an issue? Why did the discussion focus on black people? Fully 62.5 million Americans, 25 percent of the U.S. population, would fall into Murray and Herrnstein's lowest IQ categories, "dull" and "very dull," those with IQs under 90. And obviously, all "dull" and "very dull" Americans cannot be black, because there are only 35 million black Americans in all. And no one says all blacks are "dull" or "very dull." So if "dull" or "very dull" people are indeed such a problem, it is most likely white people will be the problem's largest component. Let's consider that for a change.

Still, black people are the ones haunted by stereotypes about intelligence, and it is all too easy to jump from this stereotype to others that are related. Washington, D.C., became a case in point; the misadventures of local government were frequently cited in a way that made them seem like an object lesson on what happens when you let black people run things. Similarly, in surveys on prejudice regularly conducted at the University of Chicago, black people are still rated less intelligent, less ambitious, less willing to work, and more prone to violence than whites—all the classic stereotypes still functioning.

And the logic of these expectations invades day-to-day situations: if whites are supposed to be more intelligent, then what white people say will make sense. And if blacks are less intelligent, then what blacks say is likely to be stupid or unintelligible.

Exactly this pattern of thought seems to make it all too easy for whites to dismiss what black people say or do as illogical or unfathomable, relying on assumptions that that is the way black people are supposed to be. How can you figure these people out? Many whites seemed to conclude from the first O. J. Simpson trial—or had their preexisting belief reinforced—that black people can't think straight or see conclusions that are obvious to more rational beings.

Perhaps, some claimed, black thought processes are strangely different from those of whites, an idea that hovered about us in the aftermath of the Simpson case. But was this notion something new? Maybe it's been there all along.

I am often struck by "Afrocentric" comments about such things as thought processes—some writers say that the black cultural perspective on experience is different from that of the "Eurocentric" perspective of white-dominated America. It is engaging to explore such approaches, even if more mainstream American writers—most of whom happen to be white—insist that facts are facts, and that objectivity and a color-blind version of universal truth should be our goal. I remain drawn to the idea that blacks and whites can benefit from seeing themselves as others do.

When I heard that a Hunter College professor of African studies named Marimba Ani had written a book called *Yurugu: An African-Centered Critique of European Cultural Thought and Behavior*, I ran off to get a copy at a D.C. bookstore where she was appearing. She autographed it, "To Jim Myers, We are making an Afrikan victory—The Afrikan World Order! Marimba Ani."

How "Europeans" See Themselves and Others	
"Europeans"	**Others**
rational	irrational
critical	noncritical
scientific	superstitious, magical
logical	illogical
civilized, advanced	uncivilized, primitive
modern	backward
	(continued)

How "Europeans" See Themselves and Others (continued)	
"Europeans"	Others
lawful, orderly	unlawful, unruly
responsible, adult	childlike
energetic	lazy
active	passive
enterprising	apathetic
creative	imitative
white	black, colored

Source: Marimba Ani, *Yurugu: An African-Centered Critique of European Cultural Thought and Behavior*

In *Yurugu*, Ani writes that the belief in white supremacy has traditionally been based on assumptions that whites are the rational, scientific, logical, civilized, advanced, modern, lawful, orderly, energetic, and enterprising people. And blacks or "others" are irrational, superstitious, backward, unlawful, unruly, lazy, and apathetic.

Ani's point is that this worldview has encouraged whites to view themselves as the saviors of the world and other peoples as "objects to be controlled and manipulated." These themes still arise in America's relations with the rest of the world, and they can be found floating around in news about crime, welfare, poverty, failing schools, urban blight, or the plight of cities like D.C. And they certainly showed up in those arguments in the Simpson case that the black-majority jury did not act rationally. Or, as Jeffrey Rosen wrote in *New Republic* magazine, that Simpson's acquittal was a "celebration of subjectivity over objectivity, of emotion over truth," which fits another set of recognizable patterns in the way whites tend to look at black people, down to a common belief that blacks often lie. This thought parallels a similar belief blacks have about whites—they don't tell the truth either.

Perceptions Whites Have of Themselves and Blacks	
Blacks	Whites
subjective	objective
emotional	reasonable
illogical	logical
uneducated	educated
untruthful	truthful

Yet it is common that whites and blacks consider themselves in terms of opposites—*we* tell the truth and *they* lie—and this pattern extends to our understanding of behavior, temperament, and values—whites are cool and rational; blacks are emotional and easily overwrought; blacks are loose and uninhibited; whites are rigid and repressed.

Both sides might even generally agree that in terms of temperament, blacks are "hot" and white are "cold." Both might agree on these premises, each seeing themselves in flattering terms as opposite from the other. Blacks could agree they are "hot," meaning they are people of compassion and feeling (while whites are "cold," heartless and scheming). Whites could agree that they are "cold," if it means they assess problems calmly and reach logical conclusions (while blacks are "hot," always getting worked up over things). Once again, it's no wonder why we hesitate to cross the color line that divides these differing worlds. Whites could conclude they would be out of place in a "hot" environment and blacks could conclude they would be out of place in a "cold" world. And these are logical conclusions in both cases, because neither can expect to be at their best in environments where the rules and values are not their own.

Black people might doubt their ability to function under the rules of reason, calm, and detachment that seem to predominate in white culture. Or white people might doubt their ability to function amid the intense drama of emotions that seems to be common in black culture.

Whites and blacks may sense it is safer to stay in their own worlds, that crossing the color line will always produce a measure of uneasiness and self-doubt. Author Shelby Steele described a variant on this predicament in his 1990 bestseller, *The Content of Our Character*: "I call this *integration shock*, since it occurs most powerfully when blacks leave their familiar world and enter the mainstream. When blacks move into integrated situations or face challenges that are new for blacks, the myth of black inferiority is always present as a condition of the situation, and as such it always threatens to breach our denial of racial vulnerability. It also threatens to make us realize consciously what is intolerable to us—that we have some anxiety about inferiority."

This interesting insight may be accurate on one hand. But it misses half of the equation of race relations by suggesting that black people are the only ones who feel inferior. Let's admit right off that whites also have feelings of inferiority. If black people are uneasy about measuring up to "white" standards, so are white people uneasy about measuring up to "black" standards. And, to paraphrase Steele, whites have their own integration shock. When whites move into integrated situations or face challenges that are new for them, the myth of white inferiority in the activities at which blacks are supposed to excel is always present as a condition of the situation, and, as such, it always threatens to breach their denial of racial vulnerability. It also threatens to make whites realize what is intolerable to them—that they have some anxiety about being inferior.

Perhaps some white Americans have not pondered this possibility— that they feel inferior, unable to perform at the level of black people in some aspect of human endeavor. And if we press this idea further, some whites might admit to feeling doubts about themselves in one way or other.

We can be dead sure that whites have *some* feelings of inferiority, if only because all God's children feel inferior to their circumstances at some time or other. But if whites have quiet feelings of inferiority, they are just that—quiet, rarely cited as an issue in a white-majority society. White inferiority has not been an issue on the covers of news-magazines. Yet I sense that white Americans are ceding territory in their thinking to black people, even as they recognize the entry of blacks into areas of American life that were once exclusively white.

You doubt this is happening? Just consider the activities at which whites might suspect they are being outperformed. Whites can't sing like Whitney Houston or Aretha Franklin. Whites can't preach like Jesse Jackson. Whites can't play basketball like Michael Jordan. Get the picture? These are areas of endeavor—art, sports, entertainment, politics—that whites might consider are no longer completely theirs. These are human activities where whites now must compete against others who, some might argue, have special aptitudes or "gifts." And these examples alone represent human efforts involving sound, music, movement, feeling, and the forceful expression of ideas.

Some whites may disagree with the idea that whites are ceding territory such as basketball playing to black people. Obviously, some whites still play ball or play jazz. Some whites even sing the blues. Yet ceding territories like basketball to blacks may be much easier—and less painful—than it might seem. A concession to black superiority is inherent in the idea that "white men can't jump." And it doesn't bother white

Americans to make this concession, because it corresponds with another distinction that is often basic to white—and hence mainstream—thinking about race:

Mainstream Assumptions About Race	
Black	**White**
body	mind

Here's how that works: even if whites grant black people physical superiority—if they say blacks can jump, run fast, or dance—this thinking still does not cede superiority in endeavors that whites consider of higher importance.

As long as whites believe that functions of the mind are of a higher order than functions of the body, they can still see themselves on top. In fact, some whites might conclude that since functions of the mind separate humans from lower animals, whites must be more human and blacks more animal-like. And all the athletic glories involving running and jumping, even the 100-meter Olympic finals, only serve to prove that whites can feel superior as long as they believe they have a mental edge.

Whites can well afford to be cavalier about the inability to jump. What's so important about jumping? World leaders don't jump. CEOs of major corporations don't jump. What serious profession outside sports requires skill at jumping? Thus it becomes easy to concede that black people are good at jumping because it is an act of no consequence. Let blacks run and jump. White people don't need to jump or worry about it, because they have faith they can excel otherwise.

In fact, the stereotype might be rephrased. Instead of, "Whites can't jump," it could be said, *whites don't jump.* And the reason is simple: jumping is something black people do. Most whites don't even try.

4

A DIVIDED LANDSCAPE

Where We All Want to Be

White and black Americans often have fixed assumptions about what the world looks like on the other side of the color line. In this stereotyped vision, white America is new and shiny; black America is old and shabby. White America is spacious and clean; black America is crowded and strewn with trash. Well-to-do neighborhoods are assumed to be white; poor and run-down big-city neighborhoods are assumed to be black. And even if we know these fixed notions are overly broad and often wrong—white America can be shabby, too, and black America opulent—we are trapped in them. They are powerfully reinforced by images on television or in the movies, which tell us that crossing the color line can be unwise and dangerous.

Crossing the color line is not always an easy thing to do. For many Americans even getting near the color line requires effort; millions of whites and blacks live many miles from the point where their lives might intersect. To each other, they are out of sight, out of mind. The forces of race—or the rule of the color line—have functioned so well as to propel blacks and whites in opposite directions. Meanwhile, the images we have of each other's worlds work to keep us apart, so much so that millions of white and black Americans would need to battle their own basic instincts to bring themselves closer together. At times, we move in opposite directions without even realizing it is happening, without understanding the forces—try suspicion of cities for one—that are dividing us.

For some whites, a look of urban decay warns that dangers lurk in the shadows. For some black Americans, a look of suburban newness or space warns that cops or surveillance cameras will be watching for those who don't fit into these surroundings. To many whites, graffiti-ridden walls, abandoned and trashed-out buildings, gaping windows, and rundown houses announce the presence of black people or the idea that "that's how *they* live." Some white Americans—and even journalists, which is no surprise—make this assumption, and a few journalists insist on it. After a screening of Spike Lee's *Do the Right Thing* at the 1989 Cannes Film Festival, *USA Today*'s gossip columnist, who is white, vigorously protested at Lee's press conference that Lee, who is black, had misrepresented black neighborhoods. "It's too clean," she proclaimed. "There's no garbage, no drugs. Where's the rape? Where's the crack?"

This was a demonstration of stereotypical assumptions at work. Yet some scenes in my Washington, D.C., neighborhood might easily come up to her expectations—corners where idle men congregate near dilapidated liquor stores or take-out eateries in which the proprietors face the public from behind bulletproof shields. Other nearby stores are boarded up, a few turned into storefront churches.

By contrast, much in the suburban sprawl of white America usually looks arrestingly different: fresh, new, verdant. This white America, so new, clean, and spacious, it dazzles the eye—a world of serpentine streets, plastic shutters, atrium foyers, minivans, and lawns so lush they seem artificial. Much in my neighborhood is worn and shabby by this measure. And this wonderful, modern white America doesn't have street-corner gatherings or obvious signs of unemployment, either. This white America of the newest malls doesn't have its alcoholics, drug addicts, or poor in plain view. Sometimes this white America appears to have no evident problems at all, while back in my neighborhood, all of life's possibilities, both good and bad, are on public parade.

Still, nothing more upsets some of my black friends, including those who live in million-dollar homes, than suggestions that race determines the way things look on the American landscape, especially when contrary examples—black neighborhoods that look upscale or white neighborhoods that look rundown—are easy enough to find. But assumptions about race, place, and economics are so fundamental to our thinking that it is difficult to extract the image of urban poverty from white thinking about black Americans; a fundamental and undeniable economic disparity is so much a part of what we see. Yet we also have an odd tradition of not seeing this reality—or rather of romanticizing that the poor are somehow sometimes better off.

Given the choice of living in a world where the per capita income was $12,351 in 1997, as it was in black America, or a world where it was $20,425, the white average, why would anyone choose the former over the latter? Black neighborhoods are supposed to be more dangerous, too, but many Americans, white and black, somehow manage to imagine that black America is teeming with sound, life, and good times. On occasion, whites can seem a bit jealous. By comparison, white neighborhoods are supposed to be clean and peaceful but maybe too plastic to represent life lived to the fullest.

Romanticizing like this allows those with comfortable lives to fancy that poverty is ennobling or that the good times had by those who have little are much more richly enjoyed than the costly pleasures of the well-to-do. We alter life's balance sheet in such notions, as if to claim it is more rewarding to be poor. And it's often supposed that black people are having naughty fun, too. Whites are sometimes stereotypically convinced that life in black America is unrestrained by laws and social niceties; it is a libido-driven underworld of drugs, prostitutes, and stolen goods, with floating crap games on every corner. But to fancy that crime and sin reigns in black America does not explain all those churches that are so much in evidence, too.

But black people also contribute to these romanticized views. Some of my black neighbors insist that life in our neighborhood is more *real*, which makes it a refuge from the manner, forms, and pretenses of the white people or their tiresome behaviors and whims. That means that my neighbors consider themselves more sincere and straightforward than people on the blocks west of 13th Street, where white America starts. There's also more noise and loud voices in my neighborhood—even at 3:00 and 4:00 A.M.

Romantic Notions About Black America	
Black America	**White America**
real	phony
poor	rich
honest	dishonest
	(continued)

Romantic Notions About Black America (continued)	
Black America	**White America**
used	brand-new
variety	sameness
feeling	unfeeling
soul	soulless
sound	silence
struggle	ease
city	suburbs
turmoil	peace
danger	safety
alive	dead

Over the years, white people have looked from their distance at this world of black people and occasionally concluded that something is missing from white experience. Some whites believe that there is not enough hard reality in their lives to produce the blues or whatever other artistic greatness might emerge if life were more of a challenge. This starry-eyed notion surely fueled white enthusiasm for rap music in the 1990s, and in the 1950s, the noted beatnik writer Jack Kerouac succumbed to such musings in *On the Road*. "At lilac evening," he wrote, "I walked with every muscle aching among the lights of 27th and Welton in the Denver colored section, wishing I were a Negro, feeling that the best the white world had offered was not enough ecstasy for me, not enough life, joy, kicks, darkness, music, not enough night."

What a perverse form of envy this was! James Baldwin, the noted black writer, called Kerouac's reveries "absolute nonsense . . . and offensive nonsense at that." Baldwin noted, too, that Kerouac would be hooted out of the hall if he read these words before a black audience.

Yet—again, odd as it may seem—whites can feel left out, uninitiated into the mysteries that are supposed to accompany black experience. Sensing this, whites believe the world of black Americans is endlessly exotic. Many whites assume that black people know dark, esoteric secrets that whites do not—things like how to smoke crack, run a drug gang, find a prostitute, or cast a voodoo spell—as if such information automatically comes with being black.

Black people—any black people—are supposed to know lingo and low-life lore from which whites are excluded. Of course, this assumption is ridiculous, but white journalists often turn to black colleagues for information on matters pertaining to poverty or street culture. And their black colleagues, frequently products of the middle class, often don't have a clue. Whites often believe black people talk about their secrets when they gather in the school or office cafeteria. And it makes these conversations seem all the more distant and forbidding to whites who watch and imagine what is going on.

Fancies like these only serve to deepen the belief that blacks and whites come from different worlds. But there is, in fact, a fundamental divide:

- 56 percent of black Americans live in cities—they are city people.
- 70 percent of whites live in the suburbs or in rural America— they are not city people.

Often blacks and whites *do* come from different worlds, which can produce differences in attitude and lifestyle. One world, the suburbs, where 52 percent of whites live, is a much whiter place than the national norm, with a white-to-black ratio of about 12 to 1. And cities are much blacker than the national average, with a white-to-black ratio of 3 to 1.

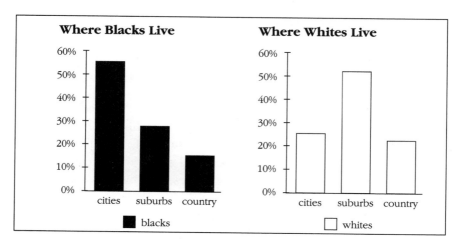

City dwellers and noncity dwellers have a long history of looking at each other with suspicion. We would assume that white suburbanites and white city dwellers might see things differently, not to mention differences that might occur between white suburbanites and black city dwellers. Mistrust of cities is an American tradition, as old as the Founding Fathers. Thomas Jefferson believed that virtue was more likely to flower among those who communed with nature and corruption was more likely a product of city life. Jefferson noted, "Commercial cities are as different in sentiment and character from country as any distinct nation."

We assume that nature—or that which is "natural"—is good; cities are poisoned, corrupt, and artificial. We assume country life breeds honesty and hard work, cities corruption and crime. This view of cities is well-documented in *Batman* movies, where all manner of twisted values lurked in the shadows of Gotham City.

The vehement disdain with which many Americans view cities is shocking. Many suburbanites swear they wouldn't live in a city. Others proudly state they don't even visit cities and wonder about the sanity of those who do. Saying you live in Washington, D.C., often raises eyebrows in America's heartland, because Washington—*black* Washington beyond the marble monuments—is often considered a strange and scary place.

Do these impressions of cities involve race? Surely the "darkness" of city residents—real or imagined—is intermixed with notions about city corruption. The habitat of noncity dwellers, which includes 70 percent of the white population, is wonderfully spacious, with trees, ball fields, and acres of free parking, while the habitat of city dwellers is crowded, with more people per square yard and tough competition to play at the nearest basketball hoop. Inevitably, city dwellers develop a different sense of personal space from that of noncity dwellers. Crossing the frontier from one to the other triggers predictable discomforts.

Cities, to noncity dwellers, teem with people living in close proximity, almost on top of one another. In black neighborhoods, children are to be seen everywhere, because—remember this?—the black population of America is much younger than the white population. Cities can represent a threat of clashing personal space to noncity dwellers of whatever color; some will surely hope to escape this press of strangers quickly. And race, meanwhile, might only exacerbate such discomfort.

On the other hand, the very spaciousness of white-majority suburbs has its own daunting aspect to those more accustomed to the press of people. And if suburbia is a whiter place, black Americans are likely to sense themselves more isolated there. But it may be difficult for whites to appreciate how their world could be intimidating to outsiders; after all, white America is where they feel most comfortable.

But from this spaciousness of white America, black Americans draw various conclusions about what white people are like. In a world where the human interaction is less immediate, it is easy to wonder: Where are all the people? Where is the interaction? Where are the laughter, the noise, and the fun? Why is everything so quiet?

It might seem, too, that there is something hidden and secretive about much of white America or that hidden surveillance cameras are watching. And understand that this sensation is no paranoia, because the police and the surveillance cameras are indeed watching. Yet whites sometimes scoff when blacks claim whites are spying. Some whites even cite this as crazy, forgetting the impression whites get when they find themselves alone in a group of blacks or in a black neighborhood. In those moments, whites experience that same sensation—of being watched.

White America can be truly daunting in its sweep and grandeur. It is the wonder of the 20th-century world. In its upward reaches, in the gleaming towers that grace the skylines of our cities, it might seem that the higher you go in white America, the whiter it becomes. Black people might inhabit the streets below, but the white world literally extends into the heavens. And imagine the isolation a black person is likely to encounter in these upper altitudes. Where are the black people? Often, there are none.

Similarly, pervasive whiteness has spread into office towers in the new satellite or "edge" cities, the office clusters in the suburbs and along interstate highways almost supplanting traditional cities as centers of life and commerce. Tysons Corner, Virginia, once a crossroads hamlet outside D.C., has more office space than the cities of Richmond or Baltimore, following an overall trend since the 1980s. Commerce, too, moved to the suburbs, closer to the center of the white population and farther from that of black people.

This contributes to another overlay on our thinking about race. Much in the ever-expanding universe of white America looks brandnew; much of black America looks old, worn, and secondhand. It has evolved that both blacks and whites associate white America with growth, progress, and change and black America with decay, decline, and death. What we see on the American landscape causes us to assume that whites build, as if that were their nature, and blacks destroy, as if that were theirs.

In fact, millions of black Americans live in hand-me-down neighborhoods that were once white. At the same time, the great movie palaces and elegant downtown department stores, once the showpieces of white America, are boarded up. Americans of all races now shop and go to the movies at suburban megamalls and cineplexes. The abandonment of center cities is another invitation to conclude that decline accompanies blacks wherever they may go. Black people are similarly blamed for the gutted, windowless hulks of public housing, invitations to conclude that efforts to help black people are a waste of money, too.

Across the nation, many white Americans believe that black America cannot be helped—that welfare, public housing, and antipoverty efforts produce contrary results. And a simple drive across almost any city will likely fuel these negative impressions. It may even be that many whites see the blight of American cities as evidence of the character flaws of black people, adding a new indictment to an already ominous list.

Millions of white Americans tend to consider themselves refugees, as if they were driven from cities by the coming of black hordes. Many white Americans grew up in neighborhoods that are now black; they look back upon idyllic youth, believing that black people were among the forces to expel them from Eden. Such tales are often insinuated: "It was a nice neighborhood, full of decent people, until *they* moved in."

What is usually overlooked in these reveries is that most of these neighborhoods, constructed in building booms between 1890 and 1910 or between 1920 and 1929, were declining before whites left. And then powerful forces involving race, the automobile, and changing times intervened. One such force was called white flight.

No one ordered whites to abandon their old neighborhoods, but they left in a rush, sometimes much like the exodus that produced black Harlem in the early 1900s, as described by the noted black writer James Weldon Johnson:

They took fright, they became panic stricken, they ran amuck. Their conduct could be compared to that of a community in the Middle Ages fleeing before an epidemic of the black plague, except for the fact that here the reasons were not so sound. But these people did not stop to reason, they did not stop to ask why they did what they were doing, or what would happen if they didn't do it. The presence of a single colored family in a block, regardless of the fact that they might be well-bred people, with sufficient means to buy their new home, was a signal for precipitate flight. The stampeded whites actually deserted house after house and block after block.

And then what happened? With the exodus of white people, the basic economic circumstances of these communities changed drastically. Banks were less likely to grant loans for homes and businesses, which led to further decline. As recently as 1988, the *Atlanta Journal-Constitution* won a Pulitzer Prize for articles on the "redlining" that made black neighborhoods off-limits for loans. Whites in the Atlanta area were five times more likely than blacks to get home mortgages, and nationwide, they were twice as likely.

Money flight of this sort—call it green flight—meant that poverty soon became concentrated in cites as everyone who could, including the black middle class, headed to the new suburbs, making "housing starts" a signal of the nation's economic health. So to the degree that whites ran away from black people in their neighborhoods and moved into new houses in the suburbs, fear about race was even seen as contributing to the nation's economic vitality.

The powerful push of white flight and green flight transformed the landscape of America in ways that are still rarely recognized. In fact, it made the North more physically segregated by race than the old South. Northern whites truly ran from black people as no one did elsewhere.

A 1976 Detroit Area Study by sociologists at the University of Michigan is often cited as evidence of the psychological dynamics—or the herd instinct—of white flight. According to this study, white flight begins when a neighborhood becomes 8 percent black and keeps on going thereafter. This result even suggests that residential inte-

gration cannot succeed in America, because as more blacks arrive in
a neighborhood, increasing numbers of whites will leave and fewer
whites will move in.

For example, in the Detroit study, 7 percent of whites said they will
leave when the neighborhood is 8 percent black, and 24 percent of
whites will not move into a neighborhood that is 8 percent black. This
is how the 8 percent figure came to be known as the *tipping point* at
which white flight begins. Then, once the neighborhood is 8 percent
black, the factors are present that will eventually make the neighborhood all black. Whites start to leave, then when the neighborhood
becomes 21 percent black, 24 percent of the whites will leave. Then
when it becomes 57 percent black, 64 percent of whites will try to
leave. And other whites will not replace them, because by that point,
84 percent of whites would refuse to move into a neighborhood that
is 57 percent black. Eventually, the neighborhood becomes almost all
black, and integration will have been, as a Chicago alderman once
reportedly claimed, "the hiatus between when the first blacks arrive and
the last whites leave."

The Neighborhood Tipping Point: When Whites . . .			
	Are uncomfortable	**Try to move**	**Won't move in**
8% black	24%	7%	27%
21% black	42%	24%	50%
36% black	57%	41%	73%

The tipping-point theory was very bad news for those who hoped
that integration could proceed quietly and that we would all some
day wake up in an integrated America. If the tipping-point theory is
correct, we will keep waking up each day to an increasingly more
segregated America. Some might argue, however, that the Detroit study
is old, and we've all changed since 1976. But other studies have found
similar patterns. One, in Cleveland neighborhoods where antiblack
sentiment was strong, found a tipping point starting at 3 percent.

It also may surprise some readers to hear that the partitioning of
America is now more extreme in the North than in the South where segregation was once the law. In the North, white flight propelled whites
and blacks farther apart, leaving a greater actual distance between the
black and white worlds. Meanwhile, segregation in the South evolved

in circumstances under which the black and white worlds were often closer together or overlapping. In D.C., a formerly segregated city, many black families lived in alleys while white families lived on the surrounding blocks; despite the legal strictures of segregation, blacks and whites actually lived in closer physical proximity.

Currently, 9 of the top 10 most segregated metropolitan areas in America—that is, with blacks concentrated in the cities and whites in the suburbs—are in the North. They are Gary-Hammond, Indiana; Detroit; York, Pennsylvania; Buffalo; Syracuse, New York; Lima, Ohio; Youngstown-Warren, Ohio; Rochester, New York; and Lake County, Illinois. Chattanooga, Tennessee, is the lone exception. This Northern-style segregation, sometimes referred to as "chocolate cities, vanilla suburbs," also produced a phenomenon called "hypersegregation," a term coined by sociologists Douglas S. Massey and Nancy A. Denton in their book *American Apartheid.*

Pay attention to this description, particularly if you believe integration is working or that blacks and whites are coming closer together:

> Typical inhabitants of one of these ghettos are not only unlikely to come into contact with whites within the particular neighborhood where they live; even if they traveled to the adjacent neighborhood they would still be unlikely to see a white face; and if they went to the next neighborhood beyond that, no whites would be there either. People growing up in such an environment have little direct experience with the culture, norms, and behaviors of the rest of American society and few social contacts with members of other racial groups. Ironically, within a large, diverse, and highly mobile post-industrial society such as the United States, blacks living in the heart of the ghetto are among the most isolated people on earth.

By the authors' reckoning, large sectors of Atlanta, Baltimore, Buffalo, Chicago, Cleveland, Dallas, Detroit, Gary-Hammond, Indianapolis, Kansas City, Los Angeles, Milwaukee, New York, Newark, Philadelphia, and St. Louis are hypersegregated. And these same 16 cities alone contain 35 percent of the total U.S. black population. Millions of other black Americans live in largely segregated cities but in black neighborhoods not quite as totally isolated as to qualify as hypersegregated. "Racial segregation," say Massey and Denton, "still constitutes a fundamental cleavage in American society."

And how are *race relations* in hypersegregated neighborhoods? There aren't any. Whites and blacks do not interact in these circumstances. Whites are so rarely seen in many black neighborhoods that residents assume whites only bring trouble—they must be cops or someone looking for drugs and prostitutes or something of that nature. What else would white people be doing in a black neighborhood?

Washington, D.C., my hometown, is not on the list of hypersegregated cities, but there are vast sections of the city where you rarely see a white face. It should be noted, too, that the description of hypersegregated neighborhoods might, if the words *black* and *white* are switched, apply to large sectors of white America. Many whites also live in a separate world in which they are unlikely to come into contact with blacks; even if they traveled to the adjacent neighborhoods they would still be unlikely to see a black face.

Overall, millions of black and white Americans reside in worlds so separate that they might as well be citizens of foreign countries—black and white America can *look* like foreign countries, too. Indeed, black and white attitudes may actually be shaped by the degree to which blacks and whites actually think of each other as foreigners—that is, people who come from some other, strange place. If, for example, white Americans think of black Americans as foreigners, even in some small way, then white Americans might feel greater cause to protest affirmative action. What kind of country would pass over its own citizens to grant jobs or other opportunities to foreign nationals? That wouldn't make sense.

Meanwhile, both blacks and whites say—or tell pollsters—that they would prefer to live in neighborhoods that are more integrated, even if they don't actually do so. In a phenomenon that needs explanation (because it may not mean exactly what it seems), most black Americans say they would prefer a neighborhood that is half white and half black.

What Neighborhood Do Blacks Want?		
1st choice	**2nd choice**	**5th choice**
all black 12%	5%	27%
70% black 14%	55%	2%
50% black 63%	20%	73%

In that same Detroit study, 63 percent of black respondents made a neighborhood that is 50 percent black, 50 percent white their first preference. As their second choice, 55 percent listed a neighborhood that is 70 percent black, 30 percent white. But 66 percent of the black respondents also listed an "all-white" neighborhood as their *least* favorite choice, so bear that in mind, too. While most black Americans say they would prefer a neighborhood that is half white, they strongly want to avoid a neighborhood that is too white. In 1989, more than a decade after the Detroit study, 71 percent of black respondents in a *USA Today* poll said they would prefer a neighborhood that is "half and half," and only 4 percent said they would prefer a "mostly white" neighborhood.

So what's going on? Most black Americans appear to want whites around—but not too many whites. And their choices indicate that a perfectly integrated neighborhood with 6.4 whites for each black person would be too many whites for most black tastes. But why the distinction? Why do so many black Americans say they want a neighborhood that is half white, then reject a neighborhood that is any whiter than that?

Possibly, the choice being made here is not as much about living near white people as it is about gaining access to the quality of services whites are believed to get. Wanting to live in a 50-50 neighborhood does not reflect a fondness for white people as much as a desire to live in a neighborhood with better houses, stores, schools, and services. But to get such a neighborhood, black Americans still don't want a neighborhood that is so overwhelmingly white that they will feel isolated or like outsiders.

Whites, on the other hand, are less clear about what they want. In the 1989 *USA Today* poll, 41 percent of whites said they would prefer a neighborhood that is "half and half," while 40 percent said they would prefer a "mostly white" neighborhood. No whites said they wanted to live in a "mostly black" neighborhood.

Meanwhile, because so many Americans, black and white, say they want a 50-50 neighborhood, that option bears examination. Actual 50-50 neighborhoods are rare, so all those who say they prefer a 50-50 neighborhood would have a hard time finding one. For example, the 41 percent of whites who say they want a 50-50 neighborhood would be 89 million white people, and the 71 percent of blacks who want a 50-50 neighborhood would be 23 million black people. And if 89 million whites shared neighborhoods with 23 million blacks, the average result would be 80 percent white and 20 percent black, not 50-50.

Applying similar calculations to a 1996 ABC *Nightline* poll, in which 12 percent of whites and 33 percent of blacks said they live in neighborhoods that are 50-50, indicates that somebody must be mistaken. If the resultant 26 million whites shared neighborhoods with 11 million blacks, the average neighborhoods would be 70 percent white, again not 50-50.

And where do black and white Americans actually live? And how does this reflect on the possibility of contact along the color line? In 1990, 35.6 percent of white Americans lived in census tracts that were less than 1 percent black, and 47.1 percent lived in tracts that are between 1 and 10 percent black. Hence, 82.7 percent of the white population lived in census tracts where blacks are underrepresented in terms of the national average.

At the same time, 15.6 percent of whites lived in tracts that were 10 to 50 percent black, and 1.7 percent lived in tracts that were more than 50 percent black, meaning that whites who live in black-majority neighborhoods were relatively rare. And many are city dwellers who do not necessarily have high degrees of social contact with their black neighbors; their social lives can still be very white.

Among black Americans, 53.9 percent lived in tracts that are more than 50 percent black and another 12.9 percent lived in tracts that were between 10 and 50 percent black. Only 13.7 percent of black people lived in neighborhoods that are 10 percent black.

These statistics showed that slightly more blacks were moving into white-majority neighborhoods, although very few moved into extremely white neighborhoods. A 1997 Gallup survey also found that only 8 percent of whites said they would "object" if blacks moved into their neighborhood "in great numbers," a percentage that had dropped way down from the 80 percent in 1958 who said they would object.

Two other trends deserve note. One is that white flight and racial fears were not the only factors emptying American cities. Some smaller cities are dying at the core with no black people in sight. The downtown areas have declined and commercial buildings are empty, not because of black people—these cities don't have many black people—but because of the automobile. Commerce and vitality left these cities—author Witold Rybczynski cites the case of Plattsburgh, New York, in *City Life*—for malls outside of town where there was easier access and plenty of parking. Black people had nothing to do with it.

The other trend is that black people are also leaving cities; a black flight, too, has been taking place in cities like D.C. Race is less the issue in this trend than economic class. Black families, too, want space, newness, better schools, less crime, and green grass. The first sign of this exodus comes in the choice of where to shop, which becomes another important step in the flight of money from black neighborhoods.

Black people are the first to assume that the stores and branch offices in black neighborhoods are inferior. Even when supermarkets and department stores are part of national chains, blacks assume that the best goods will be sent to the suburbs where white people shop. The tomatoes will be redder and the lettuce greener—it's as simple as that. The stores, of course, deny this premise, but it still persuades many black Americans to drive past stores in their own neighborhoods to shop in the suburbs.

Meanwhile, whites occasionally make their own foolish admissions like one D.C. bank president who assumed black people prefer rundown neighborhoods and trashed-looking stores. Sound odd? When the *Washington Post* in 1993 asked why bank branches in black neighborhoods don't look as nice as in the ones in white neighborhoods, the president replied: "People in those neighborhoods wouldn't go into a plush office. That's an intimidating environment."

Such thinking helps the green flight along. Believing that suburban stores are better—and seeing that whites won't invest in black neighborhoods—black Americans have all the more reason to shop elsewhere. Stores in black neighborhoods do less business, and some eventually shut down. Other businesses hesitate to locate in black neighborhoods because the commercial environment looks bleak. Eventually, the perception that stores are better in white America helps turn much of black America into a commercial wasteland of little more than liquor stores and hair salons, the situation in my neighborhood.

In cities like D.C., thousands of black families have followed the money flight into growing black suburbs like Prince George's County, Maryland, which now includes subdivisions described as "a showcase of African American affluence," where homes sell for a million dollars or more. Prince George's County also has malls that look like their counterparts in white America, only almost everyone you see shopping is black. And this suburb represents a speedy transition from white to black. Prince George's County voted for onetime segregationist George Wallace for president in 1968; blacks became a majority in Prince George's County in 1990, and only a few years later it is hard to find a white face in certain malls and housing developments there. Whites have vanished. Gone. Disappeared.

Meanwhile, roughly 30 percent of black Americans, about 10 million people, now live in the suburbs, but this figure can be misleading, because some of these "suburbs" are themselves decaying cities such as Camden, New Jersey, outside Philadelphia, and East St. Louis, Illinois, near St. Louis. And nationwide, black Americans lag behind Asians and Hispanics in "suburbanization"—the rate at which they are moving out of cities toward the new centers of American life.

But even the growth of black suburbs joins other trends that appear to be pulling blacks and whites farther apart. The suburbs, where most whites live, are now their own self-contained universe. Suburbanites don't need cities anymore, and many are highly pleased with this result. New traffic patterns have emerged in major metropolitan areas, with more motorists traveling between the suburbs than going to and from the big cities. Megamalls have replaced downtown avenues as America's main streets.

This suburban growth and commerce has, of course, been theoretically open to black Americans, even as the epicenter of American life shifted farther from the cities where most blacks still lived. So black Americans must now travel to the suburbs for jobs and opportunities, and the unhappy result is evident on city street corners as more black Americans become disconnected from the mainstream economy.

It also appears to be an illusion that easy transportation from cities to suburbs is readily available, because many suburbanites no longer need or want quick transportation links to cities. Some suburbanites suspect that transit links to cities only bring city problems closer. And they want city problems to stay where they are.

In the 1990s, when new Metro subway stops opened in suburban D.C., they were accompanied by news reports about residents who feared the trains would bring more crime into their neighborhoods. When a station opened in Hyattsville, Maryland, in 1993, one resident told the *Washington Post* he was putting the family home up for sale. "I just don't know what the new station is going to bring," he said.

Meanwhile, supermarket and movie theater chains have all but abandoned many cities, while some suburban malls try to discourage black customers. This exclusionary phenomenon occasionally makes news, as in the sad case of Cynthia Wiggins, a 17-year-old black woman who was crushed by a dump truck in 1997, while attempting to cross a busy highway on her way to work at the Walden Galleria Mall outside Buffalo. After her death, the mall was accused of deliberately blocking access to buses from black Buffalo neighborhoods, forcing

Wiggins to cross the highway where she was killed. After protests, the No. 6 bus from Buffalo was rerouted in 1998 to stop at the mall.

But theoretically, millions of Americans will eventually be able to live wherever they choose, work at home, and conduct their business electronically. So where are they choosing to live? Demographers reported a miniexodus of whites from crowded states that just happen—by coincidence?—to have a higher proportion of blacks and other minorities to states that have lots of space and—coincidence again?—fewer blacks and minorities.

The six fastest-growing states in the mid-1990s were all in the Rocky Mountain West: Nevada, Arizona, Idaho, Utah, Colorado, and New Mexico. Utah and Idaho, for example, have black populations of less than 1 percent. *USA Today* smelled a trend: "Something else is happening, too—a kind of national white flight away from states with large numbers of immigrants and minorities, such as California, Texas, Illinois, New York, New Jersey, and Massachusetts."

William Frey, a noted University of Michigan demographer, called it "flight from diversity, economic competition, housing costs." At almost the same time, another white exodus was reported from suburbia to small-town America. *Time* put the story on its cover in 1997.

In still another newsmaking development, more Americans were choosing to live in gated, fenced, or walled communities with sentry posts to monitor who comes and goes. Gated communities were home to 8 million Americans, and the president of the American Institute of Architects termed it a "moat and drawbridge and fortress America mentality." Even *The Bell Curve* noted that an "invisible migration" was soon likely to isolate the experiences or the social milieu of the educated and affluent from those of more limited means.

Yet none of this movement was all that spectacular. Nothing here sounds like the panic that drove whites from Harlem. Who might notice that blacks and whites are heading in directions that take them farther apart? There is something subtle, almost secretive, about this trend. It is too low key to be described as ominous or wrong. Yet it is just that; the common ground of American experience is quietly shrinking.

5

TUNING EACH OTHER OUT

Segregation in the Information Age

The 1990s introduced a new dimension to the racial divide: now blacks and whites weren't even watching the same TV shows. The information age, as it was heralded, brought wondrous new choices in news and entertainment and with them new opportunities for blacks and whites to tune each other out of the picture, particularly the video picture. This new age raised the possibility that America might soon have electronic cultures as separated according to race as are most neighborhoods where blacks and whites live. Not only was the American landscape divided and segregated, soon the airwaves would be as well.

This possibility arose from technological and commercial developments that could hardly seem ominous: an expanding marketplace for ideas that included TV, radio, publishing, movies, and the Internet. But as the new options proliferated, it also appeared that the common ground that blacks and whites shared in American culture might be shrinking. From 1993 on, blacks largely ignored the most popular TV shows among white viewers, and the shows blacks most preferred were notably absent from lists of the most popular shows among whites. *Seinfeld*, *Frasier*, and *Friends* were huge hits among whites, but black viewers were unmoved, while whites similarly tuned out *Living Single* and *New York Undercover*, the top shows in black homes.

The Clinton campaign saw its own advantages in the newly segregated airways in the 1996 election. "President Clinton," the *Washington Post* reported, "has quietly launched a unique television campaign aimed at black voters."

The curious word here was *quietly*—quietly to whom? Certainly not to black voters, the targeted audience; *quietly* had to refer to white voters, who were not likely to encounter these ads for reasons of the newly divided airwaves. "Clinton is exploiting the mushrooming number of cable networks in an attempt to pinpoint his message to a specific group," the *Post* said.

In truth, much of American life was becoming like that—a land of messages targeted to specific groups. Clinton's ads appeared on the cable Black Entertainment Network, on the syndicated TV show *America's Black Forum*, and on the African American Urban Radio Network. In each case, it was assumed that black Americans would be tuning in and white Americans would not. So Clinton could promise aid to black colleges—or whatever—and whites wouldn't know the difference. The color line was making its mark in the information age as well.

From radio talk shows to the Internet, the very technology that expanded our choices can just as easily isolate us from each other. When whites tune to "white" programs or Internet sites and blacks tune to "black" ones, black and white Americans are sharing ever less of a common body of information and experience.

This development, too, might seem to run contrary to conventional assumptions about the information age. We are likely to believe that the world is shrinking, that people are being brought closer together and that this closeness will produce better understanding. But what if we're tuning each other out instead? The proliferation of choices allows and even encourages us to take refuge in social, intellectual, or political isolation—tuning in what we like and tuning out what we don't. And the result is that Americans are even less threatened by the prospect of having to change their minds about anything or defend their point of view against challenges. Instead they can barricade themselves in ideological enclaves with conservatives listening to conservatives, liberals to liberals, whites to whites, and blacks to blacks. And when disturbing or opposing points of view arise, we can simply switch the channel.

Soon, there may be less of a media mainstream; it will be replaced by a flood of tributaries. From an era of the great general-interest (and white-oriented) magazines like *Life, Saturday Evening Post*, or *Colliers* has come a multitude of specialty magazines aimed at audiences defined by age, income, special interests—and race. These days, most white Americans may not realize the degree to which white faces are unlikely to appear—not even by accident—in classy black magazines such as *Essence* or *Ebony*.

If anything, these magazines show black people in their own world, and it is definitely a black peoples' world, too—upscale, stylish, engaging, with a full range of concerns, interests, and joys. Glancing though these magazines, you will see that white people (not that they are needed or missed) are a minority.

But publishing is only one example of increasing media segregation. The major TV networks are presumed to be the new common ground of popular culture. But their audiences are also declining as options proliferate on cable and satellite-dish TV. So the U.S. citizenry that watched *Roots* together in January 1977 was no longer watching the same shows at all in the late 1990s. Whites can watch the Nashville Network, where it's rare to see a black face, and blacks can tune in to the Black Entertainment Network, where white faces are few. And blacks and whites are in their own worlds.

This segregation in TV viewing, however, is not an isolated case of a black-white divide in our tastes. Where are the bonds of common interests that bring blacks and whites together? Black Americans are notably absent in the audiences at symphony halls or stock car races and much else in American life. What is more American than baseball? some might ask. Yet where have the black fans gone for this game, which once was a black passion?

One in five major league players may be black, but black Americans are unaccountably missing in the stands. In 1991, the *Boston Globe* counted fans in major-league ballparks, and black fans were few and far between: 0.2 percent of the fans at Boston's Fenway Park; 0.8 percent at Milwaukee's County Stadium; 2.2 percent at Detroit's Tiger Stadium; 2 percent at Atlanta's Fulton County Stadium; 2 percent at St. Louis's Busch Stadium; 1.6 percent at Cincinnati's Riverfront Stadium; and 3.1 percent at New York's Shea Stadium.

These are shocking figures for the game that once symbolized, beginning with Jackie Robinson, the ability of black Americans to succeed alongside white Americans. But not only are blacks staying away from big-league ballparks; the game is also dying among black young-sters in big cities, replaced by basketball dreams in most cases. Black youngsters aren't playing baseball; they aren't thinking about base-ball; many know nothing about the game, as evidenced by the fact that many high schools in D.C. and other cities gave up fielding teams, because of so little interest.

At Eastern High, near my house, the coach was forced to field a team of total novices. When practice began in the spring, most of his players didn't know how a double play worked, he said. In another age, not knowing how a double play works was considered a sign of social and cultural isolation; it is quickly becoming a norm in black neighborhoods.

Elsewhere, in the worlds of music and entertainment, the tendency has also been to categorize audience preferences ever more narrowly— and by race—increasing the possibilities that whites will have minimal contact with what blacks are doing and vice versa. *Billboard* magazine charts on popular music have long been racially segregated, so much so that the term *crossover* was coined to describe artists whose appeal crossed the color line.

Thanks to *Billboard*, "r&b," standing for rhythm and blues, is cur-rently the official term for "black" in the music industry. And how this came about is an odd and tormented journey across our thinking about race that is recounted in the 1990 book *Split Image: African Americans in the Mass Media* by Jannette L. Dates and William Barlow:

> When the music industry confronted the issue of r&b artists selling pop in the 1940s, their work was still listed as "race" music. As the music began to cross over into the white market, however, it was decided a more palatable term was needed. Record companies toyed with labels like "ebony" and "sepia" for a while, but these, too, were obviously distinctions of color, not musical style. Eventually *rhythm & blues* became the ac-cepted term. The rhythm & blues charts were actually discon-tinued altogether from the end of 1963 until the beginning of 1965 and replaced with the term "soul" in 1969. In some ways, the industry came full circle when the soul charts were renamed "black" in 1982. At the time, *Billboard* felt that "'soul' was too limited a term to define the diversity of musical styles appear-ing on the chart, and that 'black' was a better tribute to the

music's origins." Ultimately, however, the term "black music" was vulnerable to the same criticism as the term "race music" four decades earlier. Thus, in 1990, *Billboard* went back to the future of 1949 and retitled the chart, once again, "rhythm and blues," explaining that it was "becoming less acceptable to identify music in racial terms."

Black preferences—and spending power—are reflected in *Billboard* charts for r&b and rap and are a major influence on charts for jazz albums, "contemporary" jazz albums, blues, and reggae—all categories in which black artists are always a significant presence. But this strict segregation of musical tastes in the charts is further projected into the so-called formats of radio stations, which further limit explorations across the musical color line. Fans of country music are unlikely to hear black artists, and for fans of rhythm and blues, most country stars might as well live on another planet. Yet once again, this musical apartheid is created out of nothing more sinister than an expanding marketplace and a proliferation of choices. So who is likely to say there is something sinister going on?

An expanding marketplace clearly affected trends in TV viewing. The golden age of network TV viewing as the nation's cultural common ground appears to be over. This is not to say that Americans don't watch TV. In fact, black Americans watch much more TV than white Americans. In black households, sets are turned on for an average of 10 hours and 6 minutes a day as compared to 6 hours and 47 minutes in the average white household.

Theoretically, during more than 3 hours each day in which blacks Americans have their TV sets turned on, whites are doing something else. This fact also means blacks are considered the more loyal TV audience, but I suspect this data *actually* means that the TV set in many black homes is turned on even when no one is watching. Rather, it is like keeping a window open just in case something interesting happens outside.

Meanwhile for whites, what they see on TV causes them to believe America is darkening. This is curious. Whites see blacks on TV shows, including sports, dramas, and sitcoms, and consider this to be evidence that blacks are doing very well economically or that there is no shortage of opportunities for black people in America. And they're getting some of this from sitcoms! But the impression that blacks are "all over the place" on TV may be a fair comparison to past eras when blacks were nowhere to be seen on TV.

For example, the black presence on network TV in the 1950s was limited to two comedies, *Beulah* (1950–53) and *Amos 'n' Andy* (1951–53); the character Rochester on the *Jack Benny Show* (1950–77); and two variety shows, the *Billy Daniels Show* (1952) and the *Nat King Cole Show* (1956–57). That was it.

In the 1970s and 1980s, black shows became part of the cultural common ground, and this was even more so in the 1980s, when *The Cosby Show* was number 1 for five years in a row. Also note that in the 1985–86 TV season, 15 of the 20 most popular shows in black households were also in the top 20 among white households. This, too, is evidence of common ground. But in 1993, the season after the original *Cosby Show* left the air, black and white preferences in TV viewing veered in opposite directions. Suddenly, none of the 10 most-watched shows in black households were in or near the top 10 in white households.

Syndicated columnist Julienne Malveaux, who is black, called the new development "another kind of American apartheid," but the split in TV viewing habits was not otherwise widely noted or considered earthshaking. "Part of it is the general trend in race relations in this country," noted Robert Johnson, founder of the Black Entertainment Network. "People are a little bit more separate in their racial interaction than they were in the 1970s and '80s. People are identifying more with their own culture and ethnicity and feeling comfortable about doing so, without the pressure to integrate or amalgamate cultures."

In other words, blacks and whites were going their own way in TV viewing, and maybe they were heading that way in other matters, too. One might argue that Nielsen ratings described a widening gulf between blacks and whites. In 1993, the top show in black America was *Living Single*; it finished 54th in white households. The top show in white America was *Home Improvement*; it barely cracked the top 30 in black households. *Seinfeld* and *Frasier*, number 4 and number 6 in white America, failed to make the top 90 shows in black America. Whites loved *Seinfeld* and *Frasier*, treating these shows as classics. But most black Americans couldn't care less.

In 1994, a new all-white show, *Friends*, debuted in direct competition with *Living Single*. And the shows were strikingly similar: *Living*

Single was about black singles living in New York City, and *Friends* was about white singles living in New York City. But the audiences were strikingly different. *Living Single*, the number 1 show in black America, was watched by about 9 million people; and about half of them were black. *Friends* was watched by almost 14 million people, but only 3 percent were black. *Friends* finished number 17 in the yearly ratings; *Living Single* finished 54th, which perhaps only illustrates once again that whites are a much larger group to begin with.

The reason for this black-white split in viewing habits could seem obvious. If given a choice between similar shows, blacks will prefer the one with black characters and whites will prefer the one with white characters. Or is it that simple? Beyond skin color, there is an issue of how blacks and whites talk and act—the issue of different cultures—and also the matter of how blacks and whites look upon each other and the amount of experience they have dealing with people on the other side of the color line.

Since whites generally have less experience with black people than vice versa, they often find the way black people talk or gesture— or black culture—to be exotic. TV can give whites a glimpse across the color line that they don't normally get. However, blacks may not find white mannerisms and behavior quite so intriguing. Usually they've seen lots of it. Sometimes they've seen more than they want to. Maybe their office or workplace is full of it. Maybe they don't feel like watching white behavior on TV, too.

I have noticed shows that seem overwhelmingly "white" as to manners, dialogue, or inflections. In particular, this whiteness shows when characters are bossy, self-centered, or self-involved and when they don't relate to others. I also have spotted white women flipping their hair in ways some black women read as arrogance. Characters on the *Seinfeld* show often seemed particularly quirky, neurotic, awkward, funny looking, self-involved—and "white." And on several other "white" shows—*Murphy Brown* and *Frasier* come to mind—the central characters are often obnoxious or overbearing, which fits the stereotype about whites having to be in charge or the center of attention. *Seinfeld* even seemed adamant and narcissistic about being "white." To say that the show was about "nothing," as the creators claimed, matched a classic stereotype blacks have about white people that whites are boring and are always carrying on about nothing.

Then, when the "white" *Seinfeld* characters encountered black people or members of any other minority, trouble usually followed.

Eventually, *Seinfeld* was even called "post-politically correct" in the degree to which the white characters ran afoul of blacks and minorities. Yet perhaps *Seinfeld* was an interestingly accurate reflection of white experience: whites remain uneasy about encounters with blacks and unsure they will work out well. And *Seinfeld* merely reflected this uncertainty.

Clear as it was, racial polarization in TV viewing was a product of choice. The Fox Network debuted in 1990, and Fox programmers soon targeted young viewers and black viewers, the most loyal TV watchers. As a result, 5 of the top 10 shows in black households in 1993, the year of the sudden black-white split, were on Fox. In 1994–95, only 1 of the top 10 shows in black America, *Monday Night Football*, made the top 10 in white households. In 1995–96, the new number 1 in black households was *New York Undercover*; it ranked number 122 with whites, and the pattern of a widening divide seemed ever more firmly established.

In the 1996–97 season, the racial segregation of American TV took another turn. The shows on the older major networks became whiter, while two new mini-networks, Warner Brothers (WB) and United Paramount Network (UPN), targeted black viewers. Of UPN's 9 shows, 6 had all-black casts; 5 of 12 series on WB had all-black casts. Meanwhile, NBC, the number 1 rated network, was left with no black shows when *The Fresh Prince of Bel-Air* left the air in 1996. For the 1996–97 season, CBS had only one, a newly reincarnated *Cosby Show*.

Meanwhile, stark segregation predominated in sitcoms. Of the 64 sitcoms that aired in 1995–96, only 12 had racially mixed casts that included at least one regular black or white character in an otherwise all-white or all-black cast. Another 40 shows featured all-white casts, and 12 shows had all-black casts. So most shows—62.5 percent—had no black characters, while 18.7 percent of the shows had no white characters. And all this *really* means that 81.2 percent of all sitcoms, the most popular TV format, showed no interaction across the color line.

And what kind of country does a segregated lineup of TV sitcoms portray? For many white Americans, who encounter few blacks in their lives, the all-white sitcoms mirror their own reality. And the shows would seem to confirm that it is not a disgrace to have few contacts across the color line. Meanwhile, the all-black shows would similarly mirror the lives of many black Americans who live in segregated neighborhoods. And together, the predominance of all-black or all-white shows have the effect of saying that segregation is common, and there's nothing wrong with it.

Still, the general absence of black people could also be considered strikingly odd—or revealing—in some instances. Many shows, including *Seinfeld, Friends, Frasier, Cybill, Ellen, Mad About You, Murphy Brown,* and *The Nanny,* claim to be set in big cities. But the white characters rarely encounter black people. In fact, the exclusion of black faces from these "urban" comedies would seem to suggest that many whites prefer a world that doesn't include black faces. Yet these shows may also portray the actual social surroundings of many white Americans, who live in cities with large black populations but whose social contacts are overwhelmingly white.

Segregation may also predominate in sitcoms because so many of them are set in the home, where American life is likely to be most segregated. But there must be no great audience demand for depictions of integration. Or maybe there is a feeling among those who make programming decisions that black-white relations are no laughing matter.

Serious drama shows, which are often set in the workplace—hospitals, offices, etc.—tend to be integrated. Yet serious dramas of this sort also tend to draw fewer black viewers. One exception was *New York Undercover,* a police drama with a strong minority presence, which has remained at or near the top of the black ratings. In 1997–98, however, the drama *ER* joined *Monday Night Football* as the only shows in the top 20 in both black and white households, and in 1998–99, *Touched by an Angel* joined them. And there were other anomalies in the black top 20, including two all-white sitcoms, *Step by Step* and *Boy Meets World.* Experts said that these shows clicked with black audiences merely because they were on the same Friday night ABC schedule as popular all-black shows *Hangin' with Mr. Cooper* and *Family Matters.*

Despite the growing segregation of the airwaves, Americans still get much of their information about race from the media. And this connection has to be especially important for the millions of whites whose direct contacts across the color line are limited, which gives black Americans cause to wonder what images whites will get of black people on TV. Blacks also sometimes wonder about who is controlling these presentations—and what their agenda might be.

Often, both blacks and whites view the exchange of ideas and images across the color line as dangerous. Just as blacks might gauge how whites think and behave by watching TV shows, blacks also worry that common stereotypes about blacks as criminals, gang members, addicts, or welfare mothers will dominate what white Americans see. Black Americans can be particularly sensitive on this matter, and whites sometimes view it as unreasonable touchiness. But blacks also recognize that whites—particularly those who rarely encounter black people—are likely to judge all black people in terms of the images they see.

Blacks have a point. This predicament for black Americans operates within the familiar mathematics of race. Because whites are a larger group and likely have less personal experience with blacks than vice versa, it is more likely that whites will draw conclusions from what they see on TV. Back Americans also have little faith that the window of television will work in their benefit, when the reporting of urban crime alone can seem to be an endless parade of black violence or black perpetrators. Inevitably, black Americans wonder, "What will white folks think?"

The expectation of always being judged in negative terms becomes a tension of its own. Black people sense a personal stake in the way blacks are portrayed in the media, because they expect to be looked upon the same way. Many black Americans assume that the bad news about blacks will always outweigh good news and much more so than is justified by real events. They have just cause.

Most Americans, for example, remember the 1992 rioting in Los Angeles as a "black" uprising, because it followed the acquittal of white police accused of beating black motorist Rodney King. Since the 1960s, most Americans identify rioting as something black people do, but it also happened that some of the most shocking images from the L.A. riot, such as the beating of white trucker Reginald Denny, involved black assailants.

But consider the actual demographics of the riot: 51 percent of those arrested were Hispanic; blacks accounted for only 38 percent of the arrests; and 9 percent of those arrested were white. Nevertheless, a study of TV news coverage of the Los Angeles riot found that half of the stories focused on black involvement and only 13 percent focused on Hispanics. Therefore, it could be argued America got a skewed impression about who did the rioting.

Many black Americans, however, expect that whites will unfairly stigmatize black people on purpose, almost as if they have been conditioned to do so. When the *Washington Post* published writer Leon Dash's 1995 series, "Rosa Lee's Story," about the sordid life of a drug addict and petty criminal, Dash, who is black, won a Pulitzer Prize. But the reaction from many black readers was less than laudatory.

"As an African American and an honors graduate of Stanford University," wrote an Arlington, Virginia, woman, "I'm totally disgusted with this article because you're reinforcing every negative stereotype about African Americans. I think it would have been in your best interest if you had focused on heart transplant surgeons or business people, people doing volunteer work in the community . . . something positive instead of something so negative."

"I have mixed feelings," wrote a Laurel, Maryland, woman, "when I read this story, I think: Why is the *Post* spotlighting this family instead of spotlighting African-American families who have made it? . . . Because of the climate in D.C., if you walk down the street and you're black, everyone thinks you're a criminal."

As is so often the case, the underlying assumption here is that whites cannot tell the difference between Stanford graduates and petty criminals, and that, given this disability, whites will assume that all black strangers are criminals. And even if whites protest they can tell the difference, the results on the streets of America is mixed at best.

But where do whites get these ideas? The streets around my house are full of negative images of black people. One need not read the *Post* to find them. Until it was closed in 1997 as a health hazard, Kentucky Courts, a public housing project near my house, seemed to be crammed with negative images—alcoholics, drug addicts, drug dealers, lifelong welfare cases—even though the majority of residents were nothing of the sort.

One 25-year-old man I knew, Derrick Williams, was a drug dealer there. He was a stereotype, if you will. But Derrick was conflicted over what he was doing, which was a dimension in his soul beyond the simple stereotype. He and some friends started to record rap songs that showed promise. They wanted to be rap artists. And that was another stereotype of sorts, so Derrick was a stereotype two times over.

On June 4, 1997, at about 1:30 in the afternoon, gunfire erupted at Kentucky Courts, which was nothing new. But these shots left Derrick lying in a pool of blood with seven bullets in his head. His misgivings and artistic ambitions were not enough to extricate him from a dangerous world. People immediately said he had been killed "execution-style," another common phrase in this era of violence. So some might think of Derrick as a stereotype in life and a cliché in death. Surely, some black Americans might prefer not to hear too much said about Derrick or the activities at Kentucky Courts out of fear that the images of Derrick's life and death could haunt other black people in the way white people think.

Unfortunately, they are right.

For black people, the concern about negative stereotypes in entertainment has a long and tormented history. Consider, for example, the case of *Amos 'n' Andy*, which began as a 1920s radio show, performed by whites. The characters had evolved from portrayals in blackface minstrel shows, again performed by whites. The mockery of black people in *Amos 'n' Andy* would seem to be obvious, if we see it as a white creation; black behavior and language were presented as ignorant and loutish. In 1950, black actors took over the roles for the *Amos 'n' Andy* TV show, but the NAACP protested, which eventually led to the show's demise, even though it was popular among black viewers as one of the few shows at the time with black actors and characters.

Here's what the NAACP said:

1. The show tends to strengthen the conclusion among uninformed and prejudiced people that Negroes are inferior, lazy, dumb, and dishonest.
2. Every Negro is a clown or a crook.
3. Negro doctors are shown as quacks and thieves.
4. Negro lawyers are shown as slippery cowards, ignorant of their profession, and without ethics.
5. Negro women are seen as cackling, screaming shrews in bigmouth close-ups, using street language just short of vulgarity.
6. All Negroes are seen as dodging work of any kind.
7. An entire race of 15,000,000 Americans [is] being slandered each week by this one-sided caricature.

Whites may remember the 1970s as a breakthrough era for black shows like *Sanford and Son* (1972–77), *Good Times* (1974–79) and *The Jeffersons* (1975–85), but some blacks found the antics and shortcomings of characters on these shows embarrassing. One sensitivity was that whites, in the absence of other contact with black people, would consider these portrayals to be too widely representative. But there is also the possibility, too, that black people might see themselves this way.

Again, the categories are interesting to the degree that these images and characters still survive in our thinking. But I suspect that the terminology will be more familiar to black Americans than to whites. Whites, for example, are less likely to react negatively to behavior that might cause a black person to be considered an Uncle Tom, and, if anything, these terms might sound strangely old-fashioned. These days, some of the stock black figures in mainstream entertainment or popular music are represented by a lingo—"thugs," "gangstas," "bitches," and "ho's"—widely recognized as products of black urban culture. Indeed, black Americans at times appear to be replacing Italian Americans as caricatures of choice for the fictional underworld. However, in the 1990s, black actors and actresses frequently got starring and heroic roles in the movies; alluring black models and celebrities appear on the cover of *Vogue* and other magazines; and it looks like black Americans have made their place in the world of glamour and show business.

Whites may, these days, be exposed to fewer clearly negative stereotypes of blacks. But do stereotypical ideas about the nature of black people still lurk in the shadows of our consciousness? *Washington Post* columnist Donna Britt had an interesting take on this in 1998. When strong film performances by Samuel L. Jackson and Pam Grier (*Jackie Brown*), Djimon Hounsou (*Amistad*), and Debbi Morgan (*Eve's Bayou*) were overlooked for Oscar nominations, Britt wrote: "I'd bet the same voters subconsciously feel it's easier for black performers to play stereotypical 'black' roles than for white actors to play similar parts. They suspect that a black actor's kick-butt turn—as a sociopathic hustler (Jackson), clever thief (Grier), voodoo priestess (Morgan), or slavery-bound captive (Hounsou)—isn't really acting at all."

Yet blacks are not the only ones with fears that misinformation, misimpressions—or evil—will come flying across the color line. We should all understand that clearly. Whites have worried that elements of black culture will seep into white America to corrupt white youth. A common fear is that erotic suggestions in black music will threaten mainstream decency. Early rock 'n' roll, with its obvious black roots, was considered the devil's music by some who believed it would arouse animal passions in otherwise God-fearing white teenagers.

But in many of these disputes about information and the color line, it becomes strangely unclear who is doing what to whom. For example, if Jerry Springer hosts a TV show with black pimps and prostitutes who seem shameless, exhibitionistic, and antisocial, who is to blame for these negative images of black people—the pimps and prostitutes or Jerry Springer? And if black comedians on an HBO show called *Def Jam* talk of little else but sex, who is to blame for reviving a stereotype about hedonistic black people—the comedians, the producers at HBO, or Time Warner, the corporate superpower that owns HBO?

Furthermore, some black critics will eventually ask why Jerry Springer or Time Warner are compelled to portray black people negatively—or why they want to encourage black people to do it to themselves. Many black Americans believe that whites will always hold out the enticements of money and fame to persuade blacks to play the fool, because, the theory goes, that's what whites want to see.

The dilemma for black artists, writers, and filmmakers is that every portrayal of black people faces a potential gauntlet of criticism about how this work reflects on black people as a whole. White artists needn't worry that what they do will shape the reputation and fortunes of white people; this is a special freedom whites have but rarely appreciate. White comedians can talk about sex or whatever all night. And no one will say they have betrayed their race.

White artists and performers also enjoy the freedom from additional scrutiny that comes with being a minority. Inevitably, minority artists cannot escape being viewed as representatives of their group. Whatever black artists do may be seen as a window on the soul or thinking of all black people. And blacks in particular, in creating or portraying villains, risk harvesting an angry backlash. Perhaps it will eventually be noticed that the range of black characters on TV or in the movies is being limited by this extra scrutiny. Time will tell.

In the 1990s, rap music became the subject of a gnarled argument over who was doing what to whom. But I must first recall that the young men at Kentucky Courts—men like the late Derrick Williams—firmly believed that rap was *their* voice and an expression of *their* circumstances, attitudes, and feelings. They believed—were 100 percent sure—that rap came from people just like them in circumstances like theirs. Indeed, they could not have imagined it coming from anywhere else.

That said, rap music became the subject of an argument about nothing less than where it came from—and whether whites actually inspired rap and shaped it as an art form. Early on, music critics called it an authentic voice from urban black America, but the rap music that got the most attention also seemed to mirror the angry, violent images of alienated black men that are the raw material of many white fears. And there was another claim about rap, that the real impetus behind its popularity, believe it or not, was *white* listeners and *white* ideas about what black people are like.

Here is how that was supposed to work: white recording companies promoted the rap music that contained negative images of black people, the more negative the better, because that's what whites wanted. In a 1991 *New Republic* article, writer David Samuels argued that rap was primarily driven by white stereotypes, that white kids in the suburbs were seeing the alienation and anger of rap artists as a convenient pose for their own rebellious urges. "Rap's appeal to whites," said Samuels, "rested in its evocation of an age-old image of blackness: a foreign, sexually charged and criminal underworld against which the norms of white society are defined, and, by extension, through which they may be defied."

One highly successful rap producer, Hank Shocklee, who is black, agreed with the premise: "If you're a suburban white kid and you want to find out what life is like for a black city teenager, you buy a record by N.W.A. [Niggaz With Attitude]. It's like going to an amusement park and getting on a roller coaster ride—records are safe, they're controlled fear, and you always have the choice of turning it off."

Samuels gave only passing note to the young black men who consider rap their voice: "Although rap is still proportionally more popular among blacks," he said, "its primary audience is white and lives in the suburbs."

In his way, he was also noting the mathematics of race: even a small percentage of whites—alienated teenage males, for example—can add up to large numbers in CD sales. White consumers and white tastes will inevitably dominate the marketplace because there are so many more white people. And a similar argument was eventually advanced by others who insisted that were it not for whites being enthralled by the "authenticity" of blacks parading themselves as outlaws, thugs, and "gangstas," record companies would lose interest and rap music would slip quietly from the scene. Instead, however—and this was the core charge—white record executives were encouraging rap artists to make their records as perverse and offensive as possible, because the worse they were, the more whites would want to buy them.

In 1996, C. Dolores Tucker, head of the National Political Congress of Black Women, led protests against Time Warner, claiming the company was promoting rap records that celebrated violence against women and other antisocial attitudes. Former education secretary William Bennett, a conservative who linked the violent messages of rap to a decline in American values, joined her. And, it must be said, their concerns were justified. The messages coming from some rappers were twisted and troubling. They were telling us something is very wrong in their world.

Essentially, however, the claim here, too, was that major corporations were paying black people to act in antisocial ways to please whites who wanted to view blacks as less than civilized. Eventually, Time Warner divested itself of its rap label, Interscope. But another industry giant, MCA, bought the label. And the thump of rap songs continues, still emanating from passing cars in my neighborhood. And the messages are still troubling.

Even in this heralded information age, blacks and whites have contradictory urges about an open exchange across the color line. We believe we need more interactions and should get to know each other better. But we also fear that information is dangerous when it gets loose on the other side. We fret about America's divisions, and then we worry, too, that we will be judged in terms of what others see. Americans frequently say we need to communicate more, but they are afraid of what will happen if we do. We assume our horizons must be expanding, yet some of us are more isolated, too. We say that race is becoming less an issue. But when we turn on TV or buy a magazine, we see that race is more a factor than ever.

6

IN THE MIRROR

Do We Like What We See?

When a black person walks into the room, what exactly do white Americans see? Do they merely see a person with darker skin? Do they discern the exact shade of this darkness? Do they see a person with tightly curled hair—or tightly curled hair that has been straightened? Do they see a person with a wide nose or lips? Do they really see a black person? Or do they suppress all this noticing and see, as some now claim, none of the visible differences associated with race?

In an impulse to be color-blind, Americans have entered contradictory terrain, wherein political correctness, political conviction, or general discomfort with the subject of race have caused some of us, whites in particular, to declare they no longer see race at all. I have heard this claim, "I just don't see skin color," but I don't fully believe such is true or even possible. How could one not see skin color? But those who claim they are color-blind insist it is so. What are we to say?

This insistence on being color-blind could mean that Americans want to be scrupulously fair in their dealings with each other. That would be good. It might also indicate that Americans now understand dealings across the color line needn't be color-obsessed, that friendships between blacks and whites can transcend race. Good, too. But it could also mean that whites want to avoid a subject that makes them uncomfortable and unsure of what to say. So to remove the uneasy subject of race—and all that comes with it—they adopt the pose of being color-blind. Yet if whites do not see skin color or physical features when a black person enters the room, then what, pray tell, do they see? A shadow or empty silhouette? This makes no sense. How do people who are so color-blind recognize people they know?

White Americans seem singularly uneasy on the subject of skin color and physical features and avoid it for the most part. Black Americans, however, have no such problem; they talk about these matters all the time and are experts on the subject, aware of subtleties that whites would never notice. And they're candid about them, too. In fact, I don't know any black people who truly wish others not to notice what color they are. If I read their wishes correctly, my black friends do not wish to have this aspect of their being ignored. They just don't want it to be the only aspect by which they are recognized and judged.

On July 29, 1996, the cover of *People* magazine proclaimed the black actor Denzel Washington "the Sexiest Man Alive!" This choice might have been a social milestone—a mainstream magazine promoting a black man as an object of universal desire—more significantly, sex appeal—could have marked a new level of integration in our attitudes. But *People* did not treat it as a milestone. Since it was obvious that Washington is black, *People* found no need to mention this fact.

People also did what many whites believe they should do when a black person enters the room: it pretended not to see skin color, pretended not to think about race—suggesting that, perhaps, its worldview is beyond race. The only mention of color in *People*'s description of the flesh-and-blood man came in a reference to Washington's "warm brown eyes." Nothing about the actor's good looks seems to have stirred thoughts of race—*People* made no effort to describe the color of Washington's skin, the shape of his nose, or the texture of his hair. Notably, his sex appeal was more abstract than physical, more a matter of character than color, a function of his "reserve," "aloofness," and "elusiveness," more a result of what you couldn't see than what you could. Washington, *People* said, "achieves true sexiness by keeping on his clothes—and his dignity."

These days whites shy away from noting the physical indicators of race for, perhaps, another reason. For so long, whites spoke derisively of black characteristics like "kinky" hair and "thick" lips that it now might seem disingenuous to blacks for whites to speak of these features positively. Indeed, whites inherit such a history of disdain—of treating black people as if they were irredeemably ugly—that they have not yet regained full rights to speak on these subjects. Whites themselves may even sense it does not ring sincere for them to note the handsomeness of black people.

For centuries the white majority expected the black minority to emulate white standards of beauty or face ridicule. As a result, black people ended up mimicking the values of the white majority, considering light skin better than dark skin and fine, flowing hair better than hair thickly curled.

Whites are still pleased to hear that black people make these distinctions—and this is more white folly. Black color prejudices do not mean white standards are universal; rather they reflect how whites have been an oppressive majority and forced blacks to accept views that serve white self-interest. And maybe some whites realize this and are embarrassed—they should be. So they have another reason not to mention skin tone, hair texture, or the shape of nose and lips.

The segregation of America is proof that blacks and whites do see each other's color *very well*. How else could Americans segregate themselves so thoroughly? And the pervasiveness of segregated experience raises the possibility that some blacks and whites might even find each other's physical presence odd or disconcerting.

White people can seem strikingly pale, even sickly, to one accustomed to darker faces. A gathering of black people can appear so dark that the light in the room seems dim and different. How strange looking can we be to each other? In 1993, a white *Washington Post* editor, Richard Leiby, wrote about his impression at the annual convention of the National Association of Black Journalists. What hit Leiby in these unfamiliar surroundings was the *physical* proximity of black people and their strangeness to his senses.

Of course, Leiby initially sensed he was being watched, the common feeling that accompanies crossing the color line. What he further noted was embarrassing yet also revealingly honest. Leiby's gaze fixed on the unfamiliar aspect of black skin:

> Copper, I think, studying the moist, shiny neck of the man blocking my view at another standing-room-only seminar. What does copper smell like? Back in the seventh grade, at the all-white school I attended, an English teacher announced to our class one day, for no reason I can recall, "Negroes smell like copper. If you ever get close to one, you will know it." I tried. I licked and sniffed a penny. Was that it?
>
> I never got close to a black person until my first year in college, when a black professor hired me as his work-study student and patiently mentored me in journalism. He smelled of rich cologne. But I could never get that insidious notion out of my mind. Because I am white, do I smell like a dime? Are black kids ever taught such poisonous things in school?

Leiby had seized upon several common expectations that inexperienced whites have: the beliefs that black people sweat profusely, have greasy skin, and smell strange. From such musings it would seem that whites expect close contact with blacks will be unpleasant, and they often hear how black people reek of cologne and perfume. Yet such odd notions about personal hygiene are common in the mythology of race: many black people are similarly sure whites are unclean.

Also, Leiby just happened to focus on the "moist, shiny neck" of the man in front of him, an area of the anatomy about which some black people can be self-conscious. The concern relates to a detail about straightening hair—and keeping it straight. But how would Leiby know this? In the old-fashioned lore of hair straightening, black people called the nape of the neck "the kitchen." And hairs in the kitchen were considered hard to straighten and keep that way; but the term also dates from an era when most hair straightening was done in the kitchen.

Meanwhile, the real issue here is the degree to which whites, as represented by Leiby, are unsettled by physical proximity to black people. Are Leiby's reactions common? There is little data on this question.

Leiby admitted he was uneasy, and anecdotal evidence is that other whites are as well, because they occasionally say so among themselves. But such talk, too, is suppressed in an age when one is supposed to be color-blind.

These days, even encyclopedias hesitate to describe racial characteristics, warning that the concept of race itself is suspect, because there are no clear dividing lines between races. Whites are still sometimes classified as Caucasians or Caucasoids, a reference to the Caucacus Mountains in present-day Russia, Georgia, and Azerbaijan, from which white people were once believed to have originated. That was a mistake, but the name stuck, at least until recently. According to the *American Heritage Dictionary of the English Language, Third Edition*, the word *Caucasoid* is "no longer in scientific use."

Whites are also considered to be members of a "European geographic race," and, speaking very generally, Caucasoids are expected to have straight or curly, fine hair; thin lips; straight faces; and well-developed chins. The 1993 edition of the *Encyclopedia Americana* was more descriptive than other sources:

> The Caucasoid groups have a wide range of skin color, varying from the pale, translucent, alabaster white frequent among Scandinavians through the Mediterranean light brown common among Greeks to the darker brown typical of Arabs. Similarly, the Caucasoid group has a wide range of eye color, from the blue frequent in Sweden to the dark brown characteristic in Greece. The hair of Caucasoid—yellow, red, brown, black—is usually straight or wavy. Although the structure of the nose varies greatly, ranging from high and narrow to broad and snub, the lips are usually thin. Many male Caucasoids can grow heavy beards, and both sexes have a relatively large amount of body hair. Caucasoid body builds vary considerably from the medium, short stature of Mediterranean people to the tall, rangy build characteristic of Scandinavia.

This encyclopedia also lists four Caucasoid racial subgroups:

1. Northwest Europeans
2. Northeast Europeans
3. Alpine Europeans (along a belt from France east through the Balkans)

4. Mediterraneans (on both sides of the Mediterranean and east into Arabia and Iran)

Also bear in mind that 63 percent of the U.S. population in the 1990 census claimed ancestry traceable to countries in northwestern Europe—Germany, England, Ireland, Scotland, France, Holland, Sweden, or Norway—which confirms Northwest European Caucasoids as the dominant racial group in the land.

But back to the broader definitions. Black people have traditionally been referred to as Negroes or Negroids, words derived from *niger*, the Latin word for "black." But *Negroid* is another term that is "no longer in scientific use." Instead, black people are recognized as part of an "African geographic race," which includes people with woolly hair or hair that forms spiral tufts; yellow, dark brown, or black skin; a slim, angular body build; broad lips; broad noses; minimal body hair; little male pattern balding; and sometimes pronounced buttocks. In extreme forms, this latter phenomenon is called "steatopygia."

Again, from the *Encyclopedia Americana*:

The Negroid racial aggregate is characterized by color and body build. Color of skin ranges from brown to black, as does that of the hair and eyes. The hair on the head is often tightly curled and on the body is sparsely distributed. Full lips, broad noses, small close-set ears, and relatively rounded heads are common in these groups. One finds a greater spread of height than that encountered in the Mongoloid or Caucasoid racial aggregates. Individuals within the Negroid group include the towering Tutsi, some of whom are as tall as 7 feet, and the Pygmies, small people of the African forest, whose adult height is under 5 feet.

Among six subgroups of Negroes, the encyclopedia lists North American Blacks, "the population resulting from an African-European hybridization, the majority of whose genes (approximately 80 percent) are from Africa."

No matter what words we use to classify each other, physical characteristics linked to distant European or African ancestry will determine our recognition of who is black and who is white—unless our attempt at being color-blind is ultimately successful. And from these encyclopedia descriptions, the possibility arises that blacks and whites might find each other strange looking, even if we don't want to admit making such distinctions.

Take the example of body hair. A Negroid with limited body hair might—secretly, at least—view a Caucasoid with lots of body hair as an unusual phenomenon. A Negroid with limited body hair might even wonder if a hirsute Caucasoid is more closely related to monkeys or gorillas. And some black people do, in fact, admit finding heavy body hair odd or even distasteful. Differences in body hair also lead to different habits in personal hygiene. Many black women, for example, do not shave their legs, because they don't think they need to. And some white women, who shave their legs religiously, find it very strange that black women have few concerns in this regard. I've even heard white women profess great shock. "Goodness, you never shave your legs!"

Although it might seem indelicate to ask, what are Caucasoids whose buttocks are flat to make of Negroes whose buttocks are more in evidence? In fact, many whites and blacks *do*, at least occasionally, notice this obvious—and, some say, interesting—difference in rear ends. Many black Americans note with puzzlement that white people can seem insufficiently endowed. Or as some put it, "They ain't got no ass."

Some white Americans, however, find the prominence of some black people's buttocks grotesque. On occasion, some whites even conclude that black women are loose or flaunting themselves when they dress in ways that reveal the shape God gave them. And that attitude could be reexamined.

On the matter of appearances, it is obvious that the standards of the overwhelming white majority—and of Northwest European Caucasoids, too—predominate in American culture. Merely being the majority has allowed whites to consider thin lips, fine hair, straight faces, and thin rear ends—what *they* see in the mirror—the all-American ideal. And whites have also determined which deviations from these norms are unattractive or even gross.

At this, whites did a thorough job. They revealed how they looked at black people in endless cartoonlike depictions of blacks with huge mouths, balloon lips, bugging eyes, and hair that seemed to shoot straight out from their heads as if from electric shock. White preferences, however, were enshrined in maxims like "blondes have more fun."

And the advantages that accrued to those who looked right were extensive. On the average, Northwest European Caucasoids and the sub-subgroup, WASPs (White Anglo-Saxon Protestants), make more money, live longer, own better houses, and send their children to better schools. And only in the past 30 years or so have WASPs begun allowing others into their club.

Meanwhile, across the color line, the dominant white values were perversely mirrored. Black society also favored light skin, so much so that in some instances a paper-bag test—you had to be lighter than a common paper bag—was a standard for those wishing to join exclusive churches, groups, or social circles. However, if whites hope this relieves them of exclusive blame for color prejudice, they should think again: Whites *are* most directly to blame. They set the rules.

Even in the 1920s, the extent to which black Americans had adopted white attitudes was the subject of academic studies. In *The American Negro*, published in 1928, the noted anthropologist Melville Herskovits uncovered an apparent link between skin tone or the width of noses and lips and economic and social success among black men in New York City's Harlem. "The average nostril width of the well-to-do male Harlemites," wrote Herskovits, "is 37.5 millimeters, while that of the general Harlem population is 41.3; the average lip thickness of the former is 19.8 millimeters, that of the latter 20.8."

Got that? Researchers of this sort surely contributed to the notion among black Americans that white people will count, measure, and study *everything*, even ridiculous things. It is also considered likely that whites will miss the moral or spiritual dimensions to life. Whites are considered expert at splitting hairs and focusing on odd details; they can cite obscure facts and arcane data to support whatever claims they want to make. Whites would, indeed, know how the width of a black man's nostril relates to his economic fate. But according to the stereotype, whites would do nothing to remedy the social injustices inherent in the findings.

Note, too, that the average difference Herskovits found between economic success and failure, as measured in the width of a black person's lips, was about *one millimeter*—less than a quarter of an inch or less than the width of a dime. In regard to skin tone, Herskovits found "that for the well-to-do group, the average percentage of black in [the scale] used for skin color valuations is 56.7 percent, while that of the general population is 68.8 percent." Again, the difference was relatively subtle. One needed to be only 12 percent lighter than the average black person to have a better shot at joining the well-to-do. But this also suggests that even minute racial differences have impact.

The impact spreads quickly. In the 1940s, psychologist Kenneth Clark demonstrated that black children would choose to play with white dolls, rejecting black ones. These studies were used in arguments against segregated schooling in the 1954 U.S. Supreme Court case *Brown v.*

Board of Education. Clark subsequently described how quickly small children grasp and adopt the prevailing attitudes about color:

> As children develop awareness of racial differences and of their racial identity, they also develop an awareness and acceptance of the prevailing social attitudes and values attached to race and skin color. The early rejection of the color *brown* by Negro children is part of the combination of attitude and ideas of the child who knows that he must be identified with something that is being rejected—and something that he himself rejects. This pattern introduces, early in the formation of the personality of these children, a fundamental conflict about themselves.

Are these studies relevant today? Many black Americans believe that the predominance of positive white images and negative black ones, particularly in the news, still encourages black children to think negatively about themselves. The theory goes like this: America sees blacks negatively; blacks internalize this view and end up with a diminished sense of self-worth. There is a "cancer of black self-deprecation and exaltation of whites," wrote black psychologists William H. Grier and Price M. Cobbs in their 1968 book, *Black Rage*.

The 1960s produced a counterbalancing consciousness movement with its message "Black is beautiful" and brought about an awakening on both sides of the color line. Across black America, programs were undertaken to encourage black youngsters to have pride in their history and cultural heritage. Whites sometimes forget that much in the black consciousness movement was an antidote to attitudes that had previously poisoned American culture.

These days, attractive black Americans are familiar figures in advertising, publishing, and entertainment. Many Americans might assume that the era when lighter-skinned black people were favored over darker-skinned black people is past, too, if only because we now see both lighter- and darker-skinned black Americans in successful positions on TV, which produces so many of our ideas about race.

So how can shades of color still be an issue? As recently as 1990, one study found that for every dollar earned by light-skinned black Americans, dark-skinned black Americans earned only 72 cents. And the authors of *The Color Complex: The Politics of Skin Color Among African Americans*, a 1992 study on color prejudice, saw the effects of color prejudice suggested in many of America's social problems:

Drive past any inner-city housing project, and you cannot help but notice that the majority of residents are dark-skinned. Even more disturbing, look behind the walls of the nation's prisons; they are filled with a disproportionate number of dark-skinned inmates. (A telling saying in the Black community is "The lighter the skin, the lighter the sentence.") While it is possible to trace the color-and-crime connection to differing opportunities for education and success, the suspicion that dark-skinned Blacks, especially men, are more criminally dangerous lurks in the American psyche.

Let's be frank. Those who are fearful of black people are likely more fearful of darker black people. It still appears that darker skin can make many people, including some black people, too, warier of strangers. Darker skin can raise suspicions that individuals are less intelligent or more criminally inclined. Even those who recognize that these ideas are wrong—scientifically and logically ridiculous—can still find themselves affected by them. Surely these reactions to dark skin are our most basic form of racial prejudice. Yet how can we rid ourselves of it? One antidote is contained in this maxim of black folk wisdom: "The darker the berry, the sweeter the wine." But is that idea enough?

It also appears that blacks and whites have developed different skills in recognizing or talking about skin tone. Whites see the world in black or white; they don't see subtle differences. Blacks have a much more refined awareness of shades. Herskovits was surprised to find blacks used various words to describe lighter skin—*good, brown, high-brown, high-yellow, ginger-brown, fair, air-brown, red, pink, cream-colored*, and *bronze*. Another researcher found that black junior-high students in the 1940s used 145 different terms for skin color. These days, making distinctions among those who are "light-skinned," "brown-skinned," and "dark-skinned" is an everyday matter—that's how black Americans describe people as a matter of course. "He's the light-skinned guy by the mailbox. She's the brown-skinned woman in the red Toyota."

Meanwhile, whites hardly focus on differences of skin color on their own side of the color line. In the past, the lighter-skinned Northwest European Caucasoids distinguished between themselves and darker Mediterraneans. Swarthy Sicilian immigrants once found themselves on the lower rungs of the socioeconomic ladder; now they are assimilated into the mass of white people.

These days, whites seem most confused about color in regard to Hispanics, a group that in actuality is defined by language and culture, not skin color. Although Hispanics are not a race, many whites seem to imagine them as "darker" people. Yet it is possible Hispanics will eventually be seen as "lighter," as Sicilians were. And it would be no surprise if many Hispanics were assimilated into the white population.

Generally, too, whites make their stereotypical distinctions about hair color, not skin: Dark hair is supposed to indicate passion; redheads are hot-tempered; blonds are cool customers. Meanwhile, the idea that "gentlemen prefer blondes" seems clearly based in the aesthetic preferences of Northwest European Caucasoids, not some universal truth. In the late 20th century, all white skin almost seemed to be relatively equal among whites. Even Asians were called "honorary" whites inasmuch as stereotypes about Asians—they are hardworking, have strong families, and value education—were scarcely negative or menacing.

In the 1990s, whiter or lighter white skin did not confer strikingly higher status among whites, and until skin cancer became an epidemic, a good suntan was considered a marker of health and status. But perhaps in the near future, avoidance of the sun will become a health-conscious virtue that returns extreme paleness to vogue. You can watch for that.

In the 1960s, black Americans discovered huge Afro hairdos, which many whites found disconcerting. Then whites linked Afros to other ideas about race that the 1960s brought. It seemed that blacks in the 1960s were perpetually angry and accusatory, and whites began to assume that black hairdos and black anger were interrelated. So those who wore Afros were assumed to be angry, too.

But whites are generally unaware of the efforts black Americans extend to their hair. Or whites are confused about the processes involved or the *meaning* of hair, if you will. Hair belongs to the general mysteriousness whites sense about black people.

Readers of *The Autobiography of Malcolm X* were introduced to the old-fashioned ritual of getting your hair "conked," a painful process that involved a caustic brew of potatoes, eggs, and lye; but Malcolm was also focusing on the psychological wounds that accompanied this ritual submission to white values:

My first view in the mirror blotted out the hurting. I've seen some pretty conks, but when it's the first time, on your own head, the transformation, after a lifetime of kinks, is staggering. . . . on top of my head was a thick, smoother sheen of shining red hair—real red—as straight as any white man's.

How ridiculous I was! Stupid enough to stand there simply lost in admiration of my hair now looking "white." . . . I vowed I'd never again be without a conk. . . . This was my first really big step toward self-degradation: When I endured all of that pain, literally burning my flesh to have it look like a white man's hair.

This passage is a relic from the 1940s, and the process of straightening hair has since changed. Still, whites were likely to miss out on the intrinsic joy that has accompanied the rediscovery in the 1960s of the many wonderful possibilities that black hair, so long disdained, can represent. This feeling was evident in a 1994 *Washington Post* column by Donna Britt on reports, apparently premature, that 1960s-style Afros were about to make a comeback.

Maybe I only craved a Fro at age 14 because everyone who was remotely cool wore one. Or because getting one was sure to give my mom a fit. But that didn't explain its effect. I remember sitting, heart pounding and scalp smarting, as my cousin Joann washed, oiled and picked my previously straightened hair into an Afro. Halfway though, Joann whispered, "This is gonna be pretty."

It was—but it was more. Staring mesmerized into Joann's bedroom mirror, I marveled at how my basic blackgirl hair had evolved into something vibrant, neat and beautiful without being hot-combed or chemically relaxed into submission. It's impossible to explain the psychic damage that was undone in that moment. My reflection challenged years of hearing my hair was ugly in its natural state—from society and even from relatives who loved me. The miracle atop my head refuted every word.

Whites seem to take black hairstyles personally, managing to focus on their own hair rather than the interesting aspects of black hair. When they realized that blacks were rejecting white norms in hairstyles of the 1960s, a host of related ideas were planted in white minds. For better or worse, whites have continued to associate ethnic dress and hairdos with an awareness of black history and culture. And they assume an awareness of black history and culture could cause blacks to be angry and antiwhite.

A black person might be happy and at peace with the world, but from his or her hairdo whites could read anger and alienation. An ethnic-looking outfit produces suspicion that the wearer could be one of those blacks who hates whites—the ones whites cite in polls. This suspicion is unfortunate.

Black people who braid their hair or twist it into dreadlocks sometimes find that their white friends react strangely. The technical details of the hairdo, such as how long it takes, are a mystery to whites; but whites may also be confused about what the hairdo means. Does it mean the wearer is rejecting white culture? Or coming out of the closet, so to speak, on angry feelings about whites? Whites worry about such things, when—if only they could relax for a moment—the new hairdo probably has nothing to do with white people and is merely an attempt to look good.

Still, the conventional wisdom among black workers in corporate America is try to fit in. Wear what white people wear. Wear your hair like white people do. How would one know this is so? Look around. Although attitudes are evolving—Senator Carol Moseley-Braun wore a braided hairdo in 1996—many black Americans assume that hairdos of ethnic origin can lead whites to suspect you are "angry" or "have an attitude." And these results can hurt you in the long run. After five o'clock, however, when you leave the white-dominated world, you can be as "black" as you want to be. Millions of black Americans are accustomed to operating under these two sets of rules, one black and one white. When they go to work, white rules are in effect. When they go out on Saturday night or to church on Sunday, black rules prevail.

And the two sets of rules can produce noticeably different results.

On this question of differing styles, we must be cautious. Nothing irks my black friends more than the suggestion that all black people are alike, that their experiences are the same, and that they all have the same tastes. And it would surely annoy many white people to realize how frequently it is claimed that white people can't be told apart.

Often, blacks and whites share values and preferences. Still, I sense the black or white worlds occasionally operate on different standards about what looks good and what does not. Attitudes about hair can help explain some of the difference. Because black hair and white hair are usually different in texture and curl, blacks and whites see different "problems" with their hair, but the "problems" usually involve curliness. Often, whites want more than God gave them, and blacks less.

Black Americans may refer to hair that is thick with tight curls as "bad"; white Americans have "bad hair days," when curliness goes every which way at once. At the same time, whites with the long, straight hair that is often envied have their own woes: if it is *too* straight, it just lays there, a disaster. Some black people might imagine it's wonderful to have long, flowing hair, an all-American ideal extolled in shampoo ads. But those with long, flowing hair have a devil of a time keeping it under control. Almost any physical exertion or encounter with the elements produces a mess. A solution is to grease the hair, lacquer it, or stiffen it with hair spray. But this move nullifies the flowing quality. Another solution is to incorporate dishevelment into the hairstyle, eliminating the need for every hair to be exactly in place. And the high-fashion variants on windblown disarray can be elaborate indeed.

More commonly, too, white Americans affect airs of indifference toward their hair, as if to say, "My hair? Oh, I just ran a comb through it." This illusion of minimal effort is often admired and envied as a white ideal. In 1996, for example, Carolyn Bessette Kennedy, then the recent bride of John Kennedy, Jr., was described by the *Washington Post* as "model tall and a perfect size six" and "just sloppy enough to make people think you aren't obsessed about your looks."

This is a version of white perfection involving a flirtation with *sloppiness* that suggests that looking good requires no effort—looking good evolves naturally without worry or work. Either one is born with perfection or not. Many black Americans find such an attitude phony or condescending; they refuse to believe that anyone looks very good without trying, a view that points to an important difference between black and white attitudes. Whites often try to make things look effortless, understating the work involved. But many black Americans are more likely to believe good appearances result from effort and attention to detail. As a result, black men and women are less likely to affect the casual airs that the *Post* admired in Mrs. Bessette Kennedy. They are also less likely to say they don't care how they look. In fact, this focus on appearance is evident in black neighborhoods, if only in the number of beauty parlors and barbershops you are likely to see.

Whites sometimes see this focus on appearances in black America as odd—almost a triumph of style and surface over substance. Some whites claim that looks are only skin-deep—but this notion ignores how deeply skin color has affected the lives of black Americans. So that argument doesn't wash.

In our stereotypical impressions about race, it is likely whites will be assumed to be more affluent and blacks less so. And with this stigma of poverty following them, black Americans sense a need to demonstrate evidence to the contrary. Many blacks also firmly believe that good grooming pays off. You feel better. You are treated better. Better opportunities come your way.

And it turns out that fleeting fashions will often reflect these values. While white youths may adopt a sloppy style, as in the "grunge" look of the 1990s, it is hard to imagine black youths deliberately seeking to look poor or ragtag. Black fashions are often costly, as in the case of $150 sneakers. Black youths may take an idea like baggy pants, as was popular in the 1990s, and exaggerate it, pushing it to an extreme, pants so baggy or worn so low so as to cause others to look twice. And when jeans with tears and holes became briefly popular, black women made sure they were torn artfully in *exactly* the right places for maximum impact. Even in the torn-jeans look, nothing was left to accident.

Similarly, it is no secret that many black Americans spend vast amounts of time and money on their hair; some complex or braided black hairstyles take hours to produce. But black hair also presents opportunities for elaboration that white hair doesn't, and centuries of African culture produced a multitude of decorative variants, including braids, cornrows or plats, dreadlocks, and others. Straightening hair, or "relaxing" curls, the current term, can involve attention to details that whites won't even notice. Since the tiny hairs on the nape of the neck—the kitchen—and along the hairline on the forehead are difficult to straighten and keep straight, they get extra attention, and other black people will notice if the curl returns there. Whites probably won't notice because they don't know those hairs are considered an extra problem.

Dealing with problems that force you to pay attention to almost every single hair is a quite different approach from pretending you don't have to pay your hair much mind. Hence, even on the subject of hair, we have two differing sets of values—two versions of what looks good. The "black" version announces that effort is important; the "white" version pretends no such concern. The "black" version can focus on details; the "white" version ignores the details in favor of emphasizing the overall effect.

Sometimes, too, it can seem that whites favor simplicity and under-statement, while blacks will be drawn to complexity and exaggera-tion. Blacks tend to dress up for an occasion, while whites tend to dress down. There are, of course, countless exceptions to such gen-eralizations, but they are, at least, interesting to note. Still, whites may look upon the variety and inventiveness of black hairstyles as puz-zling. Why do they do that? Or they may conclude blacks love to be different, to stand out in the crowd, which can also seem to be true. Black Americans seem to admire originality in style. It has made them style leaders in America and around the world. But black people may find it just as puzzling that whites *don't* stand out. Why do whites want to look so plain and nondescript? Or why do they pick up black styles, like wearing your baseball hat backward, so long after it was new in black America?

And let's not forget the buttocks. God appears to have endowed blacks and whites differently. By and large, blacks and whites appreciate what-ever God has given them. If it is true that a breast fixation holds white America, as is claimed, black Americans often appear to be looking else-where. They seem to give the rear end particular notice. They have spe-cial words for the buttocks—*booty, bumper,* and *back*—which seem to inspire aesthetic consideration as well. For example, linguist Geneva Smitherman, in *Black Talk: Words and Phrases from the Hood to the Amen Corner,* defines the word *back* as, "a woman's buttocks; if round and large in proportion to a woman's body, viewed as sexy."

In Zora Neale Hurston's 1937 novel, *Their Eyes Were Watching God,* an interesting moment occurs when all eyes were actually on something else: "The men noticed her firm buttocks like she had grape fruits in her hip pockets." But the general idea should be relatively clear. While whites might say, "Get your ass (or your butt) in the house," blacks are more likely to say, "Get your *black* ass (or your *black* butt) in the house." There's a subtle distinction.

Biographer Phyllis Rose notes in *Jazz Cleopatra: Josephine Baker in Her Time* that black entertainer Josephine Baker, who was the toast of Paris in the 1930s, had special regard for her derrière: "She handled it as though it were an instrument, a rattle, something apart from herself that she could shake. One can hardly overemphasize the importance of her rear end. Baker herself declared that people had been hiding their asses too long. 'The rear end exists. I see no reason to be ashamed of it.'"

In the 1960s, Ray Charles sang of the woman who could "shake that thang." And the same focus of interest produced dances and songs in the early 1990s like "Doin' the Butt," or "Baby's Got Back." A moment even arose during the 1994 football season when—perhaps for the first time in American sports—a well-shaped butt was noted as the mark of a good running back, a position that is over 90 percent black in the National Football League. In his assessment of a prize rookie, a Philadelphia Eagles vice president exclaimed, "Look at Garner. He's a little thicker than he looks. Look at those arms, thighs, butt. He's a running back!"

Meanwhile, on the other side of the color line, shapeliness in the buttocks draws less interest. Shapely rear ends are not a valued attribute in the white-dominated world of stick-figure fashion models. And some white attitudes appear to be anti-ass: In her exercise book *Bottoms Up!* fitness maven Joyce Vedral lists "the parts you hate" as "thighs—hips—butt—stomach" and confesses, "I'll never have narrow hips or tiny buttocks, but I've achieved the perfect look for my body shape."

So here is another image of white perfection: narrow hips and tiny buttocks. But this assessment is logical because white people are less notably endowed in this regard. And also, if you "hate" specific parts of your body, as Vedral suggests, you would want them to be as small as possible.

The idea that whites hate parts of their body suggests another instance in which blacks and whites see things differently. Studies show that white and black women have quite different attitudes about their appearance, most markedly in their attitudes about weight and body shape. In simple terms, whites see themselves as heavier than they actually are (and they are unhappy about it). And blacks see themselves as lighter than they actually are (and they are happier about the way they look).

A 1989 study found that adolescent white girls believed they were overweight, even when their weight fell within the medically determined "normal" range. But adolescent black girls did not see themselves as similarly overweight. In a 1995 follow-up study, University of Arizona researchers found that adolescent white girls often have a circumscribed vision of ideal beauty—something along the lines of Barbie dolls or extremely thin fashion models. White girls even formed important social bonds when they fretted together about their weight—all in pursuit of an ideal that was virtually unreachable for most white women. So white women inevitably faced degrees of dissatisfaction or even self-contempt.

Adolescent black girls, on the other hand, were more accepting of themselves as individuals with different shapes and didn't fixate on one image of beauty. And the social bonds between black girls often involved reinforcing the view that each woman should make the most of what she has. They would plot strategies to highlight the good and hide the bad. It should be noted, too, that few black women suffer from anorexia or bulimia, usually linked to obsessive preoccupation with weight. The few black victims tend to be women who spend more time in white surroundings. But it has also been found that in their lessened concern about weight, some black women are less health conscious in their eating habits.

The results of these studies invite interesting comparisons. Do they mean that white people are unhappy because they cannot be perfect? Are black people happier because they accept the way they are? Such realities would seem to represent a turnabout from the older view that black Americans suffer from self-contempt in a society where norms are all white. It would seem to be the opposite of choosing the white dolls over the black ones or of that cancerous exaltation of white ways. Now it's white people—or white women—who hate themselves.

The Arizona study also found that black girls recognize the difference between their approach and that of the white girls who sensed themselves falling short of their ideal. And the black girls did not want to join the white girls in their fruitless pursuit of perfection. The studies also seemed to confirm a common observation: if black America is riddled with self-contempt that's centered on the way black people look, why doesn't it show up more clearly? In fact, in my experience, black people enjoy they way they look. It is a joy to be around such people.

Many blacks also recognize that whites can seem strangely capricious—and two-faced—about looks in general. Whites can mock dark skin as inferior or even scary yet admire a white person with a deep suntan. Whites can ridicule thick lips as grotesque and ugly, yet years later when plastic surgeons promote "full" lips as a fashion trend, that's what white women want.

If whites don't see the irony in this behavior, black people do. In 1990, *USA Today* reported that women—and only white women were mentioned—were eager to have their lips augmented with collagen injections. Even *USA Today's* fashion reporter tried it: "It's just that I was born with thin lips and have always hungered for a full set. Having a meager mouth didn't bother me growing up, possibly because I came of age in the Twiggy and Cheryl Tiegs era. Not exactly your fat-lipped role models. But in the '90s, full, luscious lips loom large."

Strangely, all the full-lipped women she listed were white: Madonna, Cher, and Barbara Hershey were reported to have had the treatments, while Kim Basinger, Julia Roberts, Michelle Pfeiffer, and Claudia Schiffer already had the lips white women now longed for. But the article did mention attitudes that whites used to have: "It used to be full lips said you weren't white, Anglo-Saxon Protestant, which was considered negative," a Beverly Hills dermatologist told *USA Today*. "Now full lips are considered attractive, evidence of our shrinking global village."

"And why do plain [white] folks want big mouths?" *USA Today* wondered.

"A lot of people with small lips are just very self-conscious about it," said the Beverly Hills dermatologist, to which a Miami dermatologist added: "Lips are the most sensual organ we are allowed to expose, so it's very personal."

So do we follow this correctly? In the 1990s, white women desired full lips in order to appear more sensual, a transformation involving two characteristics—full lips and sensuality—that some whites once regarded as undesirable and "black." And while it may be reading too much into one fad, were whites chasing an ideal that would represent a milestone in social history? Although they didn't say it—remember they were trying to be color-blind—some whites were chasing an image they once would have considered unthinkable.

Now they desired to look more like black people.

7

THE STORY LINE

Good Guys and Bad Guys

Blacks and whites often seem to be telling different stories about who they are, where they came from, and where they are going. And some of the basic facts in these two tales are obviously different. This fundamental divide needn't be belabored to be recognized. Most black Americans' ancestors were brought to the New World as slaves, while most white Americans' ancestors had more choice in their abode.

From disparate beginnings, our stories continue in divergent directions. Blacks can argue they were forcibly brought to a land that thereafter rejected and exploited them even after they were freed from slavery. It can also be argued that greater opportunities more clearly beckoned for whites, almost from the moment they arrived. But this is not to say that whites didn't endure hardships or that they weren't exploited. The results of American experience make it easier for whites to forget the pain they once suffered. Black Americans have had a longer trek toward the American mainstream, and their arrival there is still far less complete.

One major American story line runs through Ellis Island, another through slavery and sharecropping in the old South. There is no one story of American experience that blacks and whites can totally agree on. A principal "black" critique about the way American history has been told and taught is the degree to which the "white" version ignores the presence and contributions of black Americans.

Since the 1960s, when black Americans were clamoring for inclusion in American history, whites developed their own sensitivities about this idea. Some whites sensed the inclusion of black history was artificial, requiring the designation of February as a month in which to do it. And after hearing black critiques about white-centered histories, many whites also suspected that black versions of the American story would eventually focus only on the bad things white people have done. While most whites admit whites did much that was reprehensible, they refuse to believe these "negative" events, involving blacks, Indians, Asians, and others, should be turned into the centerpiece of the American story—or the *whole* story.

This significant dispute between whites and blacks over self-image involves who gets to claim they are the good guys and who is assigned the role of villain in the American story. Blacks and whites divide sharply on this issue—everybody wants to be the good guys in their own story and make somebody else the bad guys.

White Americans want to think of themselves as the good guys on the world stage, and indeed, few nations stir their citizens with such lofty rhetoric as the United States does. Americans are regularly told they live in the richest, most divinely blessed nation on earth, which is no small load to bear. The glorious American story of how the original American colonies undertook a revolution based on principles of freedom and human equality and expanded their nation across a continent to become the mightiest nation in human history is well known. Along the way, Americans also invented the airplane, split the atom, cured diseases, explored the heavens, and won great wars. Eventually, they vanquished other competing forms of government and emerged in the dawn of the 21st century as the good guys of the world.

But another version of reality has always lain hidden beneath the glitter of America's glories, involving the ever-thorny issue of race as writer James Baldwin noted in *The Fire Next Time*:

> The American Negro has the great advantage of having never believed the collection of myths to which white Americans cling: that their ancestors were all freedom-loving heroes, that they were born in the greatest country the world has ever seen,

or that Americans are invincible in battle and wise in peace, that American have always dealt honorably with Mexicans and Indians and all other neighbors or inferiors, that American men are the world's most direct and virile, that American woman are pure. Negroes know far more about white Americans than that.

This judgment, from the 1960s, may seem angry or archaic. Yet many black Americans would today still identify with Baldwin's sentiments. This difference in perspective demonstrates that two story lines are at work. On one side of the color line, whites have their American story and heroes like George Washington and Thomas Jefferson. On the other side, black Americans immediately recognize that these two Founding Fathers owned slaves. How can black Americans celebrate Washington and Jefferson without reservations? What particular forms of respect should they bring to these figures?

There are many descriptions of this fundamental irony in the history whites celebrate, but few equal the eloquent speech Frederick Douglass gave in Corinthians Hall in Rochester, New York, on July 5, 1852, titled, "What to the Slave Is the Fourth of July?"

> I say it with a sad sense of the disparity between us. I am not included within the pale of this glorious anniversary! Your high independence only reveals the immeasurable distance between us. The blessings in which you, this day, rejoice, are not enjoyed in common. The rich inheritance of justice, liberty, prosperity and independence, bequeathed by your fathers, is shared by you, not by me. The sunlight that brought life and healing to you, has brought strife and death to me. This Fourth [of] July is yours, not mine. You may rejoice, I must mourn. To drag a man in fetters into the grand illuminated temple of liberty, and call upon him to join you in joyous anthems, were inhuman mockery and sacrilegious irony.

And if blacks and whites disagree on the Founding Fathers and the Fourth of July, other fundamental differences must lurk nearby. Perhaps what makes sense on one side of the color line will make no sense on the other and vice versa. Frequently this appears to be so. For example, when voters in Washington, D.C., reelected Marion Barry as mayor after he went to prison for smoking crack cocaine, many white Americans—and many black Americans, too—wondered what black D.C. voters (for it was assumed they were black) could have been thinking? Across white America, this election was viewed as convincing evidence that black residents of D.C., like the members of the black-majority jury that acquitted O. J. Simpson, were crazy, stupid, or monumentally confused. Or was it that blacks are easily duped by charlatans and demagogues?

It seems possible that blacks and whites see themselves as players in opposite dramas—that what is up on one side of the color line will be down on the other. Good is bad; bad is good. Across America, many whites almost automatically assume that blacks will always behave in contrary ways or side with criminals and rabble-rousers. However, black Americans often say much the same thing about white people, that whites are contrary and don't make sense. So in one world, whites are heroes and blacks, or individuals like Barry or Louis Farrakhan, are the villains and buffoons. And in sectors of the other world, blacks, or individuals like Barry or Farrakhan, can sometimes be the heroes, while whites are often villains and oddballs.

Whites have also come to notice that accomplishments by black Americans may get extra attention as history-making, while similar achievements by whites seem so much less noteworthy. Thus, when Virginia voters elected Douglas Wilder governor in 1990, the *Washington Post* said: "Virginia Democratic Lt. Gov. L. Douglas Wilder, a grandson of slaves, won a razor-thin victory over Republican J. Marshall Coleman yesterday to become the first black elected governor in U.S. history."

Wilder's victory was, of course, history-making, and it put him in unique historical terrain no white governor-elect will ever match. By comparison, the story line for Wilder's successor, Richard Allen, was downright pedestrian: he was merely the son of a pro football coach.

Perhaps, the difference is subtle here, and whites have no right to claim they are being wronged because it is assumed that whites will succeed. But the reason the white story line can seem anticlimactic is simple enough. In particular, white men have had no built-in obstacles such as slavery or Jim Crow segregation to overcome or glass ceilings to break through. And without barriers to hurdle, white accomplishments can appear almost humdrum, while successes by black people are heralded as triumphs of the human spirit.

In the 1970s whites began suspecting they were becoming forgotten players in the American drama because their accomplishments didn't inspire much notice next to the efforts of others, which were being hailed as "firsts." To be sure, whites could hardly claim to have been grievously wronged. This was a mere slight. But there was another detail whites also began to note: Black Americans were using the tale of past wrongs to explain their failures. And that didn't ring fair, either, because whites had no such excuses to fall back on.

Again, whites sensed blacks were getting a better deal, more credit when they succeeded, more sympathy when they failed—and more help along the way. This idea—that blacks were using past wrongs to lower the standards applied to them—quietly infiltrated white thinking, infecting our politics and much of what is taken for race relations. The charge was that "victimization" or a "victim mentality" was being used to gain unfair advantages for those who had been mistreated.

General bitterness about busing and other integration efforts or about antipoverty programs combined to convince many whites—and a few blacks, too—of active victimization. Lyndon Johnson's Great Society programs, in particular, were blamed for replacing individual initiative and personal responsibility with an expectation of government handouts. Conservatives accused liberals of convincing Americans they were helpless victims of a host of "isms"—racism, sexism, ageism. Columnist George Will called the phenomenon "the social science of victimology" and said, "Its specialty is the universalization of victimhood, the dispersal of responsibility into a fog of 'socioeconomic factors.'"

On top of all this, it was widely imagined that the triumph of victimization as the means to get one's way had permitted blacks and other "minorities" to hijack American values and take over the country. But how could blacks, a relatively small group, gain such colossal advantage over white people, a much larger group?

The political scene is a seemingly clear demonstration that blacks and whites see things differently. Black Americans overwhelmingly support the Democrats, while the Republican Party is overwhelmingly white. In fact, only 1 percent of registered Republican voters are black, but the Democratic Party is also white by a landslide; only 23 percent of all registered Democrats are black. So while obviously more blacks are Democrats, whites are still the overwhelming majority in both parties, and blacks are always in the minority. This means that most of the time, the two parties are telling a "white" story, or one that is primarily crafted to appeal to whites.

It is inevitable, too, that Republicans will appear whiter than the Democrats, because in fact they are. Therefore, Republicans are less beholden to black voters than the Democrats. They are, in fact, hardly beholden at all. And the whiteness of the Republican Party is no coincidence. The party inherited disaffected white Democrats from the formerly segregationist South, which became a Republican base after the federal government pressed integration against the theme of states' rights. And Republicans also appeal to whites who have fled cities for the suburbs.

Obviously, given this background, it is presumed that Republicans will seek political themes that appeal to whites. And Republicans do rail against racial quotas or affirmative action programs that seem to benefit blacks at white expense. But another means Republicans use to appeal to whites comes in their choice of heroes and villains. The Republican version of the American drama is likely to pit hard-working, God-fearing, tax-paying Americans against criminals, welfare cheats, and unqualified minorities using victimhood to get unfair advantages. Get the point? It can very easily seem, in accordance with standard racial stereotypes, that blacks are the bad guys and whites the good ones.

Many black Americans believe that Republicans, who were identified with Willie Horton ads and the like, are scandalously prowhite or shamelessly antiblack. Most black Americans maintain an affiliation with the Democrats, even if it is an unhappy one. Often, the Democrats ignore their black supporters, because white people are still their prime constituency; they need white votes to win. And for black people, loyalty to the Democrats has at times produced insulting results.

Early in the 1990s, the "new," middle-of-the-mainstream Democrats—the almost Republican-sounding Democrats—often sought to push "black" issues to the side. As a presidential candidate in 1992, Bill Clinton actually sought out opportunities to rebuke Jesse Jackson for philosophical indiscretion in an obviously calculated effort to show white voters he was not beholden to black interests. This detail was forgotten, however, when black Americans became Clinton's strongest supporters in his later times of need, and black churches became an environment in which he was most at home.

But candidate Clinton didn't want to pander to black voters in 1992. He made gestures to push them away, while figuring they also had no other place to go, which was true. Yet while Democrats were so self-consciously pushing their prominent black figures aside, in effect hiding their black support, Republicans pushed the few notable black Republicans to the fore, if only to show that theirs was not exclusively a party of whiteness.

Republicans also didn't have the slightest worry that anyone would say the Republican Party was *too* black. And they eventually had a prize catch—the extremely popular Colin Powell, the former army general and chairman of the Joint Chiefs of Staff. Polls showed that Powell was more popular among white Americans than he was among blacks. Late in 1995, however, Powell was the early-line favorite in the 1996 presidential race, with polls showing him beating incumbent Clinton—but with a curious twist: among black voters, Clinton was ahead by as much as 62 percent to 28 percent. What was that all about?

What was different about Powell was the story he told as a black American: He spoke of America as a land of opportunity, not the familiar rhetoric of black experience. Powell's parents were Jamaican immigrants; he was not a product of the old South. As a son of immigrants, Powell cited a family history that was common to millions of white families. "My parents came to this country as immigrants over 70 years ago," he told the 1996 Republican National Convention. "They came here, as had millions of others, with nothing but hope, a willingness to work hard, and a desire to use the opportunities given them by their new land. A land which they came to love with all their hearts."

This was not the familiar "black" story. There was no mention of slavery or segregation and no mention of rights and opportunities denied. "My parents found here a compassionate land, with a compassionate people," Powell said. "They found a government that protected their labor, educated their children and provided help to those of their fellow citizens who were needy. They found their dream in America and they passed that dream on to their children." In short, Powell told the Ellis Island version of the American story that so many whites recognize as theirs.

One can only wonder what Powell's speech would have been like if he had descended from generations of sharecroppers in Mississippi. Would it have been different? Would he have spoken of a benevolent, protective government? Would whites—and Republicans—have liked what he said nearly so much?

Still, American politics seems to play out in terms of basic themes that are common as well in terms of race. In the late 20th century, Republicans tended to be the party of the haves, wishing to defend against encroachment of the have-nots. Democrats tended to be the party of the less fortunate, one drawn to strategies for gaining the have-nots a little more. In this regard, Democrats claim they are the party of feeling and compassion, while Republicans often get involved with *things*—like the flag.

Much in these basic themes fits into the feeling-unfeeling, liberal-conservative, black-white dichotomies that haunt our thinking. But in reality, are blacks and whites all that different in their political views? Maybe less than we think. Blacks are supposed to be very liberal, right? And whites are supposed to be more conservative. This assumption is so common as to be inescapable in our understanding about race.

Yet on many issues, polls reveal that black and white views are strikingly similar, with black Americans describing themselves as more moderate or conservative than is commonly assumed. In a 1997 Gallup poll, for example, 27 percent of black Americans said they were "conservative," 37 percent said they were "moderate," and 28 percent said they were "liberal," while 37 percent of whites said they were "conservative," 46 percent said they were "moderate," and 21 percent said "liberal." So really, what's the big difference?

The largest number of both whites and blacks consider themselves "moderate," a stunning similarity that is generally overlooked. Also, a majority of black Americans are "conservative" on many issues. For example, 58 percent of black Americans in 1996 favored limiting welfare benefits to single mothers who have additional children; 73 percent favored mandatory sentences for drug dealers; and 90 percent favored increased enforcement of child-support laws.

Black Americans are also conservative in another regard. They are a minority, which brings a built-in sense of conservatism that comes with the understanding that one is always being watched and judged by members of a much larger majority, which means having to be careful about what one says and does.

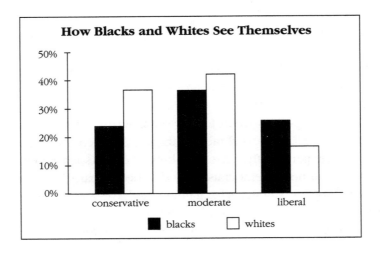

This conservatism becomes wariness about trying new things, going to new places, or trusting too thoroughly anyone outside one's circle. This way of thinking prefers the old and tried to the new and unproven. It accepts less on trust and long remembers bad examples, seeing the past as concrete evidence of what the future is likely to bring. Those accustomed to such thinking believe it's best for members of minority groups to go about their business quietly—the less notice they get, the better.

Hearing these themes of caution frequently expressed in black America might well make one puzzle about the claim of blacks as liberals. Black people can appear to be more forgiving on occasion—sometimes too forgiving—but this is an admirable, Christian virtue others might do well to match. It should not be taken to mean that blacks are starry-eyed liberals all the time. That's a huge misunderstanding about black Americans.

Where whites and blacks seem to divide most fundamentally is on the basic details of black American experience. Is there equal justice for all? Are there equal opportunities for all? Blacks and whites give a contradictory account of the American experience. Most whites describe a country that gives everyone an equal chance, while most blacks believe race still intrudes. And this disagreement reflects another racial divide—over the very existence of the racial divide. Black Americans are more likely to see America as two worlds, one white and one black. White Americans are more likely to believe that this is one nation indivisible.

Most white Americans also assume the philosophical issue of integration versus separation is now settled. Integration is the law of the land. Yet millions of black Americans still confront daily choices involving integration and separation, an experience that subtly alters their point of view. Integration may be the law, but America is not integrated. The choice, integration versus separation, confronts millions of black Americans daily in decisions big and small. Some might justifiably claim they face this choice every time they go out the front door: which way will they go—white America or black America?

The choice is inherent in decisions about where to live, worship, or send children to school. Whether they recognize it as a philosophical divide, white Americans make similar choices in avoiding black America; yet they are not likely to realize how prevalent these decisions are in the lives of many black Americans who see America as two worlds. Indeed, as W. E. B. DuBois wrote in *The Souls of Black Folk*, the divide can cause black Americans to sense themselves as two distinct beings:

> It is a peculiar sensation, this double-consciousness, this sense of always looking at one's self through the eyes of others, of measuring one's soul by the tape of a world that looks on in amused contempt and pity. One ever feels his twoness—an American, a Negro; two warring souls, two thoughts, two unreconciled strivings; two warring ideals in one dark body, whose dogged strength alone keeps it from being torn asunder.

Therefore, it should be no surprise that 50 percent of black Americans agreed in a 1994 survey by researchers at the University of Chicago and Wayne State University that black America is "a nation within a nation," and 50 percent also said they would support a separate black political party. Similarly, 55 percent said they support the idea of black-only institutions; 68 percent said blacks should control government in black communities; and 74 percent said blacks should have economic control in their own communities.

These opinions are a reflection of the continuing "twoness" in America. The assumption of two worlds echoes across conversations in black America whenever it is said that black people must solve black people's problems. Indeed, most calls for blacks to be responsible for their own lives and their own communities assume twoness— that blacks and whites do not live in the same place.

An even more extreme form of separationist rhetoric is found on any corner where the Nation of Islam newspaper, *The Final Call*, is sold. Always, on the penultimate page, *The Final Call* lists the late Honorable Elijah Muhammad's "program," including this: "We want our people in America, whose parents and grandparents were descendants from slaves, to be allowed to establish a separate state or territory of their own—either on this continent or elsewhere. . . . We want every Black man and woman to have the freedom to accept or reject being separated from the slave master's children and establish a land of their own."

Of course, not every black person in America subscribes to this call. Indeed, most do not. But the conflicting impulses about integration and separation that black Americans feel can confuse white Americans who often hope for a simpler explanation of what black people want.

Don't blacks want integration? Isn't that what Martin Luther King, Jr., marched for?

No, actually, it appears that black Americans sometimes want to be by themselves. And they want to be free to join white Americans at other times. These wishes are not as contradictory as they might seem. They are a product of a nation with two stories to tell, even though the people involved may not be as different as they are wont to believe.

Black America exists; it is real even though as a nation we are confused about it. And white politicians—even Bill Clinton—regularly inveigh against the concept of two nations. Here's what Clinton said about it on the day of the Million Man March: "Here, in 1995, on the edge of the 21st century, we dare not tolerate the existence of two Americas. Under my watch, I will do everything I can to see that, as soon as possible, there is only one."

Still, it is often asked, "Who speaks for black America?" Journalists ask this all the time. And the answer is no one. Black America has no official spokesperson, which can confuse white people even more, because if they want to know what black people think, whom are they supposed to ask?

This reality makes black America a paradoxical place with no capitol, president, or parliament. Meanwhile, the U.S. Senate, sometimes called the world's greatest deliberative body, currently has no black senators, so there's nobody to ask what black people think. If blacks were represented in proportion to their numbers in the population, we would have 12 or 13 black senators.

Nor, of course, has there ever been a black president, vice president, secretary of state, or Speaker of the House. But if blacks got a turn in proportion to their numbers, we would have already had five or six black presidents. And blacks are underrepresented in the House of Representatives, too. Even after the 1994 election, when there were 40 black representatives, the all-time high, blacks were less than 10 percent of all 435 representatives. Now there are 39, and 2, the representatives from the District of Columbia and the Virgin Islands, can't vote.

Furthermore, with this evident shortfall of representation in America's political mainstream, one might wonder how black Americans gained the tremendous advantages over whites that many white Americans imagine. How did they manage to get all those advantages from victimization? Why didn't whites just say no? That takes some explaining.

At the end of World War II, white Americans were truly on top of the world. They had vanquished evil empires in Europe and Asia, harnessed the atom, and were poised to move into the suburbs in massive numbers. Yet one discordant theme remained for those who saw themselves as promoters of liberty and progress, which came to be known as "civil rights."

Looking back on World War II, whites were the good guys. But in the drama about civil rights, they were emerging as the bad guys, and blacks were becoming the new heroes. And blacks had immeasurable help from whites in this heroic transformation: Ku Klux Klan terrorists; cretinous white mobs; and Southern police, who turned fire hoses and attack dogs loose on seemingly peaceful black demonstrators, all did their part on TV.

The world also saw whites—seemingly ordinary whites in Little Rock, Arkansas, Selma, Alabama, and outside Chicago, too—shouting vicious epithets at black schoolchildren or throwing rocks at black marchers. And whites burned and bombed black churches, killed black children, and assassinated black leaders. An ugly picture of white Americans indeed. Even the white Americans in the North, who briefly appeared to be on the sidelines of these struggles, eventually sensed themselves under assault on the issue of race.

Indeed, a unique transfer of moral authority had taken place. The heroes of World War II were the villains in the new drama. Black Americans, a hidden presence in World War II, became the heroes around the world for standing up to white oppressors. And when A. Philip Randolph introduced Martin Luther King, Jr., at the 1963 March on Washington as "the moral leader of America," this was no idle assertion. It was close to the truth.

King gave one of the most memorable speeches in American history, a simple yet eloquent plea for fairness for black people. "I have a dream," King said, "that this nation will rise up and live out the true meaning of its creed, 'We hold these truths to be self evident, that all men are created equal.' . . . I have a dream that my four little children will one day live in a nation where they will not be judged by the color of their skin, but the content of their character."

Around the world, black Americans were seen to have seized the moral high ground, heroism in the face of long odds. Yet the righteousness in their cause overcame their disadvantage in numbers, and they turned whites into the bad guys.

For a time white Americans were almost automatically assumed to be racists, as if this flaw was rudimentary to their nature, almost an original sin. It was claimed that white racism was a reflex incorporated into the workings of society at every level. White thought, speech, and action were infused with racism. Whites, it was claimed, could no more rid themselves of racism than they could live without air. And this view of white people as racist was retroactive as well.

Suddenly, history seemed open to drastic revision: Columbus was no visionary; instead, it was said that he initiated a chain of events that wiped out most of the indigenous population on two continents. Then the fabled opening of the American West was a bloodbath, a continuation of the horrors Columbus had started. Even as Americans were landing on the moon, the country was embroiled in a war that was widely reviled as evil. In this period, which would subsequently be recalled as the time when America doubted itself, white Americans were hard-pressed to see themselves as the shining knights of history.

On the lead of black Americans, other Americans also realized that their rights had been abridged. Women demanded new opportunities in the workplace and an end to male dominance. Other ethnic groups demanded their own rightful place. The handicapped demanded access in the mainstream; the elderly demanded fairer treatment; and gay people demanded basic respect. Far and wide across American society, there was a clamor for rights.

In fact, it might have seemed that almost everyone in America was demanding rights of some sort. The U.S. population includes 139 million females, or about 51 percent of the total, and 114 million of these females are white, 42 percent of the total population. And they all had rights to call for. Hispanics represent 30.4 million people, or 11.1 percent of the U.S. population that sensed it also had rights. Together, Hispanics and white women add up to 144 million people, 53 percent of the total U.S. population. Adding another 35 million black Americans, the group grows to 179 million, or the equivalent of two thirds of the U.S. population that under this new consciousness could consider itself an aggrieved "minority." Toss in the elderly—the 36 million or so who are above age 65—and the disabled, and the numbers keep growing.

Of course, millions of Americans might have "minority" rights from several sources, such as being both elderly and Hispanic. Presumably one could even be elderly, Hispanic, disabled, black, and female, all at the same time. This demonstrates how overwhelming the demand for rights could seem. Virtually everyone other than white males under age 65 could claim broadened rights in the wake of a movement black Americans began.

And because white males run just about everything, from the government to major corporations, it seemed like white males were catching hell for all the ills of the world. And perhaps, they blamed black Americans for starting all this, but black Americans were hardly the problem.

White males, who number about 110 million, or about 40 percent of the U.S. population, are a powerful group. But their own mothers, daughters, sisters, and wives outnumber them. So massive forces were allied against white males, who were, in fact, losing some of their control. Only it wasn't to black people, who only number 35 million; it was to just about *everybody* who wasn't a white male. And black people themselves were even getting lost in the shuffle.

But whites had another problem: they had never been absolved of those original charges of racism. Some whites protested that they had never owned any slaves or slaughtered any Indians, so why should they be blamed? But the argument sounded lame, and it discounted any advantages that might have accrued from 400 years of slave labor and millions of acres of expropriated Indian land. Other whites swore they had no bad thoughts about black people—that they were totally color-blind—but they often protested this too much. Nothing whites said could remove the stain of racism and turn them into the good guys again.

It may, therefore, have been no coincidence that Ronald Reagan excelled at telling stories. And the stories he told were often about good guys and bad guys. The way Reagan told it, Americans were boundlessly good, and the Soviet Union was the "evil empire." It could easily be inferred from Reagan's stories that white Americans were hardworking and black Americans were riding around in "welfare" Cadillacs.

Black Americans were uneasy about the coming of Ronald Reagan; white Americans were said to be feeling better about themselves. Reagan and conservatives were engineering a new shift in moral authority, "the Reagan revolution." As white Americans reassumed their role as good guys, black Americans were increasingly associated with problems—crime, violence, civil disorder, corruption, drugs, declining cities, and moral decay.

And if storytelling wasn't important, why did so many Americans tune in to Rush Limbaugh? He railed against "multiculturalism," which he summarized as: "Indians are good. White Europeans are bad. Blacks are good. Asians, we're not so sure about." Limbaugh, who has a sense of humor, also warned against the rewriting of history by "Columbashers, who turned the 500th anniversary of Columbus's landing in the New World into an irrebuttable (in their own minds) presumption of prejudice against Western culture."

Limbaugh concluded that this prejudice involved—note the words—"a not so subtle racism so insidious and pervasive as to be almost unspeakable."

Surely, this idea represented another sea change in the American story line. In the civil rights movement, blacks charged whites with racism; now many whites were convinced that they were victims and Limbaugh called the racism "unspeakable." Was this hyperbole? Maybe not. In a 1991 Peter Hart poll, a majority of whites said "qualified whites" were being more hurt by the reverse discrimination of affirmative action programs than "qualified blacks" were hurt by the discrimination these programs sought to remedy. In other words, a majority of whites said whites were now the primary victims of discrimination in America.

If whites had once felt helpless against charges of racism—how can one deny it?—they were now claiming to be its victims on many fronts. Limbaugh and others swore that an oppressive orthodoxy, "political correctness," was depriving whites of their constitutional right to free speech. Jokes about blacks or any other group that had "minority" status were off-limits. Idle remarks about these same people were thought to be extremely dangerous. And serious observations that these "minorities" might not like were suppressed, because truth was no defense. Limbaugh termed *political correctness* "a threat to free expression and the constitutional limits on government" and championed a University of Pennsylvania student accused of "racial harassment" after he shouted, "Shut up, you water buffaloes!" at a group of black women making noise outside his dorm window while he was trying to study.

But frank discussion about race was also said to be impossible. "We will never have the candid dialogue and real debate we should have," lamented former New York Mayor Ed Koch. "If [white Americans] talk honestly, they'll be called racists."

Speaking unguardedly about black people, in fact, has cost a few white people their jobs. In 1987, Los Angeles Dodgers Vice President Al Campanis was fired for saying on ABC's *Nightline*, "I truly believe [blacks in baseball] may not have some of the necessities to be, let's say, a field manager or perhaps a general manager." The next year, CBS fired Jimmy "the Greek" Snyder for his comments on black athletes and slavery.

It was claimed—and widely believed among whites—that these were dangerous times for whites to open their mouths. At the same time, many whites believed that blacks had carte blanche to say what they pleased about white people—a double standard. Some whites were even disturbed that black people regularly used variants on the word *nigger* among themselves, but whites were not allowed to use the word at all. This seemed symbolic of the restraint whites regularly faced, and this notion of oppression of white people has not gone away.

As recently as 1998, a writer in the newsletter of the Council of Conservative Citizens issued this "Call to White Americans" for an end to such double standards:

Among all the races . . . the white American alone cannot feel pride in, defend, or even define his racial identity without arousing suspicion or outright hatred. He cannot form a Congressional White Caucus. He cannot hang the works of white artists on a gallery wall and identify them as such. He has no month, no week, not even a day set aside to teach his children, his neighbors and his countrymen about the origins of the white race, ancient and modern white history, and the accomplishments of white individuals and the issues facing modern white people.

Isn't it ironic that the victims of this new "racism" were among those who previously claimed blacks were using victimization to get themselves a better deal? And these new "victims" were members of the overwhelming white majority in America, which raised the question of how "minorities" could oppress the majority in a democracy?

Eventually, it would seem, the majority will have its way. So if political correctness was *really* silencing the white majority, several other phenomena needed to be explained. One was Howard Stern. For

Stern, saying the "wrong" or politically incorrect thing on the radio was obviously the right thing to do. Stern never obeyed the laws of political correctness. Of beaten L.A. motorist Rodney King, Stern commented, "They didn't beat this idiot enough. He should be beaten every time he reaches for his car keys."

And how much did Stern suffer? Among his devotees, Stern is considered brilliant—and valiant, too—for saying whatever pops into his head, and he has been fined or punished in other ways for his act. But if political correctness was truly such an awesome barrier, how come Stern and others breach it so profitably? Slaying the dragon of political correctness, if anything, helped make Stern rich. Without it, how could he earn a reported $7 million a year?

And if political correctness is such a deterrent to free speech, how come *The Bell Curve* spent months on the bestseller list? In *The New Republic*, coauthor Charles Murray claimed that other scholars and journalists were "scared stiff" of the book's subject matter on IQ and race. But this claim looked more like an attempt to promote a heroic pose; many thought Murray's ideas were merely bad. And who would claim that political correctness was such a force as to prevent Murray from being heard? He was heard all over the place.

Perhaps amazingly, a key turn in the story line that made whites the good guys again involved Martin Luther King's 1963 speech in D.C. This famous plea for the rights of black people—"I have a dream that my four little children . . . will not be judged by the color of their skin, but the content of their character"—was rediscovered for its value to white Americans, too.

These very same words became the means to free whites from the stigma of their past sins. And it worked like this: if whites are not judged by the color of their skin, then they could not be held accountable for the sins of white slaveowners, segregationists, and old-time racists. And if whites are not judged by the color of their skin, they need not be called upon to redress wrongs done by whites in other times and places. Perhaps whites need not even feel guilty about the evils of the past and instead could claim a clean slate on matters involving race, slavery, segregation, and discrimination, starting here and now.

King's standard of character not skin color cast immediate doubt upon remedies undertaken in the name of righting past wrongs.

Affirmative action would be wrong by this standard if it recognized people by the color of their skin. Instead, whites argued, it was time to put race behind us and be color-blind. Let's not see color at all, they said.

Perhaps white Americans chose character over skin color because they also believe they are well stocked in this regard and others are not. That might be the case. But it also seemed that the landscape of racial discussion—the charges and countercharges—had shifted without anyone much noting the event. The old charges of white racism from the days of the civil rights movement were heard much less, and they were given less credence when they arose. Sometimes, they didn't work at all.

Many whites assumed that blacks who made such charges were "playing the race card" or seeking to blame others for their own failings. Meanwhile, the charge of unfairness to whites in affirmative action and other programs was heard much more. Almost any discussion of race was likely to center on that. Blacks were no longer given great recognition as victims in the American experience. Whites had usurped that role for themselves. Once again the tribulations and struggles of white people were center stage.

8

DOGS AND MONKEYS

Tracking Our Worst Thoughts

Any dictionary of the English language is full of insidious messages about race. A scene in Spike Lee's film *Malcolm X* demonstrated this disturbing truth. At age 20, a bitter, angry Malcolm was sentenced to a 10-year prison term. Another inmate, soon to emerge as his mentor, entreats Malcolm to reject the hold of white thinking. When Malcolm is skeptical, especially about the mentor's belief that freedom is found in knowledge, the mentor reads from *Webster's Collegiate Dictionary* the definition for *black*: "Black—destitute of light, devoid of color, enveloped in darkness, hence ultimately dismal or gloomy, as in, 'The future looked black.'"

"You're pretty good with those words, ain't you?" Malcolm notes.

The mentor continues to read: ". . . Soiled with dirt . . . foul . . . sullen . . . hostile . . . forbidding, as in 'a black day' . . . thoroughly outrageous. . . . Wicked—as *black* cruelty . . . indicating disgrace, dishonor or culpability . . ."

But Malcolm still doubts how this knowledge can set him free, so the mentor suggests, "Let's look up *white*," and hands Malcolm the book. Malcolm reads: "White—the color of pure snow, reflecting all the rays of the spectrum. The opposite of black, free from spots or blemishes . . . innocent . . . pure."

"Huh," the awakening Malcolm says. "Ain't this something?"

He continues reading: "Without evil intent . . . harmless . . . honest . . . square-dealing and honorable . . ."

"Hey," he exclaims. "This is written by white folks, ain't it? This is a white folks' book!"

Are dictionaries "white" books? If they are an objective record of the meaning of words, how come a dictionary—any ordinary dictionary—offers such a host of positive associations for words like *white* and an even longer list of negative associations for words like *black*? Is it some kind of plot?

Anyone can investigate this puzzle. Take the word *dark*, for example. The definitions in *Webster's New World Dictionary of the American Language* include "not fair in complexion, brunet or swarthy; hidden, secret; not easily understood, hard to make clear, obscure; gloomy; hopeless; dismal; angry or sullen—as in 'a *dark* countenance'—evil; sinister; ignorant, unenlightened."

Most of our problems about race are there in a nutshell. This simple list includes the most common stereotypes about blacks: sullen, angry, sinister, ignorant, not easily understood. And white people *do* seem willing to consider themselves innocent, pure, without evil intent, harmless, honest, square-dealing, and honorable. *Webster's* also lists *blackball, black book, Black Death, black flag, black hole, blacklist, black magic, black sheep*, and *black widow*. Is this part of a grand design—a conspiracy?—to make whites look good and blacks bad? Is the dictionary supporting white supremacy?

Now hold on. The dictionary defines words as they are commonly used—usage determines the definition. We cannot alter fundamental realities of life on Earth: day and night, light and dark, sunlight and shadow. When the sun goes down, darkness comes, and it's impossible to see clearly—that's a given. Could the laws of physics be conspiring to favor white people? No way.

But as Malcolm X asked in the movie, who writes the dictionary? In a country that is 82.1 percent white and 12.9 percent black, whites will dominate the evolution of language. Blacks might reasonably expect the dictionary to reflect white beliefs that black people are sullen, angry, sinister, ignorant, and unfathomable.

Nation of Islam members, for whom Malcolm became a spokesperson, argue that whites have manipulated the language so that black people have a negative view of themselves. The Honorable Elijah Muhammad, founder of the Nation (which came to be known as the Black Muslims) coined the word *tricknology* for white manipulations that cause black people to believe false propaganda about them. He said tricknology was the work of "white devils." Some black Americans have tried to reverse the effects of tricknology—hence, for the word *blackmail*, they use the word *whitemail*. But this movement has not had wide impact.

In the world of sports, the *color* black is thought to be loaded with "dark" and "sinister" associations. Teams that wore black—among them the powerful Pittsburgh Steelers and Oakland Raiders football teams in the 1970s and 1980s—were identified by a hard-hitting, aggressive, "outlaw" style of play that sometimes crossed the limits of the rules. But it was never clear whether black uniforms caused the hard hitting or the hard-hitting teams caused this association with the color black.

An epidemic of black sportswear ensued. Team after team bought black uniforms and black sportswear came into vogue. Would teams play more aggressively in black and win more games? Well, lousy teams wore black, too. Then black sportswear also became the rage among "outlaw" street gangs.

At Cornell University psychologists Thomas D. Gilovich and M. G. Frank found that black-clad teams did seem to play more aggressively than white-clad teams. They also found this correlation was not necessarily an advantage: referees also viewed black-clad teams as more aggressive and called more penalties. The Cornell researchers found National Hockey League teams that had switched to black in midseason suddenly got more penalties after the change. Why did it happen? The Cornell researchers didn't know. Others, however, insisted that any links between the color black and "outlaw" imagery was surely learned behavior. Generations of Americans had watched Hollywood cowboy movies in which the bad guys wore black hats and the good guys wore white hats. And generations after that were exposed in *Star Wars* to dark figures like Darth Vader, whose memorable voice emanating from a black visor was that of black actor James Earl Jones.

Language and popular culture aside, for centuries the tendency was to portray black people as closer to the animals than to civilized Europeans who were making these assessments, even among those who considered themselves scientists. For example, Georges Cuvier (1769–1832), a Swiss anatomist sometimes credited as the founder of paleontology (the study of prehistoric fossils), was one of various observers who believed he saw links between black people and apes. In 1812 he wrote:

> The Negro race is confined to the south of mount Atlas [a mountain in Moroccan North Africa]; it is marked by a black complexion, crisped or woolly hair, compressed cranium and flat nose. The projection of the lower parts of the face, and the thick lips, evidently approximate it to the monkey tribe: The hordes of which it consists have always remained in the most complete state of utter barbarism.

This stupid notion still survives today, as both apes and black people are commonly associated with Africa or because apes have dark skin. It survives, too, in epithets such as "porch monkeys," referring to black people gathered on a front porch, or in occasional statements that whites usually explain as slips of the tongue. These blacks-as-monkey incidents keep happening, such as the night in 1983 when Howard Cosell exclaimed on *Monday Night Football*, referring to Washington Redskins wide receiver Alvin Garrett, ". . . that little monkey gets loose, doesn't he?" In 1995, a New York Yankees executive got into trouble when he cited the destruction of basketball hoops in a nearby park as an example of neighborhood decay around Yankee Stadium. "It's like monkeys," he said. "Those guys can all go up and hang on the rim and crack the rim and bend the hoops. It's a continuous maintenance problem."

But this question of which race is more closely related to apes could be viewed quite differently. Whites may *think* they see a link between blacks and apes, but those in the know, so to speak, make a different connection. "If racists would take the trouble to visit their local zoo and for a moment drop their air of superiority and take a dispassionate look at one of the apes," anthropologist Ashley Montague once noted, "they would find the hair of these creatures lank [straight and limp, not curly], that their lips are thin, and that their bodies are profusely covered with hair. In these characteristics, the white man stands nearer the apes."

Meanwhile, it is curious—surely a coincidence—that the dictionary definitions for *white* refer to "purity" in terms of *milk* and *snow*. According to old folklore among black Americans, white women are supposed to smell like sour milk. Black stereotypes also inevitably link white people to cold—both cold weather and coldness of temperament. White people are thought to be cold-weather people, just as blacks are hot-weather people. From a black perspective, the Winter Olympics could look like a sports festival dedicated to white peoples' affinity for ice and snow. Very few black people are involved, and no black athlete has ever won a Winter Olympics gold medal, although figure skaters have come close.

To some black Americans, the sight of white people frolicking in snow remains a prime example of strange white behavior: Keep me away from that. But to many whites the idea of black people frolicking in snow is odder still, almost an automatically humorous premise. It was the underlying comedic gambit of a Hollywood movie, *Cool Running*, about the true exploits of a bobsled team from Jamaica. Of course, they did not win; just participating was considered an accomplishment.

Yet for all the alleged purity that surrounds the idea of whiteness, white Americans are surprised—shocked—to hear the very common stereotype among black Americans that white people are dirty; whites are believed to be messy in their personal habits and lax in their personal hygiene. How could this be? It's an idea that could easily have its roots in the era when blacks were frequently hired as janitors or domestic help, and it could even be as old as slavery. Those who have spent their lives cleaning up after whites were not likely to claim it was an easy job. When they came home, domestic workers most likely described in intimate detail the work involved in cleaning up after white people.

The idea that whites are unclean remains surprisingly common. In a February 1995 *Essence* magazine article "A Marriage in Black and White," Katrina La Throp noted: "It was difficult for me to make peace with myself and to ignore the stereotypes I'd learned in the past. As a child, for example, I was told that white people were untrustworthy and dirty. So what possible justification could there be for interacting—not to mention sleeping—with a white man?"

Some black Americans can't help but recall these stereotypes when they notice white people acting in a way that seems disgusting. They see evidence that at least some white people don't wash their hands after they go to the toilet or that they pick their noses at the dinner table, or that they scratch their rear ends in public. Henry Louis Gates, Jr., recalls in *Colored People: A Memoir* the discovery that his mother had a long list of negative ideas about white people:

White people, she said, were *dirty*: They tasted right out of pots on the stove. Only some kind of animal, or the lowest order of trash, would ever taste out of a pot on the stove. . . . Tasting right out of the pot was almost as bad as drinking after somebody on the same side of the cup or glass, or right after them on a Coca-Cola bottle without wiping their lips off real good. . . . One thing we always did was smell good, partly because we like scents, but partly because white people said we smelled bad *naturally*, like we had some sort of odor gene. "Here come you niggers, funking up the place"—even we'd crack that kind of joke a lot. So one thing colored people *had* to do around white people *was smell good*. . . . But it was white people who smelled bad, Mama always said, when they got wet. When they get wet, she said, they smell like dogs. . . . That these doggy-smelling white people should cast olfactory aspersions upon *us* was bitter gall for her.

Gates admits to having "done a lot of sniffing of wet-headed white people in my time" to disprove the wet-dog premise. But he is by no means the only black American to have heard it. The same theme is raised somewhat coyly—a black audience would surely get the reference—in *The Autobiography of Malcolm X* as Malcolm recounts his old message as a spokesperson for the Nation of Islam:

Few white people realize that many black people today dislike and avoid spending any more time than they must around white people. This "integration" image, as it is popularly interpreted, has millions of vain, self-exalted white people convinced that black people want to sleep in bed with them—and that's a lie! Or you can't tell the average white man that the Negro man's prime desire isn't to have a white woman—another lie! Like a black brother recently observed to me, "Look, you ever smell one of them *wet?*"

Another view of whites suggests they have an unusual relationship with their dogs; it is noted that some whites kiss their dogs on the lips, while black people look upon their dogs in more practical terms, as hunting dogs or guard dogs. Some suspect that white people would willingly lavish more attention and resources on their pets than on children who are suffering elsewhere in the world. That notion also returns us to the stereotype that white people are cold and unfeeling toward the misfortunes of others.

This judgment can be the underlying theme in almost any charge that white America is ignoring the pain and suffering in black America or anywhere else. And historic examples of this alleged white characteristic are easy to cite. Start with slavery; continue with segregation; add World Wars I and II, including the Holocaust and the dropping of the atomic bombs.

Only occasionally are whites aware of such charges or do they take them seriously. Whites, of course, will protest that they *do* have feelings, that it is ridiculous to say whites are heartless by nature. Some white Americans got a small taste of these ideas through a 1991 controversy over lectures delivered by Leonard Jeffries, a professor at City College of New York, who referred to blacks as "sun people" and whites as "ice people." Hot and cold again. "Our thesis is that the sun people, the African family of warm communal hope," he said, "meets an antithesis, the vision of ice people, Europeans, colonizers, oppressors, the cold, rigid element in world history."

News accounts reported that black students on several campuses wildly cheered Jeffries, especially after he became the target of white critics. But what brought Jeffries the most notoriety were his accusations against Jews—that Jews played a major role in the slave trade and later used their influence in the entertainment industry to promote negative images of black people. He was soon hounded by accusations of anti-Semitism, but his view that whites are "dastardly devilish folks" tended to be more of a laughing matter among many whites who heard about them. But understand, too, that Jeffries was hardly the originator of the ideas linked to him. Many others have sensed that the history of blacks and whites is a clash of cultures that could loosely be described as hot and cold. And there is little argument that black Africans have been victimized by white Europeans at various points in history, enough to justify a suspicion that there might be something inherently violent or demanding of power in the nature of white people.

Whites often consider such accusations unreasonable and irresponsible, likely to stir up trouble among those—here's another stereotype—who lack the ability to judge them rationally. Hence, the suspicion often is that blacks who hear about past sins against themselves are likely to lose control of their feelings—that also being their suspected nature.

Understand, too, that whites are not all that used to having themselves viewed as a group. They tend to see themselves as the norm and others as odd, but they are also used to thinking of themselves as a group involving a great variety; all whites are not the same. In short, they are used to looking at others—at blacks—as odd, but they are not accustomed to having others look at them as a group with quirks and curious propensities. Whites usually don't expect that others are watching them and drawing conclusions from everyday white behavior. But various theories and claims have been advanced about the origins of white behavior that include speculations, learned and otherwise, about prehistoric times. In these theories, which whites generally ignore, the common stereotypical assumptions whites make about themselves are reversed: blacks—or people of color—are the humane, civilized builders of stable societies, while whites are aggressive, marauding, violent, nomadic people driven by urges to conquer, pillage, and destroy.

Meanwhile, according to most credible accounts, the human race originated in equatorial Africa, and the initial human beings were dark-skinned, which protected them from the effects of ultraviolet rays. But some early humans eventually migrated northward into Europe where there is much less direct sunlight, and dark skin can be a disadvantage if it blocks the sunlight needed to synthesize vitamin D required for strong bones. Hence, over thousands of years, the skin color of the humans in northern climates gradually lightened with the survival of individuals with less of the melanin that darkens skin. They survived because with less melanin, they absorbed more sunlight, synthesized more vitamin D, and were less likely to contract the disease called rickets.

But this analysis does not claim to explain anything related to temperament or character. And it certainly doesn't bring good and evil into play, which seems to be the prime intent in other less credible claims about human origins. Some in the old South claimed, without much evidence in the Bible or elsewhere, that black people were descendants of Ham, the son of Noah who was cursed by his father for looking upon his father's nakedness. Meanwhile, Elijah Muhammad preached that white people were the creation of an evil Mr. Yacub, who selectively bred lighter black people in the isolation of an island off Africa until he had created a white population. According to Malcolm X in his *Autobiography*, Elijah Muhammad clearly delineated who were the good and bad people in this story: "On the Island of Patmos was nothing but these blond, pale-skinned, cold-blue-eyed devils—savages, nude and shameless; hairy like animals, they walked on all fours and lived in trees." When Mr. Yacub's whites returned to Africa, black people quickly realized these whites were more like animals—nothing but trouble—and expelled them to the north toward Europe and Asia, where the white people donned animal skins for protection against the cold and took up residence in caves.

Most Americans, of course, are familiar with depictions, from school texts or from fanciful creations such as *The Flintstones* cartoons, of cavemen as hairy creatures in animal skins. But this portrayal of cavemen and cavewomen as "our" ancestors gives cause for black people to take exception—to say, "That wasn't us." In most cases, the caves referred to were in Europe, so black Americans could look upon the depictions of hairy cavemen in animal skins and conclude: "Thank goodness, these aren't our ancestors. Our ancestors didn't live like that. Our ancestors came from Africa where the climate is warm."

Hence, it became easy to imagine that this experience of living in caves somehow shaped white people in ways that led to slavery, colonialism, white supremacy, and other evils. For example, in a 1992 volume, *Making of the Whiteman: History, Tradition and the Teachings of Elijah Muhammad*, author Paul Lawrence Guthrie attempts to show that Elijah Muhammad's story of Mr. Yacub parallels evidence about the ways of cave dwellers and confirms that white people developed an aggressive, violent nature. "With the arrival of the Caucasians into that cold and sparsely populated area of the world," says Guthrie, "the few older communities, which earlier had been established there in Europe, were either abandoned or destroyed. The evidence clearly suggests that the original inhabitants of those settlements either fled or were killed off."

So in this line of thinking, we are to imagine two trails of development, one black and one white. Darker people came from Egypt and Africa, the warm-weather cradles of civilization and knowledge, while whites came from cold, foul-smelling caves where they lived in shameless filth, which just happens to be a reaffirmation of the stereotype that whites are dirty. Indeed, Guthrie creates a particularly disgusting portrait of cave life:

> At the end of the tunnel was an underground nest or den. Like the natural cave, the hollow offered the whiteman a place of refuge and safety, where he could hide, eat and sleep. . . . In times of bitter cold, the inhabitants of the hollow could cover

the entrance with excrement or manure. This was a popular way of keeping warm during the winter months. In addition to blocking out the cold air, the steam produced beneath rotting excrement served to warm and humidify the inside of the hollow. . . . Ancient sources indicate that keeping warm by staying beneath massive piles of stench was common throughout many parts of Europe.

Again, this view of white people as savage cave dwellers is long-standing. Marcus Garvey, the black nationalist who proposed to move black Americans back to the safety of Africa, made reference to whites and caves in a 1923 essay. "Every student of history, of impartial mind, knows that the Negro once ruled the world, when the white men were savages and barbarians living in caves; that thousands of Negro professors at the time taught in the universities in Alexandria, then the seat of learning."

Garvey even put these ideas in poetic form, adding suggestions that whites were cannibals and vampires, too:

Out of cold old Europe these white men came,
From caves, dens and holes, without any fame,
Eating their dead's flesh and sucking their blood.

Still others give prehistoric origins to "white" behaviors. In a 1978 book *The Iceman Inheritance: Prehistoric Sources of Western Man's Racism, Sexism and Aggression*, Michael Andrew Bradley claimed that whites were descended from an old line of European Neanderthals. "A uniquely aggressive creature shivered beside his caves during the icy [glacial period]," he writes, "a uniquely alienated creature, a creature uniquely conscious of physical differences among people . . . and distrustful of those differences."

This may seem like an obscure theory—or an obscure book—but I was surprised how many black people had heard of it or suggested I should look it up. And I would note this only as an indicator that these ideas are not hidden in the stacks of a library but still circulating in the real world. Some writers also assert—and Professor Jeffries seemed to agree—that black people are biologically, intellectually, and even spiritually superior to white people. One such claim attempts to explain the relatively common black stereotype that black people are more spiritually and morally attuned than whites. The theory is that the presence of melanin helps open pathways to activity on the right side of the brain, which in turn enhances the development of intuitive faculties, holistic thinking, and the ability to comprehend spiritual truth. In contrast, the absence of melanin in white people has the opposite effect: They are less intuitive, less holistic in their thinking, and less aware of spiritual truth.

OK?

The point here is not to claim these theories are accurate or backed by credible research. Nor is it to claim that most black people subscribe to them. The important point is that these ideas are out there, perhaps even as subconscious accompaniment to the daily interactions of race. But white Americans, largely because of their relative isolation from black people, are less likely to realize that their behavior could be watched and judged in these terms. Yet how often might it be that black people sense coldness in white people or a lack of empathy with the suffering of others? It could happen every day, even by accident or misunderstanding. How often might it be that black people see whites as unclean and casual about their personal hygiene? That, too, might be a daily occurrence. How often might it be that whites seem overly aggressive and hungry for power and control?

To whites who may be familiar with the assumption that blacks are a problem, it could be surprising to realize that others are likely to view *white* people as the problem. Remember the 1994 poll in which 79 percent of black respondents said whites believe they are superior and can boss others around and 76 percent said whites don't want to share wealth and power with others? And among these were many blacks who said they had white friends.

Meanwhile, Bradley concludes in *Iceman Inheritance* that whites are "maladapted," while others says whites have inferiority complexes involving sexual inadequacy and other matters. Bradley argues that the genitalia of white males must necessarily be small to have survived the rigors of cold weather without frostbite. Frances Cress Welsing, a Washington, D.C., psychiatrist, author, and lecturer, argues that whites sense a genetic inferiority, because any mating with darker people produces darker people; and whites fear their own genetic extinction will come about in this mix.

In *The Isis Papers: The Keys to the Colors*, Welsing also examines white behavior, in general, in terms of the psychiatric disorder known as narcissism. She writes:

The third *Diagnostic and Statistical Manual of Mental Disorders* (1980), published by the American Psychiatric Association, contains a description of the narcissistic personality disorder, with the following stated criteria:

A. Grandiose sense of self-importance or uniqueness

B. Preoccupation with fantasies of unlimited success, power, brilliance, beauty, or ideal love

C. Exhibitionistic: Requires constant attention and admiration

D. Responds to criticism, indifference of others, or defeat with either cool indifference or with marked feelings of rage, inferiority, shame, humiliation, or emptiness

E. Two of the following:

    1. Lack of empathy: Inability to recognize how others feel

    2. Entitlement: Expectation of special favors with reactions or surprise or anger when others don't comply

    3. Interpersonal exploitiveness: Takes advantage of others to indulge his own desires for self-aggrandizement, with disregard for personal integrity and rights of others

    4. Relationships characteristically vacillate between the extremes of over-idealization and devaluation

Welsing concludes: "Any non-white person who has had extensive experience with whites, collectively or as individuals, will find in the above a description of those relationships." And many black Americans will agree with her.

    Whites can dismiss all this as craziness, warped pseudoscience, or thinly disguised race hatred, just as blacks might dismiss as warped pseudoscience or race hatred much of the so-called scientific evidence that was used in the past to describe white supremacy and black inferiority. Not unexpectedly, Welsing's theories have not been widely accepted in the white world—or even widely circulated there—but I know many black people who consider her wise. And she is not the only observer to see narcissism in American culture. Author Tom Wolfe labeled the 1970s the "Me Decade," and author Christopher Lasch produced a much-praised book called *The Culture of Narcissism: American Life in an Age of Diminishing Expectations*. We must also recognize that America is a huge nation of millions of whites and blacks, enough people—or enough kooks and crazies—to provide evidence to support almost any theory. Evidence of white hatred or belief in white supremacy will regularly surface in isolated Klan and neo-Nazi rallies, in white supremacist Internet sites, or in hate crimes enough to fuel any belief that there must be something seriously wrong with white people.

A critical gulf between black and white perceptions also opened over the specific realities of life in black America, where AIDS, drug abuse, and street warfare were becoming epidemic in the 1980s and 1990s. Blacks, of course, would be most likely to know about this reality; those whites who rarely visit black America are getting most of their information on these subjects at long distance. But whites are often quick to label as crazy—outlandish—any claim that whites are responsible for this reality or that it is part of a white conspiracy against black people. And whites are likely to ridicule claims that AIDS, drug abuse, and street warfare have resulted from the designs of ice people against warm, spiritual, peace-loving people of the sun.

That such conspiracy theories arise in black America, or gain credibility there, is one of the most difficult phenomena in race relations to explain to white Americans. Many whites think it is simply crazy. It doesn't matter to them that some elements of past conspiracy-like behavior on the part of whites have been proven, from slavery to FBI spying on Martin Luther King, Jr. Whites view as delusional any claim that whites are trying to control or wipe out black people or that whites are targeting black Americans in any way. And surprisingly often, whites cite a perverse logic to explain how this is impossible: if whites really wanted to get rid of black people, they would surely have done a much better job of it.

Meanwhile, the calamitous results of the AIDS epidemic, drug abuse, and street warfare are undeniably real, if not so clear to those outside black communities. In some black neighborhoods, even in my own, the costs in death and incarceration or fatherless and motherless children are incalculable. My neighborhood and many others in black America have lost more sons and daughters to these plagues and street wars than were taken by Vietnam or any other war. And recognizing this truth is pivotal to understanding the power and strange logic, if you will, of conspiracy theories: they involve horrible events that have already occurred.

There has been—and still is—a plague of AIDS, drug abuse, and street warfare in black America and it has been devastating. Can we at least agree on that? And to scoff at conspiracy theories that attempt to explain how these evils happened runs perilously close to scoffing at the awful events the theories seek to explain. And this is not quite right either. Whether it was a conspiracy or not, the terrible events did occur.

Still, for many white Americans, claims that whites are to blame for AIDS, drug abuse, or street warfare seem so outlandish that they cannot contain their contempt. Since they cannot fathom such possibilities, many whites conclude that black people must be jumping to unwarranted conclusions or that charlatans and demagogues have fooled black people. And we are back to the same old beliefs that black people can't think straight. Forgetting that many whites also imagine government or other conspiracies are all around them, too, many whites conclude that blacks must be crazy.

It is also worth noting that when whites claim an outside force has targeted white communities for an evil onslaught, the claim is taken seriously—and it may even turn out to be true. In the 1990s, Mexican drug lords targeted cities in Iowa as potential markets for methamphetamine, variously known as "crank" or "crystal meth." Could outsiders introduce a drug plague in white communities much as blacks believe their neighborhoods have been targeted? Apparently so. Methamphetamine and crimes related to it became the top law enforcement problem in Iowa and surrounding states. "Our greatest problem today is illegal aliens and drugs," said Tom Pagel, director of Wyoming's Department of Criminal Investigation. "The vast majority of this is being transported up from Mexico, and we're getting our butts kicked over it."

So how can we resolve this racially charged disagreement over awful events in black America? First, remember—keep reminding yourself—that the awful events at the center of black conspiracy theories have already happened. Then, while it may seem a stretch, at times, picture the conspiracy theory as more of a metaphor or simile; it is an attempt to describe awful events that would otherwise defy belief. To say that the CIA introduced AIDS or crack cocaine into black America could be considered similar to saying that it is *like* the CIA did it; the results are such that it would take a powerful, unseen force like the CIA to produce them.

Yet whites still must not discount how easy it is, given the realities of American society, to imagine that white Americans must have much to do with events in black America, if only because wherever one looks, one is likely to see whites in pivotal positions of power. That alone helps theories about white conspiracies appear real. We must understand, too, that frustration and rhetorical excess might easily arise if it looks like powerful whites were ignoring calamities in black America or white Americans in general were focusing on something else.

Finally, it helps to examine the simple illustration of America divided by race in accordance with mathematics of race.

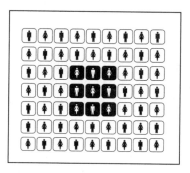

Look at it carefully. From the black side of the color line, it becomes hard to imagine that anything, good or bad, could be visited upon black America without first having to pass through white America. Therefore, it becomes hard to imagine anything getting to black America without some form of white involvement.

Yes, most Americans, black or white, know that white people are not all-knowing, all-seeing, and all-powerful. Yet look at how reality might appear in the circumstances portrayed in the illustration. How could drugs, guns, or AIDS be introduced into black communities without first having to pass through the surrounding white community? And if this was happening, it looks almost impossible that whites would not know something about it.

Various forms of this assertion that whites are involved in creating black problems have long been heard in black America. Malcolm X made a suggestion of this type at Nation of Islam rallies on 125th Street in Harlem in the early 1960s—that blacks don't have the boats and don't have the planes to bring drugs to America. So someone else must be doing it.

However, there is an opposing viewpoint that clearly emerges in our illustration. If members of surrounding white communities hear that a misfortune such as AIDS or crack cocaine has hit black communities, they are likely to assume that black people, themselves, also have something to do with it. Even if it were a white plot, black people should have the capacity to avoid the behaviors that make AIDS, drugs, and guns so dangerous. Doesn't it *look* that way?

Inevitably, we end up with two seemingly irreconcilable claims about who or what is responsible for AIDS, crack cocaine, or nightly gunfire in many black neighborhoods. Talk about seeing things differently! One viewpoint comes from the communities that have been devastated, another from the communities that might seem to have escaped relatively unscathed. Those from the devastated communities are likely to argue no community would deliberately inflict these torments on itself—or see this in white claims that blacks bring death and destruction upon themselves.

"Do they think we're crazy?" some black Americans ask.

And the unfortunate answer is, yes, many whites, who probably have little contact with black people, believe blacks are crazy, irrational, easily fooled by nonsensical arguments, or unwilling to take responsibility for their own actions. Yes, they often believe the problems in black America are particular to black people and black communities. And if these problems are particular to black people—or to the nature of black people—whites shouldn't have cause to worry about the same problems arising in their own world, too. The same problems do, in fact, plague white America as well.

Before the Oklahoma City bombing, journalists periodically tried to explain that black people are particularly and peculiarly mistrusting or paranoid about whites, the government, or the police. But black people should have seemed a little less strange in this regard after the events in Oklahoma City, which highlighted how alienated or paranoid a segment of the white population has become.

But the focus often returns to black America as the odd place. A 1995 Associated Press dispatch from Chicago attempted to describe "black mistrust" as a phenomenon isolated among black people. "It doesn't take much asking," the article said, "to reveal widespread black distrust of authority. In inner cities, rumors abound of vague government conspiracies to destroy black America by pumping in drugs, spreading AIDS or locking its young men in jail." It continued:

> Other circles, though, can point to concrete examples of government persecution. They cite documented FBI harassment of Martin Luther King Jr., Malcolm X and the Black Panthers in the 1960s. And they update their lists of grievances with recent federal prosecutions of black elected officials, notably Marion Barry, the mayor of Washington, D.C. . . . . "There's a folk notion in the black community that black people are more heavily

scrutinized than whites, and there are people out to get you," said Elijah Anderson, a sociology professor at the University of Pennsylvania.

This comment encapsulates the view that whites, in one way or another, are out to thwart black people at every turn. However, in their true-life behavior—bottom line as I see it—white people usually appear much busier keeping their distance from black people than actively plotting to do them harm. And recognizing this urge to keep their distance, many whites don't see themselves reflected in the evil intentions and deeds that many conspiracy theories would entail.

In their fleeting glimpses at the world of black Americans, what they see on TV or driving across cities, whites are more likely to worry that what they see will get out and spread than to scheme about how to make these bad realities worse. Whites worry about crime, drug abuse, or messages in rap music—and how to contain them. Perhaps some old suspicion lingers in the white psyche that fear of corruption from across the color line will infiltrate the white world or spread like a stain. Despite their best intentions, some whites will worry about the opening of rail and bus lines that will bring the center of big cities closer to suburbia where so many whites have taken refuge.

So were I to offer suggestions on this matter of conspiracies, I would list several. First a simple one for black Americans: if the CIA, FBI, or any other government agency or their representatives offer you the opportunity to smoke or sell crack—or to perform any other act that will be destructive to you or your community—don't do it. Do not participate in white conspiracies or anything you even suspect could be a white conspiracy.

I would note, too, that a pledge taken on October 16, 1995, at the Million Man March included the following ideas, which I have myself taken to heart: "From this day forward, I will strive to improve myself spiritually, morally, mentally, socially, politically and economically for myself, my family and my people." This is an excellent strategy.

Beyond that, I would suggest that we all, blacks and whites included, take more serious note of those who would divide us and separate our worlds. And I don't refer only to hate groups. I would look for the seemingly benign instances—on TV shows, in churches, or whatever—that are telling us it is OK to isolate ourselves and be alone with our own kind. I would pay attention when these choices are offered as inevitable or the easy way out, because they keep taking us in unfortunate directions.

Meanwhile, because isolation is already our continuing reality, some whites will always worry that someone will stir black people up, filling their heads with hatred and "dangerous" ideas. Whites have a long, reprehensible history of perpetuating this worry. At one time or another, whites have fretted about Marcus Garvey, Elijah Muhammad, Malcolm X, Martin Luther King, Jr., Louis Farrakhan, and others, because they feared that black people would—and this is truly strange—be alerted to the negative realities surrounding their own lives.

Whites continue to fear that agitators, demagogues, and hate-mongers will stir black people up about circumstances blacks would notice only with outside help, as if blacks would otherwise ignore their surroundings. And the deepest, most secret dread that many whites must have is that black Americans, driven by an understandable, logical, and *justifiable* rage, will break from the confines of their world and take revenge in the white one.

Altogether, it is one sad and crazy dance.

II
CLOSE ENCOUNTERS

9

DISCUSSING RACE
Some Silence Isn't All That Golden

One of the common prescriptions for America's race problem is for blacks and whites to do more talking—tell each other what they really think and feel. Get to know each other better. Try it sometime. Early in planning this book, I frequently discussed my ideas with Deborah Mathis, a syndicated columnist and correspondent with Gannett News Service in D.C. Mathis is black. I am white. She is married to a white man. I am married to a black woman. Perhaps these circumstances loosened the rules of what we can say to each other, and we often had rousing conversations about race in the *USA Today* office in Arlington, Virginia.

We covered lots of ground, too. We talked about the dreadfulness Mathis had seen and heard as a little girl in Little Rock, Arkansas—and the joys, too. And we talked about the strangeness of whites and blacks toward each other—and the suspicions they still harbor. Sometimes we laughed. Or, perhaps, I should note, we laughed with gusto, because it occasionally caused white colleagues to look askance at us. Here was a white person and a black person talking about race. And laughing about it. Still, others did not hurry to join in our discussions; instead, they gave us a wide berth, as if we were playing catch with live hand grenades. And on one occasion, one colleague—a white woman—said, "You better not let anybody hear you talking like that."

Even today, I am not sure who "anybody" was—maybe the powers that be—but the warning wasn't exactly in jest, either. Talking about race was widely considered risky business in the early 1990s, an attitude that persists across the American mainstream. Whites often imagine that blacks will overhear an offending remark, take it "wrong," and all hell will break loose. There are cases to cite such as one involving Texaco, where in December 1996 a secret tape recording was believed to have caught executives referring to black employees as "niggers" and "black jelly beans," as they plotted to destroy evidence relating to a class-action lawsuit brought by black employees. Texaco rushed into a $176 million settlement, the largest ever in a racial case.

Thereafter, corporations might reasonably worry that offhand remarks could fuel class-action lawsuits, which means that every mention of race, no matter how oblique or trivial, could be a chancy affair, if someone took it "wrong." And certainly, no one is supposed to have fun talking about race. Such discussions must not be fun. That's almost a rule.

It is likely, then, that white Americans by the millions have never participated in a serious, intense, and honest discussion about race with a black person, because to most white Americans, this is a scary proposition. Most Americans remain wary about it, even if they also believe that blacks and whites should talk more about race.

Whites, in particular, fear that they might say the wrong thing—without intending to do so or knowing what made it wrong. (This fear is related to the belief that black people are mysterious and unfathomable; you just can't figure them out.) And when I ask black people how often they discuss racial issues with whites, most say rarely or never, another measure of the current racial dialogue. Blacks and whites don't discuss race, because they're afraid to. As a result, both blacks and whites often hold their tongues in each other's presence.

Other reasons why race isn't discussed across the color line are segregation and the mathematics of race, both of which minimize opportunities for such discussions. Across much of white America, there is a shortage of black people with whom whites might have the discussions. And in many black neighborhoods, there are too few whites to hold much of a discussion. Occasionally, journalists organize "town hall" meetings on race, but that move only shows that exchanges between blacks and whites are so rare as to be considered newsworthy. And when President Clinton proposed a "national dialogue" on race in 1997, it had to mean that there wasn't much dialogue already going on—a common Clinton theme. Two years earlier, on the day of the Million Man March, Clinton had urged that Americans "take personal responsibility for reaching out to people of different races, take time to sit down and talk though this issue, have the courage to speak honestly and frankly, and then have the discipline to listen quietly with an open mind as others do the same."

I quote this here as a description of what was *not* going on. And Clinton added: "This may seem a simple request, but for tens of millions of Americans this has never been a reality. They have never spoken and never listened—not really, not really." Yet when Clinton's "national dialogue" finally began, it hardly captured the nation's imagination. Besides being lost amid the president's scandals, few whites were excited about it or eager to join in. Apparently, most felt discussions about race would be painful. And few blacks seemed very excited, either. In fact, few Americans thought the dialogue, though a noble idea, would lead to much. And journalists quickly complained that the reality of the discussion did not match their anticipations for the event.

After the first town hall meeting in Akron, Ohio, in December 1997, journalists appeared disappointed that there had been no shouting—all hell did *not* break loose. The *Washington Post* suggested that its expectations for the event were unfulfilled in a front-page headline: "Explosive Issue Fails to Ignite at Town Hall Meeting on Race."

Operating on a similar premise, a *New York Times* editorial noted that "Mr. Clinton was visibly frustrated that the participants were less open and candid than he had hoped, but full candor would be difficult, given the delicate nature of the subject."

The newspapers had clearly described journalists'—and perhaps most Americans'—expectations for a discussion between blacks and whites that we have a difficulty speaking openly to each other. If we do, it will very likely be ugly, with centuries of pent-up anger pouring forth. Yet in such expectations, we also have also put forth the very reasons why blacks and whites might want to stay away. Who in their right mind would want to put themselves though all that?

For example, we know from polls that 57 percent of whites believe that "many" or "almost all" black people do not like white people—one good reason why whites might want to avoid discussions. But whites have other reservations, too. They expect the discussion will inevitably focus on black accusations against whites—and whites will be forced to defend the actions of slave owners and segregationists or admit some manner of defeat or inner failings.

Many whites often look upon discussions about race as situations where whites cannot fare well, because whites imagine that black people have all the critical advantages:

- Blacks are better prepared. Race is *their* subject. They have all the expertise.
- Blacks have better arguments, involving obvious wrongs done them in the past.
- Blacks are more practiced at the passionate give-and-take of such discussions.

Thus whites cede special psychological advantages to blacks as quick-witted speakers, who partake of an oral tradition that teaches them to think on their feet. This aspect of black culture can intimidate whites, because it defines activities at which whites sense they could be out-classed. Whites believe that orating, what Jesse Jackson does, is a black people's art form where they hold forth best on their subject.

A notable exposition on the differences in black and white discourse is found in Thomas Kochman's *Black and White Styles in Conflict*. I have long admired this book even though it is sometimes a bit heavy on social science jargon, and it occasionally suggests that all blacks or all whites are alike. But it is still well worth reading.

According to Kochman—and everyday observation confirms this—black Americans often expect passionate, animated, and even confrontational discussions, while white discussions are more dispassionate and calm, governed by a style that seeks consensus rather than confrontation. "The first," says Kochman, "[is] characteristic of involvement; it is heated, loud and generates effect. The second is characteristic of detachment and is cool, quiet and without effect."

If black discussion tends to be loud, animated, and passionate and white discussion tends to be calm, ordered, and dispassionate, the differences are also in line with stereotypes we have about blacks and whites. Indeed, perhaps these tendencies in discussion have engendered some of the stereotypes.

And within these norms, certain expectations are common. For many black Americans, a sense of feeling and conviction is required to convince listeners you are telling the truth and care about what you are saying. But many white Americans prefer calm, reasoned discourse and are uneasy when the discussion gets too heated. As a result, blacks can wonder if whites who try to sound calm and reasonable are sincere. They suspect duplicity; whites don't seem to be saying anything they really believe in. Meanwhile, whites can worry that blacks who speak with passion are letting their emotions run riot. Maybe they aren't thinking rationally. Maybe they will turn violent if they don't get their way.

Whites fear discussions with black people will careen out of control. "Please calm down," they plead. "Let's talk this over reasonably." Occasionally, I have discovered my wife insisting into the telephone, "I'm *not* excited," or, "I'm *not* yelling." And I assume that the person on the other end of the line is white.

This idea that blacks are yelling or getting too excited is also a key indicator of why whites can sense themselves disadvantaged in discussions about race. As Kochman describes it: "White culture values the ability of individuals to rein in their impulses. White cultural events do not allow for individually initiated self-assertion or the spontaneous expression of feeling. . . . Because white culture requires that individuals check their impulses that come from within, whites become able practitioners of self-restraint. However this practice has an inhibiting effect on their ability to be spontaneously self-assertive. Consequently [whites] find themselves at a disadvantage when engaging in debate with blacks."

According to Kochman, whites find the animated and passionate aspects of black discourse "disabling." For example, many whites tend to believe that passion and reason are incompatible forces; therefore, as passion rises, hope of rationally resolving the issues decreases. Some whites believe that too much passion is dangerous and signals a loss of objectivity and control. But many blacks find white insistence on calm to be suspicious, because it seems to say that feelings are out of place in the discussion. And for many black Americans, the issue of race precisely involves how you are made to feel.

One product of these cultural differences is that whites expect to be overwhelmed by the intensity blacks can bring to a discussion. Whites are intimidated because they fear blacks will have more ammunition and more firepower, especially in a discussion about race, *their* subject. And this makes it likely whites will want to avoid the discussion altogether. Indeed, discussions about race are another activity, like playing basketball, dancing, or singing the blues, at which whites sense themselves overmatched. Even when whites are a majority in the room, they believe that one powerful black speaker can negate whatever advantages number may bring.

And whites are likely to be the majority in the room, a reality that plays out in most integrated situations whites encounter. And this, in turn, gives blacks cause to be wary about joining in a discussion about race, for they can expect to be outnumbered by whites.

Immediately, some black Americans might opt out of the discussion, although others might agree to participate, recognizing that this is the integrated circumstance they encounter most of the time anyway. Odds are that the racial makeup of a discussion about race will be much like that encountered in the office, the school, or anywhere else where blacks and whites come together. And the numbers of blacks and whites in the room will likely shape the dynamics of the discussion about race just as it does discussion on other topics in our schools, offices, or workplaces.

Idealists who believe that blacks and whites should march forward "arm in arm" must recognize that the mathematics of race won't permit this, because there aren't enough black people. Nor can whites and blacks sit next to each other checkerboard fashion. The numbers simply won't allow it. In any seating arrangement that follows the prevailing mathematics of race, about 70 percent of white participants cannot sit next to a black person. They have to sit off by themselves. And it is inevitable that if many blacks sit together, they will be seen to be segregating themselves, even if whites are more segregated at that very moment nearby.

Outnumbered as they usually are, some black participants will wonder if it is wise to speak openly in an integrated discussion about race. Some blacks will decide that silence is the best option, on the theory that you never know how whites will react. Other blacks will choose their words carefully, opting not to say what they might have said in black surroundings.

Indeed, this is an area of great misunderstanding between blacks and whites. Whites believe that black Americans will speak out—orate and hold forth when their interests are at issue. Kochman says blacks are more "spontaneously assertive," and whites have a similar picture. They picture all blacks to be like Jesse Jackson, Al Sharpton, or Louis Farrakhan—ready to speak out at the slightest cause, particularly if the subject is race.

And this is not so.

Whites sometimes act as if they expect blacks to accuse them of complicity in slavery or conspiracies to perpetuate injustice. And in these white fears, black people are pictured as shouting, gesturing, and menacing. And, yes, variants on this theme have happened—no question. However, the most common reality in American race relations is the exact opposite. Black Americans don't say anything to whites—not about what bothers them, not about what they have on their minds. They say nothing to whites or only the most innocuous remarks. Instead, they speak about their thoughts and feelings among other blacks. To whites, they are mum, even to the point of giving whites the impression that everything is going just fine.

I cannot count the number of times that black friends have insisted to me that it is dangerous for blacks to speak honestly to whites. A common prescription: "You have to tell white folks what they want to hear." And the logic of this conventional wisdom, widely shared among black Americans, is that the slightest hint of anger, assertiveness, or deviance from the white way is likely to cause mistrust. Whites will then work against you, and it can destroy your career or anything else that depends on getting along with white people, because whites can't handle deviations from the way they think.

The rule about telling white folks what they want to hear also has corollaries. You must, for example, never appear to be smarter than white people. You must never appear to be correcting white people's mistakes. You must never assert your opinions too strongly. In each of these cases, it is said that whites will react badly. Meanwhile, whites are often oblivious to the widespread reluctance of black people to speak their minds in white surroundings.

To avoid being labeled as "angry," "different," "too black," or "having an attitude," many black Americans believe it is best to say nothing, particularly when the subject is race. And this reluctance occurs even in cases when blacks may have a good point to make or just cause to be offended—they say nothing. And it happens more often than whites think. Blacks frequently decide not to challenge whites on any matter, not just those pertaining to race, because they are convinced that whites still have difficulty treating blacks as equals.

Several negative consequences can result. Whites who believe that hiring of black workers will increase racial understanding, as newspapers often do, will never hear black perspectives if black employees don't feel free to express themselves or if they feel their opinions are treated as a nuisance. Often, whites do not even know that black colleagues disagree or have a different perspective, because the black colleagues keep it to themselves.

Whites assume that the silence of black colleagues signals assent and agreement. And blacks then go off by themselves and say, "Can you believe what *they* said? Can you believe what *they're* doing?" And when things go wrong, whites often say, "But *they* didn't say anything. Why didn't *they* speak up?"

But whites should also understand that the silence of black people is not mysterious. Whites can be silent when they are in the minority or when they're facing the boss or higher-ups. Whites don't express everything they think in such situations. They clam up, too. And foolish bosses sometimes conclude that everybody agrees, just as whites conclude that their black colleagues agree.

Eventually, however, the silence of blacks around whites has a major impact on white perceptions about race. When whites hear no complaints from black friends and colleagues, they assume that other black people have few complaints. And this could happen, too, in a discussion about race. Will blacks speak out? Naturally, what happens can depend on where the meeting is, who is running it, and how comfortable black participants are. But if black participants say little—or say what they think whites want to hear—whites will conclude all's well along the color line.

Columnist George Will drew such a conclusion in a December 11, 1997, *Washington Post* column after Clinton's initial town meeting at Akron. According to Will, the lack of fiery exchanges in Akron did not mean the discussion had failed; it meant the extent of the problem is being exaggerated:

> Proponents of the hypothesis that Americans need government-supervised attitude adjustments say: Proof of Americans' dysfunctional racial attitudes is their successful determination to disguise that dysfunction.
>
> That is the lesson some people drew from the disappointing, to them, failure, as they saw it, of participants in Clinton's "town meeting" in Akron.
>
> Participants supposedly refused to be candid. Proof of their dissimulation was, presumably, the absence of anger and alarm. . . . [that is] unless the subject is decreasingly delicate for increasing numbers of Americans. Unless the frustration arises from the annoying difficulty of trying to cure the healthy. In fact,

abundant data concerning attitudes about interracial recreation, education, employment and marriage indicate steady improvement in race relations.

Really? It is those polls on friendship all over again.

At the same time, it seems possible that the results of a discussion about race could be governed by something so mundane as where blacks and whites sit. And while this might seem a trivial concern, it involves dynamics that function in most integrated settings.

Since it is likely that whites will mathematically dominate the scene, blacks will more likely sense they must be careful about what they say. Some seating arrangement might increase this effect, while others might produce different results. Three examples:

If blacks sit together or occupy one corner for the discussion, they might be emboldened by group solidarity. Or perhaps they might be moved to common defense by a sense they are cornered. And Kochman noted that blacks take up common cause when they are outnumbered in the room; under those conditions they are less likely to disagree with each other, while the white majority does not feel as inhibited about disagreement.

But if black participants are clustered off in a corner, whites may also be emboldened by the power of their numbers to press claims they would otherwise not raise if black participants were closer at hand. Clustered together, black and white participants might speak out more adamantly or find less interest in compromise than if they were spread around the room.

Proximity seems to have its effect on discussions about race. Some of the most angry, vitriolic—and pointless—discussions of race are on talk-radio programs that allow anonymous callers, insulated from any real contact with others, freedom to say anything they please. Both black and white callers are free to hurl accusations, insults, and challenges; and little else gets done. But it also could be that radio exchanges draw more hotheads because of the inherent lack of consequences. And maybe we behave more responsibly when we intermingle with each other and the conversation is face-to-face.

Even if whites were convinced that the discussion about race would be civil, calm, and ordered, many whites still believe that blacks have better arguments on their side—that is, the history of race relations gives blacks cause to be angry. Many whites recognize that they, too, would be angry if they had been victims of slavery or segregation.

Against this background, whites also expect that blacks will try to be the accusers in a discussion about race, and whites will be the ones accused. Whites expect that blacks will seek to impose this pattern on the discussion, despite important changes that have occurred since the civil rights movement.

Most significantly, many whites now believe that whites have legitimate accusations to make against blacks—about crime, welfare abuses, or claims that whites are to blame for the plight of black people. In a September 27, 1998, *Washington Post* column, George Will made an accusation that is typical of those now regularly made against black people: "Today the principal impediments to upward mobility are not institutionalized repressions but certain behaviors (principally illegitimacy) best understood in terms of class rather than race." And what is the accusation here? That poor black people are having too many illegitimate children—and that this is the primary reason so many black Americans are mired in poverty.

In fact, there may be some truth here. Many blacks contribute to their own problems. Whereas in the past, whites and racism might have been blamed, the tide has turned in mainstream America so that in the public debates of the 1990s whites are making more of the accusations and blacks fewer.

This change was symbolized by the O. J. Simpson case. Whites sided with the accusers and blacks were seen to side with the accused. Whites eventually blamed Johnnie Cochran, a black-majority jury, and "playing the race card" for what they deemed a miscarriage of justice, while many blacks blamed white racism, symbolized by Mark Fuhrman's apparent racism, for falsely accusing a black man. However, in this exchange of accusations, the "white" side eventually predominated;

Fuhrman was, to a degree, rehabilitated; Simpson and the "black" view were not.

It is fundamental to human nature to favor being the accuser over being the accused. The accuser is in the more righteous position; the accused bears the taint of the accusation, even when the charge is proved false. The accused also has the difficulty of trying to prove a negative—that something is not so—that he or she is not guilty. White Americans should recognize the difficulty they face against the accusation that all whites are racists. This charge is hard to escape because it's practically impossible to account for every minute in one's entire life and for every word spoken and for every deed done. The charge that all whites are *unconscious* racists, even if they do not seem to be, is even more challenging to overcome. How can one claim not to have ideas or urges, if one's not supposed to be aware of them?

One may even long to be the accuser for a change, instead of facing fallacious arguments from one's accusers. That white racists killed a black person does not mean that all whites want to kill black people. Or vice versa—that a black man killed a white person does not mean all black people have murder in their hearts.

Such generalizations are dangerously wrong.

Still, the role of the accuser has its seductive appeal. Less obvious than the Simpson case was how the insidious pattern, accusers versus accused, unfolded in the case of *The Bell Curve*. One needed only to understand that the book accused black people of being less intelligent. Thus, blacks were cornered in the spotlight of an unwanted—and embarrassing—accusation, while whites weren't accused of anything.

To understand how blacks might feel as the accused in *The Bell Curve* case, whites would need to imagine a ubiquitous discussion about an embarrassing inadequacy attributed to white people. And suppose the newspapers and TV were full of black people discussing the implications of this white deficiency. How would whites feel? The real problem for the accused in such cases is the temptation to try to prove a negative when it is difficult to do so. Blacks were in the uncomfortable position of feeling they had to prove they were not stupid, not an easy task for any group. There will always be examples of stupidity to cite in any group, which makes the taint of the accusation all the more powerful.

This common pattern—accusers versus accused—is useless in discussions about race. The accusing side always gets the upper hand,

and the accused side can never satisfactorily refute the charges. How do whites prove they're not racists when examples of white racism pop up so regularly? How can blacks convince whites they're not stupid when stupidity is commonplace in any group?

The more discussions about race become mired in accusations, the less productive they will be. But eventually blacks and whites might discover that hurling accusations across the color line doesn't get us very far. And that alone would be progress.

Since whites have a major advantage in numbers, the law of averages suggests that the white point of view will eventually predominate, as it did in the Simpson case. And the accusations against whites that were a familiar part of the civil rights era were eventually supplanted by accusations of crime and irresponsibility against blacks in the 1990s.

Clinton's national dialogue also followed this pattern when affirmative action became a dominant issue. In principle, affirmative action involves women and other groups, as well, but it always comes up when the subject of "race" is mentioned, because many whites believe that affirmative action gives blacks unfair advantage at their expense. And again this shows how the mathematics of race can lift white concerns to the top of the agenda, even when race is the issue at hand.

The mathematics of race also boosts the role that ignorance plays in the discussion. It is to be assumed that some participants in any discussion about race will not know what they're talking about. But they will talk all the same. The discussion, for example, may be influenced by the mistaken belief that blacks or "people of color" are taking over the country. This idea is found on both sides of the color line. Other misinformation is likely to flourish among those who have the fewest contacts along the color line. How could they know what's happening on the other side? Yet their opinions will be part of the general mix we hear about; polls inevitably include the opinions of people who don't have a clue, like the small percentage of men who will claim, if you ask them, they've had a pap smear in the past 12 months.

As polls also show, a majority of whites will say that blacks are doing well in the American mainstream, but fewer blacks will say this is so—a black-white standoff. Whites say one thing about fairness in America; blacks say another. It might be good to ask at this point who is more likely to know what they're talking about. Whites or blacks? Might it be logical that blacks would better know how well blacks are doing?

It also makes sense that whites with no contact with black people might know less about how well blacks are doing than whites who have lots of contact with blacks. Examples of Americans living in racial isolation are plentiful, from "white" enclaves in Idaho, Vermont, or Montana to black big-city ghettos. You might wonder how much any of these people know about race relations. It is also likely that whites are the largest group of Americans who don't know about race relations. Yet they have a major—an inordinate—influence on our understanding of race relations, particularly as it is expressed in polls showing how Americans are racially polarized.

How many whites know little about race? Perhaps, the 41 percent of whites who don't have black friends is an indication. Having less contact with blacks, they are likely to know less about black people. And how would this 41 percent affect other polls on race?

Here's a possible example: When the Gallup organization asked in 1997 how fairly black people were treated, 76 percent of whites said blacks are "treated the same as whites," and only 15 percent of whites said blacks are not treated as well. Meanwhile, 49 percent of blacks agreed that blacks are treated as fairly as whites—a 27-point difference between blacks and whites—while 38 percent of blacks said blacks are treated less fairly.

It would seem, then, that blacks and whites see this situation differently.

But again, which group, blacks or whites, is more likely to know what it's talking about? Three out of four whites may believe that blacks are treated fairly, but it is also possible that more than half of them come from the 41 percent of whites who have no black friends. So how would they know about the treatment of blacks?

Do Whites Know What They're Talking About?	
Percentage of whites with **no** black friends	41 (90 million)
Percentage of whites who believe blacks are treated the same as whites	76 (167 million)
Whites with no black friends as possible percentage of whites who think blacks are treated the same	54 (90 million)

So where does that leave us? It is possible our idea that blacks and whites see things differently is unduly influenced by millions of white Americans who don't know what they are talking about. And a smaller group of isolated black Americans would have similarly little experience in race relations, too, all of which suggests that almost any discussion about race will include a share of ignorance.

But it is also likely that whites who spout foolishness will outnumber blacks who do, because the mathematics of race suggest this will be so. The 25 percent of blacks who say they have no white friends would only add up to about 8.25 million black people, as compared to the 90 million white people who say they have no black friends. Hence, the white group is almost 11 times larger. And this probability becomes another reason black people might hesitate to get involved in discussions about race with all these white people.

The 90 million white Americans who have no black friends are an important group in our nation—and if they are ignorant about race, that is also important. Having no black friends may not be their choice or fault. It could result from where they live or from the mathematics of race. Then again, they may be among the many whites who are angry about race. Maybe they grumble that blacks are taking over or that black criminals are ruling the streets. Or they are angry about taxes and government handouts. Maybe they are among those who say, like some I know, that they are sick of hearing about race. "I'm sick of hearing *them* complain," some say. But when and where, I wonder, do they hear these complaints when they have so little contact with black people?

The complaints must be in the news—and the news from black America does not always help when whites are already angry and alienated. Drug epidemics and record homicide rates do not convince whites they are to blame or that they should shoulder a burden on behalf of black people. Nor do whites see themselves as responsible for drive-by shootings, teen pregnancy rates, or the chaos in schools. After decades in which whites entertained suspicions that they might be part of the problem, they are now more thoroughly convinced they are not.

The isolation on either side of the color line now makes discussing race all the more important. We must not let the civility of the president's meetings convince us there is no problem. Most of the crazy ideas blacks and whites carry in their heads never came up at those meetings. What we say and claim in isolation suggests we are in need of basic information about each other. We just don't know how those on the other side of the color line live. How fairly are blacks treated? We just don't know.

If blacks and whites draw different conclusions, maybe we need to know less about the conclusions and more about the evidence that leads up to them. What *specifically* happens to black people that causes them to conclude they are treated unfairly? And what *specifically* do whites see that convinces them otherwise? Please tell us they're not getting their evidence about black experience from TV sitcoms.

We might hope that blacks and whites could eventually base their opinions of each other on a better understanding of each other's experiences. Then there might be fewer racially polarized opinions floating about. That is the point of holding discussions—to reconcile the information we have. And if blacks and whites are still uneasy talking about race in each other's presence, we should discuss that, too. Why is it? What makes us wary?

Also, the immediate expectation for our discussions should not be to resolve political issues. We're hardly ready for that. First, we need some agreement on what our experiences are like—the basics. Do blacks or whites get a better deal? Who encounters the most discrimination? Let's hear a give-and-take on the specifics. The more blacks and whites meet and talk face-to-face about these matters, the better off we all will be. Maybe, we can reach a consensus about what our experiences are. Then we'll be ready to take on affirmative action.

10
SLAVERY
Our Past Is Never That Far Away

Clinton says slavery was "wrong."
He stops short of apologizing to Africa, but
acknowledges "sins of neglect and ignorance."

—Headline in the *Rochester Democrat and Chronicle,* March 25, 1998

I t has been a peculiarity of the 1990s that Americans—certainly white
Americans—have continued to tread ever so cautiously when it
comes to the mention of slavery. They proceed across this terrain on
tiptoes, picking their words with such painstaking care that the headline writer at the *Rochester Democrat and Chronicle* surely considered
it significant that the president of the United States said slavery was
"wrong" in a speech in Africa, not some other word. He did not say
immoral, depraved, or *evil.* And these days we demand precision on
the subject of slavery. Clinton merely said slavery was "wrong."

For those monitoring attitudes about slavery—and there apparently were many who believed blacks or whites were seeking a semantic advantage—the headline writer also added in a subhead to further
clarify what the president said: "He stops short of apologizing to Africa,
but acknowledges 'sins of neglect and ignorance.'" You follow?

According to finely drawn lines that Americans seem to have made,
to say slavery was "wrong" is one thing but to apologize might be some-

thing else. Like what? Wasn't slavery wrong? Is there any doubt? So what is so "wrong" about saying we're sorry? But in 1998, at least, many white Americans were wary of apologies that might be made about slavery. Some thought Virginia Governor James S. Gilmore III went too far when in proclaiming April as the state's annual Confederate History Month, which it had long been, he noted that slavery "degraded the human spirit [and] is abhorred and condemned by Virginians."

Under a headline, "Slavery 'Abhorred,' Gilmore Says," the *Washington Post* reported that leaders of the state's Southern Heritage Association considered Gilmore's words "an insult" and called a press conference to say so. This indicated that in 1998 we couldn't say "slavery degraded the human spirit" without a protest. Were we out of our minds?

It is true that most Americans don't want to discuss slavery. Whites don't wish to raise the subject they fear others will still try to hold them accountable for. More than a century and a half after the fact, many whites sense that slavery still casts the shadow of doubt across their righteousness. They fear, too, that the anger of black Americans about slavery is ever present in matters involving race. And at least some whites recognize that the anger is understandable, a rational and unavoidable reaction to history. Yet others believe that the subject of slavery is merely the moral artillery that blacks roll out when they want to get their way.

In this manner, slavery is seen as a great equalizer along the color line. Whites outnumber blacks, but blacks have the issue of slavery to hold over white heads. And many whites suspect that blacks will forever hold the issue of slavery in reserve in case they need to put whites at a disadvantage. Some whites suspect that black Americans will never close the books on white complicity in the slave trade, will never forgive people with white skin, for to do so would be to forsake an ever-useful advantage in moral arguments.

But this belief is only what many white people think—to them the mere mention of slavery sounds like a losing proposition for whites. And numbers alone tell a sorrowful tale that whites might hope others would forget. Conservative estimates on the slave trade are awesome: from the 15th century to the 19th, 10 million Africans were kidnapped and transported to the Americas as slaves. Another 2 million Africans died on the awful Middle Passage across the Atlantic.

Other studies, however, note that the population of Africa remained constant during the 17th, 18th, and 19th centuries, while the populations of other continents almost quadrupled. This, the studies suggest, means that about 300 million Africans are missing from what the African population should have been. And where did those 300 million Africans disappear to?

Some suspect that many more Africans died or disappeared in the slave trade than appear in most estimates. Another suspicion—a conspiracy theory of sorts—is that white historians deliberately hold the numbers down to reduce the amount of evil that can be blamed on whites. Still, the 10 million people who survived to reach the Americas is a horrific enough tally. The slave trade could not have been some occasional, hidden scheme of a few whites—it was a massive enterprise. Note that the entire population of the United States did not pass 12 million until 1830, more than three centuries after Columbus.

Many whites suspect that any call for racial dialogue is an invitation for whites to be battered with charges about slavery. Whites fear that slavery will come up, even if it rarely does. They often say we should put slavery or "that" behind us, but discussions about slavery are hardly breaking out across the land. Since the slavery issue does not confront whites at every turn, why are whites so touchy—worrying about apologies, worrying about black anger, worrying that slavery will be *used* against them? For millions of white Americans, the subject of slavery never comes up, never intervenes in their lives. Never.

Another matter that whites do realize is the degree to which most black Americans do not wish to dwell on slavery either—at least not every day. Some black Americans find the mention of slavery demeaning or embarrassing, which should be easily understandable. Who would enjoy contemplating the circumstances under which their ancestors were owned or mistreated by white people? This would have to be a disturbing, anger-producing thought, particularly when most white people hardly seem to be of such imposing presence or capabilities that they should own other people. Hell no! White people just aren't *that* impressive.

It is also said that the survival of black Americans as a people is strong evidence of the resourcefulness and spiritual strength of Africans. Yet their suffering and slaughter should not—and cannot—be forgotten. Would it be appropriate—or reasonable—to ask black people to ignore slavery? Indeed, anger and rage seem appropriate, reasonable human responses. Yet we need not recount how many slaves were raped, beaten, and killed by white people to recognize that black Americans might not want to tour these anger-provoking themes every day—or revisit the humiliation that might accompany them. It might even take a special strength, a special virtue, not to be consumed by anger. Slavery is thus a discomfiting reality that black people, at times, also need to put behind them.

In fact, whatever feelings black Americans have about slavery—and whenever they choose to have them—must be considered their right, even if the feelings are at times inconsistent and contradictory. Black Americans have a right to be angry in one moment or unobservant—or whatever else—the next, because, plain and simple, Africans did not choose to be slaves. And what cause do whites have to fuss about whatever feelings blacks may have about slavery?

In 1995, the Library of Congress in Washington, D.C., shut down an exhibit on plantation life in the old South after black employees at the library objected that this reminder of slavery seemed demeaning, even though the exhibit had previously toured the country without stirring such a response. Some whites found this puzzling or inconsistent.

The employees objected not to the exhibit's historical accuracy but to the way it made them feel. And this reaction also confounded some whites, who wondered why the employees would want to hide the very images that blacks—this is the white view—use to make whites feel uncomfortable. And it may have been the intent of some black employees to make whites feel uncomfortable, for it was said the black employees really saw the exhibit as a metaphor for their unhappiness about working conditions at the library.

In this way, we are tempted more than a century after the fact to view slavery not as it was but in terms of how images—or exaggerations—about slavery could be used to gain advantage in today's world. Blacks and whites examine slavery for the details they want to see. For example, rather than view slavery as demeaning and slaves as numbed, passive victims, blacks might reasonably prefer to hear tales of heroic resistance or see slavery viewed as the origin of mistrust that still exists along the color line.

But when Orlando Bagwell's series *Africans in America* aired on PBS in 1998, a *Washington Post* reviewer objected: "All blacks mentioned in the series, moreover, are stereotyped as bold and heroic, including Nat Turner, whose famous rebellion consisted of chopping up 44 women and children along with 6 men. With few exceptions, like abolitionist William Lloyd Garrison, whites are portrayed as racist hypocrites, including—and most prominently—George Washington and Thomas Jefferson."

Surprise? Maybe Bagwell's effort partook of a black point of view on slavery. Is that horrible, indefensible? Once again, the issue of accuracy aside, the argument along the color line seemed to be about which side, whites or blacks, gets to look heroic or victimized in representations of slavery. Yet it should not seem strange that black Americans would seek out the rare positives in the experience of slavery; nor is it odd that whites might want to escape blame for slavery.

And feelings about how to commemorate slavery or its end have changed among black Americans over time. In the 1880s, the festive annual celebrations and parades that had previously marked Emancipation Day in Washington, D.C., were criticized by black ministers and others. Frederick Douglass said the parading and other festivities were demeaning to "self-respecting" black citizens, who hoped to put slavery behind them. The wild revelry eventually disappeared.

The fact that black Americans don't spend more time ruminating about slavery doesn't mean it was less evil or less historically significant. It is not for white people to decide when it is appropriate to claim we have at last put slavery behind us. They don't get that choice; slavery does not haunt the recesses of whites' self-image to the depth it does that of black Americans. Do whites forget? They were not the slaves.

And what is the difference? Whites are removed from the notion that their very existence—who they are and where they are—is a direct result of slavery. Whites have distance from these events. Not only do they not have to consider that their relatives were in chains; they needn't identify themselves as the product of a slave-owning culture, either. Most whites wishfully consider themselves and their ancestors to have been, at worst, bystanders.

However, it seemed that the *Washington Post* critic would have whites abandon such distinctions. In his review of *Africans in America*, he insisted that the suffering of Africans was hardly unique:

> The brutality inflicted on slaves, for example, is never compared with that commonly inflicted during the same period on laboring whites like seamen, or on British men, women and children forcibly transported half a world away to Australia for minor crimes in the 1790s under conditions every bit as horrific as— and far longer than—the Middle Passage. Among the 1,006 shipped in 1790, for example, Robert Hughes's definitive Australian history, *The Fatal Shore*, shows a mortality rate of more than 40 percent. The *Encyclopaedia Britannica* estimates

Middle Passage death rates at 13 percent, though some historians say as many as one in three blacks may have died.

Still, slavery haunts white Americans. How could we say it doesn't?
Whites can worry about cosmic irony or wonder if it can be true that
"what comes around goes around." Is there a moral order akin to
Newton's law that what goes up must come down? These could be
scary thoughts. Do entire racial groups—blacks or whites—share a
collective character and fate? Are the evils done by one generation the
collective responsibility of their descendents as the Old Testament suggests? "For I the Lord thy God am a jealous God, visiting the iniquity
of the fathers upon the children unto the third and fourth generation
of them that hate me."

But whites can believe the story of their experience has many
lines, and some lines, like those of immigrants who came to America
after 1865, are not connected with the evils of slavery. Yet on occasion, whites still protest their innocence: "I didn't own any slaves." In
such moments, whites are arguing that races do not have a collective
fate that crosses generations, time, and space—as, by the way, slavery did for generations of black people. Yet at the same time some
whites are drawn to evidence that black African tribal leaders sold fellow Africans into slavery, as if this shifts responsibility from whites to
blacks. There is also the fact that free blacks owned slaves in the old
South. Estimates are that in 1830 about 3,500 black slave owners owned
about 10,000 black slaves. So blacks did it, too.

What are we to think? Are we to say that whites should not be collectively responsible for white actions but blacks should be? And white
Americans *must* know in their hearts that many whites were not innocent bystanders on the issue of slavery. They should know, too, that
being white has for centuries been a much better deal in America,
even if the grossest inequities that occurred along the color line happened long ago. The median household income for white Americans
was $38,972 in 1997; the median income for black Americans was
$25,050; and that was still a big difference.

Perhaps naïvely, some whites also wish the shadow of slavery could
quietly pass without great efforts being made; they undertake well-
intended gestures to "put slavery behind us." In 1996, for example, the
state legislature of Mississippi was stirred, 131 years late, to ratify the
13th Amendment that outlaws slavery—of course, a symbolic gesture.
In 1997, Representative Tony P. Hall, an Ohio Democrat, proposed that
Congress apologize to black Americans for slavery. Apparently, Hall

made the proposal in simple faith that it would improve relations between blacks and whites. He was then surprised to receive hundreds of letters and phone messages condemning the idea. As the *Washington Post* reported, many whites thought it was a terrible plan. One man wrote that the government should apologize to him for stripping his great-grandfather of 435 slaves. Others said black people should be thankful that slave traders rescued their ancestors from Africa. Still others argued that beginning with the 350,000 Union soldiers who died in the Civil War, the nation has done enough to atone for slavery.

In the 1990s, it seemed that almost any utterance about slavery would be scrutinized for advantages, real or symbolic, that blacks or whites might gain. However, the idea that slavery benefited subsequent generations of black Americans is not altogether new. "Think about it," black educator Booker T. Washington once said. "We went into slavery pagans; we came out Christians. We went into slavery pieces of property; we came out American citizens."

Still, assertions that good results came from slavery miss the point. This was not the plan of slave traders and slave owners, and no one volunteered for slavery on the premise that good would come to generations as yet unborn. Nor were generations of servitude demanded from any other group as the price of U.S. citizenship.

In our attempts to "put slavery behind us," it is commonly claimed that slavery happened a long time ago. Slavery, however, is much nearer to us than we like to think. Perhaps, Americans find comfort in considering slavery a distant event, but the nearness of slavery is compelling. Today, there are no living survivors of slavery, but not long ago, they were still among us. Individuals born in slavery were still living in the mid- to late 1970s, which means that most Americans alive today have at some point in their lives been the contemporaries of black Americans who were born into slavery—the two trails have crossed in time.

Because a number of former slaves survived into the 1970s, we must now recognize that former slaves outlived John F. Kennedy, Marilyn Monroe, Elvis Presley, Malcolm X, and Martin Luther King, Jr. Former slaves were still among us when men landed on the moon and when Nixon resigned. So how long ago could slavery have been? Consider that in the year 2000, most adult Americans aged 21 or older will have been alive at the same time as former slaves.

But who were slavery's last survivors? The answer to that question is not easy to come by, for the passing of former slaves was little noted, probably because we were not eager to remember slavery in the turbulent 1960s and 1970s. It was not known at the time how many survivors of slavery there still were, but three candidates emerge from the brief mention at the bottom of old newspaper obituary columns as slavery's last survivor.

If the wild stories he told are to be believed—and many doubt this—the last survivor could have been Charlie Smith, who died in 1979, at what he claimed was 137 years. But there was no proof of Smith's age, and he told many fanciful tales, including that he was kidnapped from Liberia and sold into slavery in New Orleans when he was 12. (He also said he rode with Jesse James and Billy the Kid.) However, Smith's tale could have been true, because African slaves were illegally imported into United States as late as 1859, when the last known slave ship, the *Clothilde*, docked in Mobile Bay, Alabama. Theoretically, Smith would have arrived five years earlier.

Yet if Smith was not slavery's last survivor, then maybe Sam Brown was. Born in 1860 on a plantation in Jackson, Mississippi, Brown died in February 1978 at the age of 118. Or if Brown was not the last survivor then it could have been Nora Lee, who was born in Standing Rock, Alabama, in 1859 and died in 1977, also at age 118.

As recently as the 1930s, a federal writer during the Great Depression amassed the recollections of hundreds of former slaves. Some told relatively benign stories or spoke of fondness for masters; others told of beatings, killings, rapes, and other horrors. And there was quiet, fundamental wisdom in what many said. "Better stay free, if you can stay straight," warned a former slave named Amy Perry. "Slavery time was tough. It was like looking back into the dark—like looking into the night."

Digitally enhanced recordings of interviews with former slaves were released in 1998 and were even available on the Internet. In one interview recorded in Baltimore in 1949, the haunting voice from the past is as clear as if its owner were in the room. In three, matter-of-fact sentences, he states the American dilemma: "My name is Fountain Hughes. I was born in Charlottesville, Virginia. My grandfather belonged to Thomas Jefferson."

In the 1970s, scholars attempted to reassess some of the realities and horrors of slavery, drawing conclusions in one instance that were contrary to what was generally assumed. In 1974, Robert Fogel and Stanley Engerman published *Time on the Cross: The Economics of American Negro Slavery,* in which they argued that "myths" about the evils of slavery were unnecessarily poisoning black-white relations. The authors argued that the diet, shelter, and health of slaves in the United States were often better than that of many white workers in the North or in Europe in the same period. But their reassessment was not always looked upon kindly in this volatile time in race relations. One critic in *The Nation* called the authors the "the friends of slavery" and said they portrayed it as "as a kind of happy picnic lunch." "When it comes to slavery, good news is unwelcome," conservative Dinesh D'Souza wrote in his 1995 book called *The End of Racism: Principles for a Multiracial Society.* And D'Souza had his own visions about the benign aspects of slavery. The very fact that slaves were property, he says, must have helped insure their better treatment because people generally take care of their possessions. And this claim might seem plausible were it not for vagaries of human nature that we also witness—people who don't take good care of their houses, cars, or whatever else. Furthermore, given the example of men who beat their wives and girlfriends, how might we expect them to treat their slaves? And slaves often recounted arbitrary or gratuitous beatings.

Nor is there any evidence that Northern whites or Europeans ran off to pick cotton on Southern plantations because it was considered such a good deal. It is not really surprising, either, that black Americans might look askance at efforts—in the 1970s or at any other time—to make slavery sound innocuous. What are people trying to claim? they might legitimately wonder. That being a slave to white folks wasn't so bad?

Whites further romanticize about plantation life in their fondness for *Gone with the Wind* or veneration for the heroes of the Confederacy as grand gentlemen—all without much concern for what black Americans might think. If black Americans were a majority in the United States, the Confederacy might be seen not as a bastion of gentility but as a corrupt and evil regime like Nazi Germany.

It is curious, too, that present-day Americans imagine themselves as such good and moral people—morally more sophisticated than their 19th-century forbears. But considering the fuss over *apologizing* for slavery, what would our contemporaries have done with slavery itself? Judging from the arguments raised in *The Bell Curve*, had the slavery issue not been settled in the 1860s with a civil war, we might not have done much better.

If slavery still existed today, some Americans would surely find nothing wrong with it. They might argue that it is in harmony with natural order, because whites score higher on IQ tests, and of general benefit to mankind, slaves included, because it keeps them productively occupied. Then, too, it might be in the 1990s or beyond that slavery would be abolished because we now get cheap labor by other means. Why would we need to support slaves when the poor in other countries will work for next to nothing? It might even be argued that by working for free, the black slaves are depriving other Americans of paying jobs—a blame-the-slaves argument, of sorts.

We also forget that many of the proslavery arguments in the 19th century were not all evil-sounding; most were appeals to self-interest that have echoes in today's debates about free trade. Slavery kept prices down, its apologists said. And the economic benefits spread far beyond the old South. Slaves produced raw materials that brought jobs to textile workers in New England and Europe. Slaves furnished food and clothing for rich and poor across the world. And if the profits from slavery supported the elegant plantation lifestyle in the old South, its indirect benefits through manufacturing and international trade were an economic underpinning across the Western world. Thus, the apologists said, if you abolished slavery, millions of others would suffer.

These days, the argument that cheaper labor means cheaper goods is still heard. Corporations insist they cannot compete in the global economy unless they keep labor costs down. So if workers elsewhere in the world will work for less, companies must take advantage, so the rest of us can get more goods for our money. And we generally go along with this premise without inspecting the labels in our shirts and underwear for moral implications until we discover that cheap labor elsewhere can mean that Americans lose their jobs at home.

We would condemn slavery as wrong, yet having people work for next to nothing is of less concern. Occasionally, we discover that the far-off workers, often children, who make the clothes on American backs are laboring for a pittance under conditions we would find intolerable. But how seriously do we engage ourselves in their plight? If goods cost less because they are made in China, Malaysia, or India, we buy them and assume the workers were glad for the work. Sometimes, we convince ourselves that these workers can surely survive on less, because they are used to it. We even imagine that they are happy, and their lives perhaps more charming, as we have lost so much to the rush of modernity. In other words, we are not as attuned to the suffering of others as we might like to think.

These days, we sometimes argue about slavery's residual effects on today's society. In one view, the separate and belated economies that slavery and segregation produced have left black America far behind white America. And that gap seems a plausible description of our reality. Who would argue this is not so when economic indicators describe such a disparity? And to say that black people deserve to be economically inferior—their plight is a result of their own efforts—is to suggest that whites have more intrinsic worth and ability.

A crucial issue is at hand. If Americans, black or white, believe blacks don't measure up to white standards—that blacks are demonstrably unequal—we are still trapped in evil ideas that haunted our forebears when they tried to resolve the issue of slavery.

The lives of most whites in antebellum America may have been removed from direct involvement in slavery—they did not traffic in slaves or own them. Still, most whites didn't consider black Americans equals or fellow citizens. This often gets forgotten, except in black America where it is more likely to be noted that even Abraham Lincoln had views that did not ring of equality. On October 13, 1858, in Quincy, Illinois, in the sixth of his famous senatorial campaign debates with Steven A. Douglas, Lincoln said:

> I will say, then, that I am not, nor ever have been, in favor of bringing about in any way the social and political equality of the white and black races—that I am not nor ever have been in favor of making voters or jurors of Negroes, nor of qualifying them to hold office, nor to intermarry with white people; and I will say in addition to this that there is a physical difference between the white and black races which will ever forbid the two races living together in terms of social and political equality. And inasmuch as they cannot so live, while they do remain together, there must be the position of superior and inferior. I am as much as any other man in favor of having the superior position assigned to the white race.

And that was from Abraham Lincoln. A transcript of the debates reports that loud cheers and cries of "good, good," greeted this statement from the Great Emancipator. Audiences at the debates were divided on the issue of slavery, but not so clearly split on the question of equality. Douglas, who subsequently won the senatorial election, insisted that Lincoln really did have equality between blacks and whites in mind. Douglas pressed this charge in statements like the following exchange with his supporters at the debate in Ottawa, Illinois.

Douglas: "If you desire Negro citizenship, if you desire to allow them to come into the state and settle with the white man, if you desire them to vote on an equality with yourselves, and to make them eligible to office, to serve on juries, and to adjudge your rights, then support Mr. Lincoln and the Black Republican party, who are in favor of the citizenship of the Negro."

Supporters: "Never, never."

Douglas: "For one, I am opposed to Negro citizenship in any and every form."

Cheers.

"I believe this government was made on the white basis."

"Good."

"I believe it was made by white men of European birth and descent, instead of conferring it upon Negroes, Indians and other inferior races."

"Good for you. Douglas forever."

One might now wonder who were all these Americans shouting, "good" and "Douglas forever." They were the ordinary white Americans of their time who could not recognize the tide of history any more than we can. Douglas argued that each state should have the right to determine the status of slavery and black people. But he also said: "The civilized world has always held that when any race of men have shown themselves to be so degraded by ignorance, superstition, cruelty, and barbarism, as to be utterly incapable of governing themselves, they must, in the nature of things, be governed by others, by such laws as are deemed to be applicable to their condition."

Ever hear anything like that? Douglas was talking about black Americans. Today we generally think of ourselves as wiser or more morally attuned than to say that an entire race of people is "degraded by ignorance, superstition, cruelty, and barbarism." Or would we? George Will noted that some Americans are incapable of governing themselves in an August 14, 1997, *Washington Post* column applauding Congress for stripping the elected local D.C. government of its powers. "The withdrawal of popular sovereignty," Will wrote, "is condign punishment for those District voters who have elected many charlatans and demagogues, including Mayor Marion Barry for a fourth time, after prison. Voters have chosen to be corrupted by the culture of pandemic government, the debasement of living larcenously off wealth created by others."

Perhaps it is mere coincidence that the slaves Douglas deemed "incapable of governing themselves" and the D.C. voters who, "living larcenously," elected "charlatans and demagogues" were black. The D.C. government was, indeed, collapsing. Many city departments had ceased to function. And white-majority cities, including New York, Cleveland, and Miami fell into fiscal ruin that required outside intervention. Even the government of Orange County, California, an upscale enclave of white Republicanism, went bankrupt in 1994.

Unfortunately, though, the results of this suspicion that black people are incapable of governing themselves still haunt America. Even after Emancipation, blacks across the South were consigned to a separate world and deprived of basic rights. Do we forget this? Southern segregationists demanded passivity and servile deference from black people, terrorized black people and black neighborhoods from the 1880s to the 1960s, and undertook all manner of efforts to preserve racial segregation.

In fact, if there is anything that is unlikely to arise in today's discussions about race, it is the exact and seamy nature of segregationists' deepest fears. More than anything, segregationists worried that whites and blacks would intermarry and procreate. And this would not only destroy America, they believed, but the white race as well.

Such thinking is still present; for example, in 1998 it was reported that Georgia Representative Robert Barr and Mississippi Senator Trent Lott, two prominent Republicans, had spoken before gatherings of the Council of Conservative Citizens, a group that includes members who denounce race mixing. One widely cited article in the group's newsletter claimed "forced" integration of schools, neighborhoods, and recreation facilities was tantamount to forcing the "mixing of the races to produce a mongrel race." Said one council writer, a shadowy figure known only as H. Millard: "Anyone who wishes to deprive us of our unique and distinct existence commits the crime of genocide against us."

Barr and Lott sidestepped association with such views, but at one time—certainly within my 57 years—the claim that unchecked miscegenation would destroy America was the credo of public figures across the old South and embraced by a Mississippi senator who wrote a book about the threat of race mixing. In 1947, Theodore G. Bilbo, who was twice elected Mississippi governor and three times elected its senator, described his apocalyptic version of whites' basic fears in *Take Your Choice: Separation or Mongrelization*. The book is still available on at least one white supremacist Internet site.

"If our buildings, our highways, and our railroads should be wrecked," Bilbo wrote, "we could rebuild them. If our cities should be destroyed, out of the very ruins we could erect newer and greater ones. Even if our armed might should be crushed, we could rear sons who would redeem our power. But if the blood of our White race should become corrupted and mingled with the blood of Africa, then the present greatness of the United States of America would be destroyed."

Such visions were the cornerstone of segregation. Blacks' activities and whereabouts had to be proscribed to preserve the nation and the white race. Again, have we forgotten this? And it must be that the more laws and customs created to control a specific group, the more menacing these people seem to become, because there are so many laws and customs they could conceivably break. So if, for example, it is illegal for blacks and whites to play checkers together in Birmingham, Alabama, games of checkers can be viewed as the potential first step toward the American apocalypse.

Any society that worries about games of checkers must be nervous, indeed. And unknowingly, we may have inherited stereotypes from that sad era. Many black Americans still assume it is in the nature of white people to be obsessed with petty rules. And many white Americans still seem to worry that the very existence of black people is a threat to civilized order. Yet to maintain a faith that white Americans are the civilized, peaceful partners in race relations requires that much in 20th-century history be forgotten.

In the decades around World War I, white violence against black people was the common denominator in bloody incidents across the country. Even the term "race riot" initially emerged in those years as a reference to "white violence." White mobs attacked blacks in a host of major cities—and some minor ones, too. In July 1917, white workers attacked black neighborhoods in East St. Louis, Illinois, after hearing rumors that black workers were being hired in defense plants. The results are still sketchy, as with many of these atrocities. Estimates are that from 40 to 200 blacks were killed in East St. Louis and thousands driven from their homes.

Race rioting broke out in 26 cities during the "Red Summer" of 1919, so called because of the blood that flowed. In two weeks of rioting in Chicago, 23 blacks and 15 whites were killed, because by that point in the violent string, blacks were fighting back against the onslaught. In 1921, at least 36 people—and some say many more—where killed in Tulsa, Oklahoma, when a prosperous black community known as "Black Wallstreet" was burned down—and even bombed from the air. In 1923, a white mob, set off by false reports that a white woman had been raped by a black man, attacked black families in the tiny town of Rosewood, Florida, killing an estimated 150 people. The massacre was recounted in the 1997 movie *Rosewood*, but the events in the film were hardly unique.

Thousands of black Americans were lynched in the late 19th and early 20th centuries, but historian Lerone Bennett, Jr., in *Before the Mayflower: A History of the Negro in America, 1619–1964*, cites the 1918 lynching of Mary Turner in Valdosta, Georgia, as "undoubtedly one of the most barbaric acts ever committed in a civilized country." Though pregnant, Turner was hanged to a tree, doused with gasoline and motor oil, and burned. While she dangled from the rope, one mobster ripped open her abdomen with a pocketknife, yanked her fetus out, and stomped it to death, according to newspaper accounts.

Unfortunately, too, one need not search far in the history of many black families to find stories of white violence against black people. And this remains a basis of lingering fears about white treachery. One of my wife's uncles is said to have been killed by whites in Georgia. Yet these days, white Americans rarely imagine themselves as perpetrators of racial violence. In the updated version of a "race riot," black people loot stores, carry off TV sets, and pummel whites who happen to get caught in the midst. In the new mythology of American rioting, whites do nothing wrong.

It is odd, too—and some might say contemptible—for white Americans to speak habitually about race in terms that suggest black Americans have now, after all this tormented history, been "given" their rights and their fair share of opportunities. It is particularly insulting that the word *given* is so often used, as if whites have kindly shared from a bounty of privileges that do not otherwise extend to black people.

Apparently, this alleged generosity would mean that whites gained rights from a higher authority, but blacks gain theirs from whites.

This issue involves more than semantic detail. It highlights an aspect of white thinking that needs readjustment. First, whites did not give rights to black people, if they also maintain that rights are God given. Whites may have denied black people their rights—against God's will—but they did not give black people their rights. Got that? Next, black people were not the only Americans who gained from the ending of segregation and the opening of American life to fuller black participation. Whites also gained, and to prove this we need only imagine what the South would now be like if our apartheid system had not ended.

A segregated South would surely have become ever more socially and economically isolated. Few industries would have located—or relocated—there; the new South would never have happened. The 1996 Olympics would have been held somewhere other than Atlanta. Nor would the Braves or any other big league sports teams play in Florida, Georgia, Louisiana, or Texas. Most likely, a racially segregated South would have become such a social and economic backwater, shunned, and disconnected from the rest of the world, that it wold have collapsed under its own inefficiencies.

You don't believe this? Consider how a racially segregated Hartsfield International Airport would function—or not function. It could never be the world's second-busiest airport operating under the requirements of segregation—two waiting rooms, two restaurants, and two sets of restrooms. It barely operates at some moments under integration; the silly demands of segregation would quickly reduce Hartsfield to dysfunction. And would black people have had to sit in the back of planes flying in and out of the South, too? What airlines would accommodate this nonsense?

So it seems obvious that if blacks have been "given" anything, whites have been "given" something, too. Whites in the South have been "given" the keys to inclusion in the 20th-century world, to their own prosperity in the "new" South, and to their membership in civilized society. Indeed, whites in the South should be thankful that the civil rights movement rescued segregationists from their own foolishness.

Then, too, the civil rights movement also produced gains for women and other minorities. So many Americans gained that it sometimes seems that the civil rights movement left its originators behind in most of the markers of economic and social well-being. For this reason, among others, some black Americans do not easily relinquish the notion that justice is still owed them, now and for the centuries of slavery, too. Some black Americans firmly believe reparations should be paid for slavery.

Reparations are not a mainstream idea; you don't hear whites suggesting it very often. You hear about it most among black people. I have friends, relatives, and associates who believe reparations would be just, as were payments to Japanese citizens and others interred during World War II. My wife thinks it would be right. (And if a check came, would I ask her to send it back?)

But it is also equally clear—especially remembering the white reaction about an *apology* for slavery—that white Americans would oppose such a plan. The concept, moreover, is loaded with complexities that would be difficult to resolve. Would black skin alone be enough to qualify? Who would be considered black? Recent black immigrants? The descendents of slaves who are now considered white?

Still, white resistance to reparations might be such that some whites would surely riot if payments were made. And what would motivate whites to pay reparations in the first place? It is almost impossible to imagine circumstance in which such legislation could pass.

If any payments were made, whites would surely consider it *their* money. And bitterness over blacks being paid off with white people's money would far exceed anything seen in the O. J. Simpson case. There might be no precedent for the white anger that could ensue except the violence of the early 1900s.

Imagine the frenzy, the outrage. Journalists would report on how the money was being spent. Celebrations, parties, and other extravagances in black neighborhoods would produce more anger and outcries across the color line. White car dealers and other merchants might hold sales and "Slavery Days" specials. But black drug addicts would inevitably be found spending their reparations with drug dealers who, by the way, might also be found to have gotten payments. And how long would whites stand for that?

White bitterness could become inescapable. Whites would examine every shopping cart a black person was pushing, every car a black American was driving. Eventually, whites would claim that black people get nothing through their own initiative and ability; everything black people have—their homes, clothes, whatever—would be seen to have come from the money whites gave up.

Imagine the white fury that would ensue, if rich, superstar athletes and entertainers got reparations payments. Imagine the bitterness whites might harbor toward black neighbors and coworkers who got payments. Yet all this potential for white bitterness might make no difference if reparations enabled black Americans to separate themselves from whites, creating an independent black America. And this idea has been seized by a few white supremacists or "racialists" who suggest the reparation be paid to encourage blacks to separate themselves into a black state.

Otherwise, blacks should consider the reaction reparations might produce: whites will still be the controlling majority in the land, only now they will be a very angry majority. And would paying reparations put the issue of slavery to rest?

The problem is that we can never right the wrongs of slavery. We cannot diminish it or make it more acceptable by saying it was more benign; we cannot clear the shadow, especially if we view slavery as an issue that one or the other side is trying to use for political advantage. All that will continue is an argument.

It is obvious, too, that the mere presence of black people is an effect of slavery, and this fact adds to the complexity of the moral dilemma. A wrong that cannot be undone has produced a result we must embrace as good. We cannot reject the past so totally as to wish that black Americans were not here as Americans. So if we sense that the descendants of slaves enrich and enliven our culture, as they obviously do, or if we have friends or loved ones who are black, we are in a perverse way the distant beneficiaries of slavery.

Nor can blacks so totally reject the awful realities of slavery as to wish they were now someone else, a creation, physically, culturally, and spiritually of a totally different place. But who am I to say this? My own life is grandly enriched by the presence of people who would not be here if slavery had not been. Selfishly, I would not have it any other way.

Through the magic of technology, I have been listening to the voices of former slaves that were recorded in the 1940s—individuals like Fountain Hughes, born on a Virginia tobacco farm. Listening to the voices of those who experienced slavery puts it in a different perspective. Slavery is closer in time and nearer in space; it is infinitely more personal to recognize I could have myself spoken to former slaves, if

I had had the timely wisdom to seek them out. Why wasn't their presence noted at the great events of my youth? Why weren't they treated as honored guests among us? This was a major oversight.

"We were slaves," says Fountain Hughes. "We belonged to people. They'd sell us like they sell horses and cows and hogs an all like that. Have an auction bench, an' they'd put you on, up on the bench and bid on you jus' same as you bidding on cattle you know."

"Colored people din' have no beds when they was slaves," he says. "We always slep' on the floor, pallet here, and a pallet there. Jus' like, uh, lot of, uh, wild people, we didn', we didn't know nothing. Didn' allow you to look at no book."

Perhaps these recollections are not bad enough to satisfy our notions of slavery—or too telling to satisfy others. Our current sin is that in our rush to make slavery fit the needs of our causes, feelings, and self-imagery, we don't listen and appreciate what these exquisite voices from our conscience are saying about such simple things as slavery and freedom.

"Which had you rather be Uncle Fountain?" Hughes is asked.

"Me? Which I'd rather be?" he replies. "You know what I'd rather do? If I thought, had any idea, that I'd ever be a slave again, I'd take a gun an jus' end it all right away. Because you're nothing but a dog. You're not a thing but a dog."

11

WILD IDEAS

Can You Believe This Stuff?

Among the many notions we hear about race in America, which ones should we take seriously? Some are the stuff of jokes like the one that comedian Tom Arnold told a few years back on Showtime. "On the way over here," he said, "I saw a black man with a black woman."

Arnold paused to let that sink in.

Then he continued: "I felt bad because I knew somewhere there was a blond with a big butt crying her eyes out."

The audience laughed. Or at least *somebody* in that Showtime crowd was familiar enough with racial stereotypes about black men and white women to get the joke. But for those mystified by this attempt at humor, here are the operating premises:

1. Black men want to romance white women, hence seeing a black man with a black woman is unusual.
2. Black men like women with big butts, hence the blond would need to have one.
3. White women fall for black men. Hence the blond would be crying.

Arnold's joke was a mini-tour of all-American stereotypes about sex and race. Are they true? Everyday experience—what we actually see—indicates they are not. Most black men, in fact, appear to be interested in black women. But these stereotypical ideas have been around for eons. Segregationists were worried that they were true. But does anyone still believe they are? Does Tom Arnold believe they are? Is it wrong to laugh at such nonsense? That suggests we laugh at premises we know are *not* true? And isn't that odd?

Some claims about race are theoretically more serious, made not by comedians but by individuals with solid-seeming credentials. These individuals sound like they know what they are talking about, and their claims sound like they could be true. Some claimants are wearing white laboratory coats that suggest they are involved in valuable research. And they have a serious demeanor.

One such individual says that black people have more fast-twitch muscle fibers, whatever they are, which is why blacks run so fast. Should we believe it? Another says that whites evolved in cold climates where they needed to gather and store food for a long winter, so whites are adept at organizing and planning ahead. Should we believe this, too?

In both cases, critics with equally good credentials say these claims are nonsense. But the claims keep coming. Are we all to believe that blacks are less intelligent, because it has been widely reported that blacks score 15 points lower than whites on standard IQ tests? What are we to do? Whether black or white, most of us are ordinary people, not scientists. We have a dilemma, and I suspect that many of us hedge our bets. If a claim about race sounds like it could be true—if it seems to make common sense—we store it away. We may not espouse it or teach it to others, but it may be the only actual explanation we have for phenomena that puzzle us. So such explanations slip into our consciousness, having their effect.

We often don't even recall where exactly we got the ideas we have about race. Maybe we heard or read them long ago. Maybe we picked them up as members of one group or another. The basic operating assumptions we retain about race can be shadowy stuff. Even our understanding about who is white and who is black is puzzling and suggests we are willing to accept absolute nonsense for truth, as long as everybody else is doing so.

In particular, "white" and "black" are not clear biological or genetic concepts. There is no color line in science that automatically puts an individual on one side or the other. Some individuals we think of as "black" might be genetically more "white," while some individuals we think of "white" might be genetically more "black." And we cannot discern any of this with the naked eye. Skin color, an evolutionary adaptation to climate, is only skin-deep, so if someone looks darker or lighter, this fact does not tell the whole story.

Meanwhile, science is heading away from the idea that races are a biological reality. How many races are there? That's one major issue. Some sources list only three. More list four or five. Other sources list dozens of racial subgroups. But a pattern emerges in regard to the number of races. Those finding fewer races tend to cling to the idea of great differences between them. And those positing more races see subtle differences—and much shared—among the various groups. Yet no matter how many races are claimed, no one can point out the exact line where one ends and another begins. There are no color lines in biology, even if we are convinced we see them clearly in daily life.

We may be sure that people we meet are "black" or "white," yet we are tricked if we believe this divide mirrors biological truth. Regarding race, we often see lines that are not there.

The authors of *The Bell Curve* found it convenient to see three broad racial groups—blacks, whites, and Asians. It helped make matters seem simple: Blacks are one way; whites are another way; and Asians are something else. Dividing humanity into three huge races also was convenient for J. Philippe Rushton, a Canadian psychologist who claims that the three races differ physically, mentally, and temperamentally. Rushton's idea is sensationally simple; his three races differ in every way he can imagine, and like *The Bell Curve*, his theories invite conclusions that one or another group is superior or better suited for modern life.

The problem with viewing humankind as three groups is that each one must necessarily contain a vast range of differences—and most scientists insist that the differences *within* each group will be greater than the differences *between* them. Also, most people will fall somewhere between the extremes that Rushton or the authors of *The Bell Curve* describe.

Yet Americans are accustomed to the idea of a sharp divide between races; the stark social segregation of blacks and whites promotes this impression. Hence, it is all too easy to suspect that blacks and whites might be genetically different, even extending to their behavior. Hence, Rushton and those like him gain attention because their theories sound plausible in a society in which you are either white or black, one or the other. Never mind that there is no biological color line. Never mind that evolution has produced a scale of color from black to white; our society has no such scale of variations.

We see "black" or "white," even if nature produces infinite shades of difference that we are content to ignore. For example, biological and logical reality would place the color of a child with one white parent and one black parent somewhere along the black-white scale, possibly at brown or tan. But this judgment would present a problem for the social norms under which Americans live. Convention dictates that the child must be black or white. And saying that the child is brown, tan, or mixed will not do. The long-standing rule in American thinking—excepting Hispanics—has been to classify a child of mixed parentage as black, because unlike other societies, even other countries in the Americas, we do not have viable categories in the middle.

Black or white—that's what we've got, and my wife's grandson, who is eight, understands the deal. He told me he heard a comedian talking on TV about people who say they are "mixed" and found the comedian's version of the concept funny. The comedian said, "I'm 'mixed,' too—my mother was black and my father was black as hell."

The insidious mechanism that makes the American definitions of race work so clearly, in defiance of biological reality, is the One-Drop Rule. This rule ordains that an individual with *any* known black ancestry, no matter how distant, is black. Therefore, a single drop of "black blood" makes a person black.

The persistence of this idea is peculiar to our shores. Elsewhere, especially in Latin America, racial classifications are hardly so stark or limited, and other factors, including economic class, may enter into how an individual is classified. Often, much of the population falls into "mixed" categories—mixes of European, African, Native American, and, in some cases, Asian. A family portrait in Latin American countries often includes people who would be considered of different races in the United States. As a result, the sense of a racial divide—or of a lingering taboo against intermarriage—is greater in the United States than in Latin America. And while we speak in terms of "white" or "black," elsewhere in the world the language of identity and color admits a host of variants.

One theory about the predominance of the One-Drop Rule is that the Spaniards and Portuguese who settled Latin America were more accustomed to interactions with the darker people from North Africa. Hence they were more open-minded about race mixing than the British, whose attitudes dominated in North America. That aside, the One-Drop Rule appears to have been reinforced as the resolution to a slave owner's dilemma: what race were children whose fathers were slave owners and mothers were slaves? According to the One-Drop Rule, the children would be black and therefore slaves, an economically attractive result for slave owners. DNA tests have revealed it likely that Thomas Jefferson—or some Jefferson male—fathered a child with his slave Sally Hemmings; miscegenation was a common occurrence and a major irony in the slavery system. "There is not a likely-looking black girl in the state that is not the concubine of a white man," one antebellum planter reported. "There is not an old plantation in which the grand-children of the owner are not whipped in the field by the overseers."

Following the One-Drop Rule, however, means that *only* black blood is powerful enough to define a person's identity with a single drop. White blood cannot do that. Can a pale-skinned child with one black grandparent be considered white? Elsewhere, in Latin America, few would puzzle over the problem. But here in the United States, that child might be labeled black, because American society shuns the middle ground between black and white. Indeed, these views on identity are so fixed that we worry about such a child. Which group will accept the child? Will the child face cruel taunts? Will the child grow up confused about his or her identity? But who in fact is confused? American society—that's who. Even if the child looked white, some Americans would consider its status as "passing" for white, not the real thing.

The basic premises of the One-Drop Rule are also called the *hypo-descent rule*, which means that ethnically or racially mixed individuals are assigned the identity of whichever group in their parentage is subordinate in the given society. So accordingly, children of one black parent and one white parent are considered black, because blacks are considered the subordinate social group in American society. But pay close attention. This sense of being "subordinate" is unusual, because a drop of *subordinate* blood can obliterate pints, quarts, or gallons of blood from the allegedly *dominant* group. And how could that be? If one drop of "blackness" darkens a sea of "whiteness, "then "whiteness" must be a very delicate commodity that's easily eliminated. And "blackness" would seem to have the power to take over the world.

Bear that in mind. Odd as it may be, this concept of white frailty versus black strength is very close to what white supremacists like Senator Bilbo were worried about. They believed a few drops of black blood could eventually destroy white America, and to be sure, this would be a turnabout on our traditional assumptions about who has power in America and who doesn't. According to the One-Drop/hypo-descent rule, the power of black genes is awesome, while that of white genes is more like a fragile flower.

Similarly, if we accept the One-Drop view, one black parent can produce an infinite number of black descendents, no matter what race the other parents have been. But whiteness disappears the instant a drop of blackness is introduced into the mix. Therefore, whites can produce white offspring only if they stick together, always breeding among themselves.

Although exhortations to save the white race are rarely heard in mainstream discourse, who knows what fears still lurk in the shadows of white thinking? Some members of the Council of Conservative Citizens openly declare the white race is endangered. This same idea might inspire uneasy whites to imagine danger in the presence of black people. At the same time, prominent fears about race have often centered on sex—and apparently still do. Segregationists' fears that black men would be interested in white women led to numerous atrocities in the old South; whites would believe black men were guilty of attacking white women without any credible evidence. And even today, the idea of intermarriage troubles millions of white Americans—in polls 39 percent of whites still say they disapprove of intermarriage between blacks and whites.

Does this number reflect fears about the extinction of the white race? We don't know. Pollsters don't press that question. Still, the idea that black plus white equals black is the potential foundation for a serious white inferiority complex. If whiteness is so easily threatened, whites might sense they need to be extra careful about black people. Controversial black psychiatrist Frances Cress Welsing believes this is exactly what underlies white behavior; she considers whites to be albino mutants whose psyches are tormented by the frailty of their colorless state. She also believes whites bolster their frail egos with illusions of white supremacy, when in reality, whites are not supreme at all. They must huddle together protectively—or disappear.

Despite its deformed psychological effects, the principles of the One-Drop Rule, born in slavery, still dominate our assumptions about racial identity. Few baseball fans can quickly name the Italian American player who was three times voted most valuable player in the National League in the 1950s. The player? Roy Campanella. But wasn't he black? Didn't he play in the old Negro Leagues before he joined the Brooklyn Dodgers? Yes, his father was Italian and his mother was black. In biological terms, Campanella was as much of Italian ancestry as black.

Yet in our thinking, the One-Drop Rule prevails, and despite its origins in slavery, black Americans also embrace the rule, an acceptance that black Americans usually explain in terms of white behavior. Black Americans believe that if you are known to have any black ancestry—and certainly if you look black in any way—sooner or later, whites will treat you as black. That means that the cops will pull you over or suspicious store clerks will follow you around, and all of the various slights that whites visit upon black people will be visited on you. And there is no way to escape it—so don't even *try* saying you are not black.

Consequently, some black Americans were suspicious in 1996 when golfer Tiger Woods tried to define his race as "Cablinasian," a word he concocted to describe a mixture of Caucasian, black, Indian, and Asian ancestry. They seriously wondered what he had in mind. Was he trying to say he *wasn't* black? Or that he was *better* than black? Did he think whites would accept him as something other than black? Many black Americans closely followed what Woods said about his racial makeup. But you will also note that eventually, the world—and the media—treated Woods as black, despite his earlier protestations and the obvious common sense in Woods's view of his own identity. So the One-Drop Rule prevailed.

Yet Woods's assertion that he was something other than black also highlighted the movement to include "multiracial" as a category on the U.S. census along with the other five choices: white; black; Hispanic; Asian or Pacific Islander; and American Indian, Eskimo, or Aleut. But civil rights groups looked upon the idea skeptically. Consider that if Woods now could check off "multiracial," that would be one less "black" person in the United States. Adding a multiracial category could diminish the size of the "black" population, a prospect that generally makes black Americans wary. A drop in numbers of "black" people would, in effect, diminish black Americans as an interest group or affect the allocation of government funds. In fact, some black Americans would vanish.

So it turns out that both blacks and whites can have their worries about disappearing. Some whites fear the white race will disappear though miscegenation. Some blacks fear that whites will scheme to eliminate blacks in other ways—not to mention conspiracy theories about whites spreading AIDS or encouraging drug use. And both blacks and whites worry that their familiar cultural surroundings will change. Some whites apparently fear that a darkening population will turn America into a place that is more like Africa or Asia. Hence, Denver will look like Nairobi and Des Moines like Marrakech. Furthermore, some whites apparently fear that they will wake up one day in a land where everybody speaks a strange tongue—English will be a goner, too.

Black Americans, however, sense their cultural survival is more immediately threatened, if only by the overwhelming presence of a white world around them. This fear should be easy to understand. In simplest terms, the fear appears to be that blacks who lose their cultural identity might end up talking like whites, acting like whites, walking like whites, dressing like whites, making music and dancing like whites—in short, *being* like whites. And for millions of black Americans that would be an awful prospect. The African American ethnic identity would disappear, and black experience would cease to be unique, having drowned in a sea of whiteness.

This cultural dilemma is in part similar to that of other ethnic minorities who have found themselves torn between old and new ways but eventually assimilate over generations into the white American mainstream. Among black Americans, the tug-of-war is represented by disdainful admonitions against "acting white" or "trying to be white." "White" behavior, real or imagined, is ridiculed, and the cultural conflict turns truly counterproductive when "trying to be white" is equated with doing well in school, having a successful career, or obeying the "white man's" laws. Meanwhile, in certain subcultures, including on the streets around my house, being "black" is sometimes perversely glorified by shunning education, courting failure, and ending up in jail.

Yet unlike white ethnic minorities who emigrated from other countries, black Americans have been here for centuries. Their separate cultural identity evolved under slavery and enforced segregation. White Americans need to remember that blacks were not welcomed into white society, so it is ludicrous for whites to complain that black culture is different or for whites to wonder, "Why can't they be more like us?" Nor can black people become invisible or "disappear" into the mainstream as white ethnic groups have done. Let's face it. Black people stand out in a white crowd—they have no choice.

Estimates are that 70 or 80 percent of black Americans have white ancestry; a quarter also have Native American ancestry, and a smaller percentage have Asian ancestry, too. Because of this unique mix, black Americans are often considered a separate racial subgroup. But the white in the mix has no transforming power according to the One-Drop Rule.

It has also been claimed that up to 20 percent of the white population—48 million Americans—could have some distant black ancestry, but this estimate is usually considered fanciful. It is more likely that between 1 and 5 percent of "whites" have black ancestry, which translates into between 2.2 and 11.2 million "whites" who are "black," according to the One-Drop Rule. Might some accuse them of passing as whites or denying their blackness? How confusing our ideas about race can get.

Cultural differences can also reinforce suggestions that underlying biological differences drive our behavior, if it appears convincing that people with black skin behave differently from people with white skin. Yet as groups, "blacks" and "whites" represent such a multiplicity of genetic variants as to defy generalizations based on the few racial characteristics that we happen to notice, like skin color. Still, there are persons out there claiming that race determines the way we behave. In *Race, Evolution and Behavior: A Life History Perspective*, J. Philippe Rushton claims that Negroids, Caucasoids, and Mongoloids, his three races, differ in ways that can even include values, which is a major leap most scientists are not ready to make. In fact, most think Rushton's theory is nonsense.

Also, just about every questionable racial stereotype known to man is represented in this Canadian psychologist's views. Rushton claims the three racial groups differ in intelligence, brain size, genital size, speed of sexual maturation, length of menstrual cycle, frequency of sexual intercourse, sperm and egg production, sexual hormone levels, marital stability, infant mortality, selfishness or altruistic motivations, general mental health, and willingness to obey the law.

Got all that? From the vast smorgasbord of scholarly papers and what have you, Rushton has selected the morsels supporting his claim that there are three vastly different races. Charles Murray, in *The Bell Curve*, calls Rushton "a serious scholar who has assembled serious data." But other scholars are far less generous, saying his theories are too sweeping to be plausible.

Indeed, Rushton claims that all the evidence on racial differences follows one pattern. No matter what the issue is, Asians fall to one extreme, blacks to another, and whites somewhere in between. So if the issue is brain size, IQ, or a behavioral category like "social restraint," Rushton claims Asians have larger brains, higher IQs, and more social restraint, while blacks have smaller brains, lower IQs, and less social restraint. And whites fall somewhere in the middle.

Rushton says penis size, one of his preoccupations, works in reverse order to brain size, with blacks having the biggest, Asians the smallest, and whites again in the middle. But convincingly definitive studies on penis size are hard to find. Still, Rushton sees having a large or small penis as part of a pattern relating to sexual appetite or the amount of sex people get. Rushton cites studies that claim blacks reach sexual maturity the fastest, Asians the slowest, with whites in the middle. Then he cites studies that claim blacks have intercourse the earliest, Asians the latest, with whites in the middle. After that he claims blacks have marital intercourse more often and more extramarital partners, too. Asians have marital intercourse the least and the fewest extramarital partners. Whites are, once again, in the middle. But in dealing with a variable like sexual appetite, we also need to recognize the wide variations that might occur within each racial group.

Rushton, however, focuses on alleged differences, and many of his findings parallel standard stereotypes. Blacks are supposed to be oversexed, Asians to have a reserve about the subject, and whites fall somewhere in between. Rushton proposes that these differences in behavior, or culture itself, are governed by genetics, a highly suspect premise intimating that members of different races will find it hard to live together in accordance to the same social norms. Instead members of each group will pursue the varied behavior their genes dictate.

If anything, Rushton's ideas have a kooky consistency. He says that blacks have more highly developed secondary sexual characteristics—"salient voice, breasts, buttocks, muscles" ("salient" meaning prominent, protruding, or conspicuous), with Asians the least developed in these regards, and whites in between. Rushton cites studies that suggest black people around the world have the most "permissive attitudes" and "low guilt" toward sex, while Asians have the least permissive attitudes and the most guilt. Yet in these latter instances, it would be hard to claim these qualities and attitudes can be measured objectively or that the observations are truly representative of the vast racial groupings Rushton postulates. Most scientists would also insist that differences in culture or social customs involve learned behavior.

Here, for the flavor of his prose, is Rushton talking about sexual appetite:

> Thus Conner (1975, 1976) had found that three generations of Japanese Americans, as well as Japanese students in Japan, reported less interest in sex than Caucasian samples. Abramson and Imari-Marquez (1982) observed that each of three generations of Japanese Americans showed more sex guilt than matched Caucasian Americans. In studies carried out in Britain and Japan using a sex fantasy questionnaire, Iwawaki and Wilson (1983) found that British men reported twice as many fantasies as Japanese men, and British women admitted to four times as much sex fantasy as Japanese women. . . . In contrast, African-descended people are more permissive than Caucasians. Reiss (1967) observed this with several hundred black and white university students in the United States on scales measuring premarital sexual attitudes (e.g. approving of or feeling guilt about petting and intercourse in casual and romantic relationships).

Clearly, he is jumping all over the place and drawing broad conclusions from relatively tiny samples. But Rushton's focus on sex and guilt convinced him that evolution produced three races with differing reproductive strategies. In nature, some species like fish or frogs survive by producing great numbers of eggs out of which relatively few are likely to reach maturity. Other species, such as mammals, produce fewer offspring but nurture and protect them carefully.

So one group bets its survival on numbers. Another depends on nurturing. And Rushton believes that the reproductive strategies of his three races also differ along these lines. Black people, who originated in the warm, relatively safe environment of Africa, tend to have lots of offspring and nurture them less. Asians, who evolved in the harsh, cold climate of Northern Asia, have fewer offspring but care for them more faithfully as a more rigorous climate requires. And as usual, whites fall in the middle.

Therefore, according to Rushton, black people, wherever they are found, are genetically programmed to follow a reproductive strategy of numbers. And he believes that having large sex organs would encourage a more single-minded focus on sex, while whites and Asians would have fewer tendencies in this direction. They would have fewer kids but take better care of them and educate them well. Indeed, according to Rushton, Asians seem more civilized than whites. They have bigger brains and are more intelligent and responsible in rearing and educating their children, which, if true, might have great impact for the future of the world. If what Rushton says is true, an epoch of Asian dominance could be at hand.

Meanwhile, critics of Rushton say his theories on reproductive strategies are hogwash. Human beings are human beings; frogs are frogs; fish are fish. And the fact that some fish or frogs lay hundreds of eggs and leave their young to make it on their own has nothing to do with what humans do. Blacks are not more closely related to fish or frogs than anyone else and whites and Asians are not farther removed in their development from fish or frogs. Nor do any human beings have scales or feathers, though Rushton's theory might almost suggest that could be possible.

The real devil's work in Rushton's efforts is that his theories seem to explain the stereotypes many of us already have. For example, the idea that blacks are oversexed is not new. It is an old stereotype that appears to have originated in the days when Europeans encountered "primitive" people who were living in warmer environments and wearing less clothing. The Europeans surmised that less clothing must promote more sex. For centuries, whites have viewed black people as sexually uninhibited and Asians as restrained. Still, some might believe that Rushton's theories of evolution are in evidence in scenes of black children playing outside public housing projects. It is frequently asked why black people have so many kids often on an assumption that they do so irresponsibly. Yet any claim that this behavior stems from a genetic trait peculiar to blacks does not take into account the millions of black parents who take excellent care of their kids or, for that matter, the millions of white or Asian parents who do less well by their kids than they should.

A good example of how quick impressions work was apparent at the Kentucky Courts housing project near my house. Many neighbors assumed that all parents at Kentucky Courts did not take care of their kids, because of a few, highly visible cases of kids running wild. While most families in the project struggled to do as well by their children as possible, outsiders did not see those kids. They saw only the kids creating a ruckus.

Yet how are ordinary people who do not follow scientific debates about race to know that claims like Rushton's are widely considered wrongheaded? For sure, one is wise to be wary of simple answers; the truth is *probably* much more complex. But Rushton *sounds* complex in all the studies he cites, even if his conclusions are colossally simple: blacks are always at one end of the scale, Asians at the other, and whites are always in the middle.

When confronting the likes of Rushton, ordinary people would do well to remember that science has found more differences, more genetic variation, *within* broad racial groups than between these racial groups. This idea always bears repeating, because it is probable that many whites, blacks, or Asians will be alike in the very ways Rushton claims they are different. We should also insist, simple as the idea is, that it is both unfair and foolish to prejudge individuals in terms of their race. To assume that the next black, white, or Asian person who walks in the door will have the characteristics or temperament that Rushton or anyone assigns to his or her racial group is wrong. It is likely that the next black person who comes along will be neither oversexed nor a fast runner; the next Asian will be neither brainy nor obsessively protective of children; and the next white person will not be somewhere in the middle on these extremes. In fact, we do not know what people of any race will be like until we address them as individuals.

Still, human beings have found it difficult to resist the appeal of quick, seemingly commonsense explanations for the differences identified with race. Therefore, it may also be worthwhile to ask of any theory about race whether it is the only possible explanation. The differences that Rushton and others claim are biological in origin could be explained by environmental influences such as culture. And most theories about race tend to fall at one or other extreme in the classic debate of nature versus nurture. Is human behavior the result of our genetic inheritance, as those on the nature end of the debate contend?

Or do environment, upbringing, and education also have critical bearing on who we become—the nurture side of the debate? Or to what degree do both nature and nurture affect the results?

Rushton and the authors of *The Bell Curve* fall heavily—with a thud really—on the nature side, where true believers insist that genes determine our fate. They believe people are born with the capacities that shape their lives, and according to Rushton, our behavior. These contending theories can have political ramifications as well. Those on the nature side often believe that efforts to change biological destiny are a waste of time and money. Those on the nurture side, meanwhile, insist that much can be done to improve our lot.

Nurture partisans believe that efforts to help people overcome negative environments are a worthy function of government. But nature partisans claim there is little government can do to change the fate that DNA determines. And science in the 20th century has also left us buffeted in nature-versus-nurture arguments, involving claims and counterclaims about the origins of crime, poverty, and social problems. A rightward political shift in the 1990s brought nature-leaning arguments to the fore; *The Bell Curve* is an example. But conservatives also argued that the environment created by liberal policies like the welfare state also produced its disasters, a nurture-leaning argument that government in effect taught welfare recipients to behave in nonproductive ways.

Nor are some Americans likely to believe that blacks and whites live in such different worlds as to explain the cultural differences between them. Don't all Americans go to the mall? Don't all Americans eat at McDonald's? Don't all Americans watch the Super Bowl? Yet this view overlooks the dimensions of our separation—the segregation of our schools, churches, and social lives. In the 1990s, blacks and whites weren't even watching the same TV shows. Therefore, is it surprising that blacks and whites look at the world differently?

Curiously, the same cultural and temperamental differences identified with skin color in the United States are seen in other lands as regional characteristics applying to people of the same race. Around the world, this cultural divide usually falls between North and South, a pattern that has its tradition in the United States, as well. Usually, the North is more industrial, the South more agrarian; the pace of Northern life is more frenetic, the pace of Southern life more leisurely.

Northerners are seen as serious, sober, and hard-working, Southerners as charming, easygoing, and fun-loving. In European countries, race is involved in these distinctions only in a most subtle sense: Northerners are more likely to be blond and blue-eyed, Southerners brunet and dark-eyed. Climate is an obvious factor, too. More of Southern life is lived outdoors; more of Northern life in buildings. Southerners from warmer climes are thought to be hot-blooded and passionate, Northerners from cooler places as cold and cerebral.

Around the world, Northerners and Southerners sometimes look at each other with disdain. Wars and political conflicts are common along a North-South divide, as in Korea, Vietnam, and the United States. But other conflicts along the divide are less lethal: Northern Italians merely see themselves as vastly different from Sicilians and vice versa. Northern and Southern Germans as well. And so on. Generally, Southern societies in Europe are reckoned to be noisy and convivial, while social contacts in Northern societies are more formal and soft-spoken. Southerners live their lives somewhat extemporaneously; Northerners are more likely to make appointments. Also, Northerners see themselves as thinkers and doers—serious people. Southerners imagine they are lovers, poets, and musicians—people of passion.

In Spain, the country I know second best, stereotypes about North and South are often expressed. Spaniards from Andalusia in the South, the home of flamenco music and bullfighting, see themselves as culturally and temperamentally different from the Basques and Catalonians in the North, where flamenco and bullfighting are less important and even culturally alien in some locales. Northern and Southern Spaniards sometimes view each other as strange or inexplicable people. Southerners claim that Northerners are almost Germanic in the meticulous precision of their ways; Northerners claim that Southerners are almost African in the way they get carried away with whatever catches their fancy. But all the people we are talking about here are white. So what causes these differences—nature or nurture, genetics or environment?

It is striking, too, how regional stereotypes in Spain or elsewhere parallel American stereotypes about race: Northern (or white) culture can seem cold, calm, rational, sincere, quiet, sober, private, serious. Northerners (or whites) value a literal use of language. They see themselves as disciplined people, believing they have their emotions and other urges under control. Meanwhile, Southern (or black) culture can seem hot, passionate, noisy, public, joyous, creative. Southerners use language more freely, valuing exaggeration, inflection, and word play.

They sing, dance, and party, believing that life is best when we shed our inhibitions. Northerners (or whites) look upon Southerners as untrustworthy and irresponsible, while Southerners (or blacks) frequently regard Northerners (or whites) as cold, joyless, rigid, militaristic, orderly people who have no fun. Northerners (or whites) see Southerners (or blacks) as passionate, exaggerating, and irresponsible types who live for the moment.

Rushton might claim that such differences are genetic. But they can seem as much the product of sunlight and shadows. Southerners may appear more involved in sex and romance because of the more public ways in which they live. We see more courting in Southern environments because it is outdoors. Meanwhile, Northerners pursue these same interests privately—indoors. It might even appear that Southerners take less care of their children, because we see more children outside.

But which direction does the cultural compass point in the United States—North or South? American culture in this age of TV and carbon-copy shopping malls from Alaska to Florida seems increasingly a homogeneous mix of Northern and Southern ways. Nevertheless, Northern culture still predominates, if only perhaps because a majority of Americans trace their ancestry to countries in Northern and Western Europe. Northern culture—a hybrid of German, British, Irish, and Scandinavian ways—is still likely to predominate in most American homes and in all regions, even the South.

Then as Italian Americans and others of Mediterranean descent or Southern inclination become further assimilated into the cultural mainstream, blacks and Hispanics appear to occupy the Southern extreme in our North-South thought patterns, and the actual geographic location of where we live in the United States becomes less relevant. We are an endlessly mobile nation, which brings North to South and South to North. But black and Hispanic ways might still seem off-kilter to the Northern cultural majority and vice versa, too; surely a sense of cultural estrangement promotes fears about a "darkening" nation. It is not just that the skin color of Americans might be darker in the future; the concomitant fear many whites may have is that our cultural norms will go South as well.

Once again, it is helpful to note how misunderstandings about the ways of others show up. When race is not involved, the explanations seem clear. When Northerners and Southerners of the same race have different accents, for example, no one looks to genetics for an explanation. No one claims that evolution has endowed Northerners or Southerners with different mouths, tongues, and brains. Instead, we assume that accents are picked up in the surroundings in which individuals were raised.

Yet when race is part of the picture, some of us, blacks and whites included, tend to ignore the impact centuries of cultural isolation and economic inequity have wrought. We expect that a deep schism engendered through generations should vanish in a few decades or else we look for biological explanations, forgetting that segregation persisted for more than half of the 20th century, and the results are still powerfully evident. How then can we suddenly expect the cultures in these two worlds to merge seamlessly? In fact, the real wonder after centuries of enforced separation is how similar the two cultures are and how engagingly they complement each other.

12
WHITE CULTURE
The Ways of White Folks

The ways of Americans might seem by now to have penetrated every byway of the world. A dozen white American men have landed on the moon; several have motored about there, and one even whacked a few golf balls. Of almost greater impact, America has exported concepts like blue jeans, rock and roll, and the Big Mac, which results in McDonald's french fries being served on the Champs-Elysées or the French considering themselves lovers of *le jazz*.

What, you might ask, have Americans not done? White Americans get credit for inventing the airplane, the telephone, the television, the computer, and the movies. Planet Hollywood nightspots light up distant and allegedly "dark" continents. Americans have also harnessed the power of advertising and marketing to inspire desires most people on earth didn't know they had. Marketing and advertising made Michael Jordan the most famous and admired man in the world, but there was good material to work with. Or consider the triumph of Coca-Cola: this beverage is hardly more than colored, sweetened water and CO_2 gas bubbles. Yet Coca-Cola was listed as the number one corporate employer on the continent of Africa in the 1990s.

Exported American culture, which now includes hip-hop and rap, has such awesome power it can frighten the locals at times, as it did in 1992 when some in France feared a cultural doomsday was at hand with the opening of the EuroDisney park outside Paris. Meanwhile, most Americans thought such fears were a hoot. But the park eventually became Europe's number one vacation destination—more evidence, if you will, of the rectitude, wisdom, and inevitability of American ways.

Americans also expect things to work—an expectation not so common in other countries. As a result, Americans tend to assume others should adopt American ways, not vice versa, and some Americans— both blacks and whites—can usually be spotted wearing this attitude in Paris, Rome, or Tokyo. The giveaway: Americans swagger, assuming rights to more personal space and projecting a conviction that their ways are the norm by which all others should be judged.

White Americans, in particular, rarely have occasion to see themselves as odd or "different." They rarely see themselves as outsiders might—and why should they? Americans have been told since they could walk that the rest of the world is out of step, and white Americans see themselves as the quintessential Americans. Further, our politics constantly promote the idea that Americans are right in assertions that we are the best, blessed by God. And if you notice carefully, it is whites who most often make these claims.

Similarly, since they are used to judging others by American norms, white Americans inevitably view other races in their own land as a bit odd. In "white" surroundings, black people are occasionally viewed as a tad foreign or "abnormal," as if majority rule determines all claims on normalcy. But whites can also be capricious in their claims of being normal, appropriating other people's ways at times without bothering to say thank you.

Blacks cite Elvis Presley as an example of the white expropriation of black culture, and Presley's early music was, at least, an engaging amalgam of black and white ways—no question our popular music is indebted to black Americans. Whites, however, regularly raid black culture for fashionable words like *cool, hip, rap, uptight,* and *dissin'*. Recently the word *props*, short in black usage for "proper respect," seemed to proliferate among white sports fans who have also adopted "high fives" and other salutes originated by black athletes. Or whites mock black styles, then adopt them as their own, as in the case of baseball hats; once upon a time, black youngsters turned theirs around to be different, but now whites all over the place wear their hats backward. Or whites in recent years puzzled, "Why do they wear their pants down at their knees?"—referring to black youngsters who did this. But in short order many white kids adopted the style, too.

At the same time, blacks and whites often define themselves in terms of each other, or as opposites, each saying, in effect, "What we are is not like them." Yet it is in the nature of relations between the white majority and the much smaller black minority that black people will stand out as different, which, in turn, makes black ways seem the more defined. In this optical illusion, whiteness is the backdrop against which black stands out. "White men can't jump" only because it is believed that blacks can—and those blacks who can jump well, basketball stars and track athletes, stand out.

Yet some black observers say that if whiteness can only be described in comparisons to others—if it doesn't stand out by itself—it must lack notable characteristics of its own. So how do you describe whiteness? This becomes a curious test.

When asked, some whites will tell you what *blacks* are like and declare they are not like that. So it turns out that whites don't jump up and down in church, don't get carried away with their emotions, don't congregate on street corners—or whatever else allegedly makes whites unlike black people, even if—get this—most black people don't behave in these ways either. In fact, it might be noted that the more we look at black Americans in middle-class and upscale environments, the less likely we are to find behavior that whites consider "black."

And this can be strange. If the black people whites are most likely to encounter are the least likely to act in stereotypically "black" ways, why would whites cling to other impressions? Still, the quieter aspects of white (or Northern) culture can seem most easily defined in comparison to the noisier aspects of black (or Southern) culture. Hence, it might not be noted that whites are quiet in movie theaters except that some black Americans (and people in some foreign countries) talk during movies or shout at characters on the screen.

This is a common image of how blacks behave. But is it correct? Certainly, white teens are not silent at horror movies. Carrying on in the theater, including making comments at the characters on the screen, gave *The Rocky Horror Picture Show* a persistent cult following. So is it really blacks who do all the talking at the movies?

Inevitably minorities stand out, even when only a fraction of the minority behaves in the way the majority finds odd or annoying. Really, only a few black Americans talk at the movies, but do whites recognize that? At times, relations between blacks and whites can seem to be a war of generalizations hurled back and forth with many of them clearly untrue. Yet it is hardly possible to speak in terms of "black" or "white" without being sucked into this maelstrom of generalizations.

Further complicating the definition of "white" or "black" ways is the question of economic class. Many of the perceptions that whites or blacks fixate on as "white" or "black" are often issues of economic class as well. Does anyone claim that poor whites have the same manners or interests as well-to-do whites? The distinction should apply to poor and well-to-do blacks as well. We might, in fact, expect well-to-do whites and blacks to have more interests in common with each other than with the poor of their own race. Still, when whites focus on outrageous black styles, such as getups favored by foppish black pimps, they, in fact, single out a tiny subculture that lives far differently from the ways of most black people. (And many black people may also be equally horrified at the spectacle these individuals make of themselves.) Yet when blacks fixate on rural, tobacco-chewing whites in pickups with gun racks as archetypal white people, they are also singling out a subculture which, in many cases, other white people find distasteful as well.

Similarly, some whites disapprovingly asked, "Why do they [black youngsters] always wear their pants down at their knees?" Yet their question ignored the millions of black men who don't—including the most prominent black Americans. Colin Powell and Jesse Jackson do *not* wear their pants down around their knees—and it would be a very strange sight if they did. So why do some whites claim all blacks do this or that?

It might be similarly asked what are the defining quirks of white people? Or for that matter, where exactly do whites wear their pants? Undoubtedly, whites believe they wear their pants where pants are supposed to be worn, wherever that might be. And that's that. White Americans consider themselves an infinitely varied group, even if they fail to see blacks in these terms. Whites run the gamut from blond to brunet; they are noisy or quiet—whites would never consider it accurate to say that all whites are alike. And because whites see themselves as having such a variety of ethnic origins and ways, some insist, too, there can be no such thing as "white culture," and they might seem to have a point.

"Whiteness is not a culture," says Harvard History Professor Noel Ignatiev. "There is Irish culture and Italian culture and American culture;

. . . there is youth culture and drug culture and queer culture; but there is no such thing as white culture."

Ignatiev argues that white Americans share the inherent "white privilege" that President Clinton's commission on race also identified in its 1998 report. Here's how Ignatiev described the phenomenon in a paper delivered at an April 1997 Conference on "Whiteness" at the University of California at Berkeley:

> Whiteness has nothing to do with culture and everything to do with social position. It is nothing but a reflection of privilege, and exists for no reason other than to defend it. . . . The white race is a club. Certain people are enrolled in it at birth, without their consent, and brought up according to its rules. For the most part they go through life accepting the privileges of membership, without reflecting on the costs. Others, usually new arrivals in the country, pass through a probationary period before "earning" membership; they are necessarily more conscious of their racial standing.

But if "white culture" doesn't exist, then what are black people seeing when they sense themselves surrounded by "white" behavior? From the perspective of black America, white ways can easily seem different, odd, even laughable at times. When black comedians imitate white people, the portrayals usually have several common denominators. Whites speak in singsong voices; they don't speak forcefully. Whites are stiff in their movement and nervous, bumbling, frightened, or perplexed, especially when they find themselves outside the protective cocoon of white surroundings.

Yet do whites see themselves as flustered, nervous people? Surely not. Blacks might encounter *some* whites who are flustered or inexperienced in dealing with black people. Or whites might agree that *some* whites might act so. Blacks, however, inevitably sense a common denominator in "white" behavior—perhaps a reflection of the fact that most white Americans trace their cultural roots in the countries of northwestern Europe. Once again, the norms of Northern culture prevail. It may even predominate among black families who have lived for generations in communities where the Northern cultural tendencies are more pronounced.

For example, it is surprising how many black people in Rochester, New York, on the shores of Lake Ontario have the flat nasal accents associated with the Great Lakes region, not the Southern speech pattern usually expected from black Americans.

White and black perceptions on what constitutes "white" behavior also vary widely on other matters. Some blacks say whites are overbearing and demanding, while whites see themselves as considerate and accommodating. Some blacks picture whites as unexpressive and standoffish; most whites see themselves as thoughtful and concerned. Some blacks say that whites insist on conformity; most whites say they welcome diversity.

A lot of blacks, moreover, consider whites violent and dangerous, but whites, of course, think of themselves as orderly and peace-loving. In fact, a considerable number of whites think of *blacks* as angry and dangerous. But most blacks remember the long history of antiblack violence and note that whites seem quick to bomb their adversaries—or, these days, launch cruise missiles at foreign targets. And not only is it claimed that whites have a warring nature; blacks also point out that serial killing appears to be a "white" phenomenon.

Following the 1999 shootings at Columbine High, outside Denver, *Washington Post* columnist Courtland Milloy referred to this belief among black Americans: "Why are all the mass murderers middle-class white men and boys?" Milloy also cited a suspicion among black Americans "that as America loses its 'status' as a white nation in the next century, more and more white people will be going insane." I've heard this often. Many blacks expect violence to erupt out of white fears that the country is changing in ways that will make whites a minority.

This is bad enough, but I have also heard blacks say whites have a whole set of manners and social rituals designed to hide their devious nature behind smiles and airs of civility. Therefore, whites smile and act pleasant, but you can't trust this or tell what's on their mind. Beware of white people, I've been told. Whites are sneaky creatures who will stab you in the back while smiling in your face, which, incidentally, is quite a feat.

I can also confirm that white Americans can be strangely—eerily—quiet at times. An annual arts and crafts street festival was held outside my house, and I marveled that the only noise to be heard was shuffling feet. This particular white crowd spoke in whispers as they wandered amid the pots and macramé. If this had been a black festival, there would have been voices, music, and laughter, which made it hard not to conclude that a black event would be more *alive*.

Saying this may reveal my own prejudices. I expect more energy and noise at a black event, even though I've left white events with my ears ringing, too. And doesn't economic class also influence this perception? As we go up the economic scale, do events—black or white—seem to become more subdued?

Yet I have heard whites wonder aloud, when confronted by extremes in black dress or behavior, "Why can't they [blacks] just be more like us?" The question seems to be based on a belief that America's race problems result from black Americans' insistence on being different. For example, some whites believe that all blacks are compelled to show off and call attention to themselves while whites, apparently of an essentially subdued nature, would never want undue attention turned their way.

And, of course, while neither generalization is correct, the prospect of being more like whites makes black Americans shudder. For the most part, black Americans do not want to behave like white people. Indeed, most blacks want to be themselves, and what is wrong with that? It is also commonly noted from across the color line that being white doesn't look like much fun, another perception with parallels along the North-South cultural frontier. From the Southern perspective, many Northerners seem stiff and proper. Many put on airs or speak in hushed tones. Some pretend they're interested in dull matters. And so many Northerners seem cautious and inhibited; they just never let go.

Many black Americans also charge that whites are compelled to control everything, and losing control, especially to black people, freaks them out. (And white Americans surely do control most everything.) As a result, it is a common belief among black Americans that they must keep their views to themselves when white people are around. Consequently, black people sense they are constantly adjusting to white fears and fancies, much as journalist Jill Nelson describes in her autobiography, *Volunteer Slavery: My Authentic Negro Experience*. "I've also been doing the standard Negro balancing act when it comes to dealing with white folks, which involves sufficiently blurring the edges of my being so that they don't feel intimidated while simultaneously holding onto my integrity."

Any such balancing act can be wearing. Some black Americans complain they spend their days surrounded by the oddities of white behavior, which engulfs them as soon as they cross the color line or turn on TV. Sometimes, my black friends—and my wife, too—clearly want to protest, "Enough!" While watching TV, my wife will occasionally mutter, "I'm so sick of white folks," which led me to ask black friends if they were ever "sick of white folks," and most said they get "sick and tired" to be exact. One colleague at *USA Today*, a White House correspondent, said she regularly felt this because white people at the White House are particularly full of themselves.

Whites acting full of themselves—that's at least part of what my wife and black friends tire of dealing with. First, whites are everywhere—but we already know that. Then, it seems, whites are so self-important, as if they believe they are the only people who matter—a critical attitude to recognize. Whites seem to assume they know everything worth knowing; of course if an issue doesn't involve white people, it cannot be significant.

The impression that whites are self-centered and extremely self-involved is a frequent by-product of the news. For example, after the shootings at Columbine High, journalists said a shaken nation was "searching for answers." But black Americans immediately recognized that no such "search" takes place when violence hits black communities. Yet once one is aware of this allegation that whites focus on themselves, it is easy to spot other instances. Sometimes whites seem in such a rush to talk and listen to each other that they ignore everyone else. When terrorist bombs exploded at U.S. embassies in Kenya and Tanzania in 1998, for example, black Americans noted that it was days before white reporters found anyone other than white people to talk to. And why was that? English is commonly spoken in these countries, so that couldn't be a problem. And most of the victims of the violence were black. So why not interview black people?

Did white viewers notice this incongruity? To my knowledge, no whites commented on this discrepancy, and theoretically, I suppose, self-involved whites wouldn't see it; they would assume that only whites have worthwhile comments. Similarly, it is unlikely whites would realize that many black Americans get "sick of white folks" or find whites boring. Where would they hear such a thing? Surely, the idea might never occur to white Americans on their own. White people can't possibly be tiresome and boring. How could that be?

Nor do white Americans see themselves as an overbearing presence in their own country. Instead, whites believe they are fair-minded people who play by the rules. But, as others often see it, it is always *their* rules—white rules—which happens to be a relatively easy charge to make in a country where whites are so often in command. So if you ask black Americans about "white" characteristics, some will surely claim that whites are obsessed with rules. And some will insist that whites are always manipulating them to keep blacks in their place.

Some black Americans have the impression that whites are always citing obscure rules, as if whites expect blacks will try to break them. So in an office where all forms must be filed in triplicate, where vacation days must be applied for three months in advance, and coffee breaks or bathroom visits are clocked in minutes and seconds, it is easy to claim that this is the rigid world white people have created. Furthermore, it is easy to imagine that a world run by black people (or a group other than whites), would not encourage such pettiness; it would operate without the aggravation whites allegedly promote. But how can we know? Where is this perfect place to test the premise?

In this view, rules-obsessed whites will always say things like, "You don't expect us to have a special rule just for you, do you?" Or they will cite some obscure dictate and proclaim, "We all know that rule around here. What's wrong with you?"

In my neighborhood, a 1998 police crackdown on "quality of life" crimes like drinking in public led officers to ticket individuals sitting on their front porches drinking beer. Some neighbors immediately grumbled that this "open-container" law was white inspired, even though white people drinking Chablis on their porches were also ticketed. Furthermore, the grumbling failed to account for all the black families in the neighborhood who were fed up with alcoholics drinking from bottles in paper bags, urinating in public, or passing out on corners. Instead, some blamed the crackdown on whites and their penchant for rules.

Yet whites often appear to manipulate the rules to their own benefit—and sometimes they do so openly and shamelessly, without anticipating how others might view the situation. After Jody-Anne Maxwell, a black girl from Jamaica, won the 1998 National Spelling Bee in Washington, the eligibility rules were changed, effectively eliminating Jamaican contestants in 1999. Contest organizers claimed the Jamaicans were naming their entries early, giving them more time to study the dictionary. Yet this change in the rules also fitted exactly into a common black preconception that whites set the rules, but as soon as someone else succeeds, whites change the rules, citing unfair advantages others are getting.

Implausible, you say. In 1999, organizers of marathons and other distance running events in the United States joined forces to limit the number of foreign competitors—especially Kenyans who were winning most of the major races and prize money. Some races tried instituting rules limiting foreign competitors to three-man teams and doubling the prize money for U.S. runners who finished in the top five. Race organizers argued that corporations would want Americans to do well in races they sponsored. But black commentators derisively called it affirmative action for mediocre whites runners who usually finished far to the rear.

Such examples also make it easier to imagine that whites might regularly ordain rules that give them all the advantages. For example, it can appear that white Americans put such importance on self-control that others who raise their voices are cited for breach of decorum, regardless of what they have to say. Instead, disregarding the points they are making, whites tell them, "You don't need to shout."

At the same time, it can appear on the American scene that whites will go to lengths to avoid the appearance of unpleasantness—and that's a rule of sorts. Bitter political enemies will call each other "my esteemed colleague" and will settle their disputes behind closed doors without making a public spectacle of their conflicts. And to some black people, it would seem from such behavior that whites must be in cahoots, working together against others. But black people also work together at times and often in these same ways, meeting behind closed doors or striving to present a united front, so as not to "air our dirty laundry in public."

Some might argue that the distinctions of economic class and education, not race, are the real divide between those who engage in public shouting matches and those who honor *Robert's Rules of Order*. And it is surely not uniquely "black" to have loud arguments in the street; the phenomenon is also common to Mediterranean cultures, where life in general is lived more publicly. Meanwhile, the seeming privacy of white habits—or those scenes of white politicians emerging from their confabs smiling, shaking hands, and congratulating each other—encourage outsiders to sense a special clannishness among white people. Comedian Eddie Murphy once did a *Saturday Night Live* sketch on one black view on this: whites, when alone in a bank, grant each other credit and loans without the slightest question, virtually forcing white customers to take home bags of money.

It may also be surprising—or annoying—to white Americans to hear that some black Americans assume deviousness from white people. But this belief is hardly different from whites believing that blacks share group characteristics. And what does the white world look like from the outside? In terms of classic stereotypes, the whites world must at times appear to be very much like that of the first-class passengers in the film *Titanic*; whites seem cold, aloof, indifferent to others, phony, boring, lifeless, corrupt, and preoccupied with money and property.

With no black people on board the doomed ship, the social division in the record-breaking film had to be along class lines. Moviegoers were encouraged to side with the "real" and virtuous poor passengers against the pretentious and corrupt rich passengers. But black people can imagine a similar divide in society that pits "real" and virtuous black people against whites, who seem rich, pretentious, and corrupt.

After the actual sinking of the *Titanic* in 1912, a folklorish tale emerged in black America about a character named Shine, who in this fictional version of the disaster was the only black person aboard the ship. He was also the only person with enough common sense to recognize that the ship was sinking, even as the white passengers and crew clung to the belief that the *Titanic* was unsinkable. One version of the story begins:

> It was 1912 when the awful news got around,
> That the great *Titanic* was sinking down.
> Shine came running up on deck, told the Captain, "Please,
> The water in the boiler room is up to my knees."
> Captain said, "Take your black self on back down there!
> I got a hundred-fifty pumps to keep the boiler room clear."
> Shine went back in the hold, started shoveling coal,
> Singing, "Lord, have mercy, Lord, have mercy on my soul!"

Curious parallels emerge between the story of Shine and the 1997 movie. Shine, whose name itself is a derogatory term whites commonly used for blacks, is initially viewed by pretentious whites as a person of no account, much as was the movie hero, Jack Dawson, played by heartthrob Leonardo DiCaprio. Yet like Dawson, Shine is the only person with enough mother wit to deal with a situation in which all the money in the world won't help you. In the movie, Dawson perishes saving the love of his life. In the folklorish tale, Shine rejects the entreaties of white passengers—and particularly of the white women—and instead jumps overboard and swims back to Harlem, leaving the foolish whites to their fate.

Of course, the notion that all whites are vain and foolish like the first-class passengers in these tales of the *Titanic* are as wrong as any idea that all blacks are alike. Yet whites might realize how easy it is to draw broad conclusions about members of a given group. Furthermore, it might also be understandable that a black minority could identify certain "white" characteristics, real or imagined, as central to the day-to-day problems they face.

Because there are so many whites, relatively speaking, it could seem that whites operate as a team—a massive team that works together for its own purposes. It might seem, too, that whites consider it important to fit in, to blend into the group, and demonstrate that they put loyalty to the group above individual aims. Whites might even make frequent references to teamlike ideals, for such rhetoric was common in corporate America in the 1990s, when building a *team* became a beloved management concept.

It might similarly appear—surely an illusion!—that most white people do not like to be different or stand out in the crowd. And some blacks sometimes find it is hard to tell whites apart, because whites look alike, dress alike, and speak alike. To black people it can seem that whites put such stock in fitting in, being one of the boys—or girls— that it would seem much more difficult for people with dark skin to pass unnoted in a sea of sameness.

The easiest way to fit in might be to wear the white team uniform. Hence, it might be said that "the man in the gray flannel suit" led to "the button-down mind," which evolved into the corporate uniforms that dominate today's workplace. And because there are so many white Americans, the average American scene can appear as conformity on a massive scale, because whatever is "in" among white people is seen everywhere. But are white people incorrigible conformists? Probably no more than members of any other population group.

Specific brand names aside, certain rules in taste predominated in the 1990s, particularly, it seemed, among upscale white Americans of Northern European cultural descent. Understated fashion ideas prevailed above outrageous ones. Muted colors were favored over bright and blaring ones. Low style and barely noticeable distinctions were more common than high style or blatant attempts to be different, like wearing your pants at your knees. And comfort usually took precedence over style, if the two conflicted.

But wearing your pants at your knees was a fad mostly limited to teenagers, incidentally the most fertile age group for fads among both blacks and whites. Furthermore, the conservative, subtle styles that were the province of more upscale Americans also tended to cross the color line in the 1990s. Black men climbing the corporate ladder were also among the most avid readers of *GQ* magazine. But in upscale society, men's fashions seldom stray from a narrow range of possibilities, wherein details such as the change of a few centimeters in the width of a man's necktie or lapel can represent a dramatic fashion revolution.

Against this backdrop of conservative-seeming fashions, black men again seemed to stand out. Almost every profile of Ron Brown, the late commerce secretary, talked about his natty style, which, if anything, involved extra effort and an eye for detail. And Vernon Jordan, the Washington lawyer and confidant of President Clinton, is similarly recognized as a sharp dresser. Yet at the risk of generalizing, it might seem that black Americans, if anything, put more emphasis on appearance for the simple reason they suspect they will be judged in these terms. Whites have less apprehension that someone will mistake them for poor and bedraggled souls; maybe, they sense less urgency in the matter of appearances.

Of course, those understated values that whites seemed to prefer in the 1990s were a contrast to the more extreme fashions of earlier decades, when millions of whites—and everybody else—bought Detroit-made cars with huge tail fins and odd, rocketlike appendages. Whites also snickered at the few black people who wanted their Cadillacs to be pink. Boxer Sugar Ray Robinson had a famous pink Cadillac, but so did Elvis Presley. However, pink Cadillacs were often seized upon as the archetypal example of strange black tastes. Meanwhile, the white majority—and most black people, too—stuck to more conservative standards, insisting that tail fins should be more neutral colored.

In general, Americans of all races seem to need more space than other people—room to flex their muscles. Many Americans are so used to excess space that some get edgy when others press too near, but this disposition fits a traditional American attitude about a vast nation: give me the wide-open spaces. These days, millions of Americans, including both blacks and whites, live in houses surrounded by expanses of lawn. And many Americans will also choose the romance of open spaces over the allure of crowds. It might even seem that whites prefer space to crowds, the lonely beach to one packed with bathers. But perhaps whites have more access to lonely spots, and blacks are more wary of such places, feeling more secure when there are other black people around.

Whites can also seem to be products of a highly *literal* culture, which is to say, as a dictionary does, that white Americans expect words to be used in accordance with their ordinary meanings, not figurative meanings particular to a given situation. And as a corollary to being literal, whites can seem to put great stock in written rules—or whatever else that is written down. Sometimes, whites can seem to fixate on written details, like having your papers and permits in order. For example, when some white residents on the blocks near my house wanted to protest the noise of a revival meeting a local black church was holding, they all came, one by one, and asked to see the permits for the event, as if this was their real interest.

The literal aspects of mainstream white culture can seem much in evidence in white attitudes stirred by use of the vernacular commonly called Black English. Some whites seem to be very worried about Black English, like it is both strange and deeply threatening. "Black semantics is highly metaphorical and imagistic," writes linguist Geneva Smitherman in *Talkin and Testifyin: The Language of Black America*. "Many Black English vocabulary items manifest a poetically appropriate representation of rather mundane reality. . . . Many Black English terms are unusual, innovative ways of articulating rather ordinary events."

Is this what bothers some white people?

It must be noted, of course, that all black Americans do not use Black English exclusively; some don't use it at all; and others only stray selectively from standard English usage. Still others are most comfortable with Black English because in their isolation from the American mainstream they rarely practice anything else. Yet according to Smitherman, most black Americans are bilingual, capable of switching from Black English to standard English at will—and this, too, seems to confuse some whites.

Preferring a more precise approach to words, many whites put little trust in rhetorical devices some black Americans practice, such as the use of exaggeration for effect. Hence, while a black storyteller on the corner might claim that a snake was a hundred feet long, those who eschew exaggeration for effect might insist it was about 17½ inches, no more, no less. Some whites seem deeply perplexed by artful exaggerations from black people, viewing them as outright lies or unseemly boasting. Did Muhammad Ali really mean he was "king of the world"— or all those other claims he made? Or was he being playful? Some whites I knew actually took Ali's bantering literally and concluded he must be untrustworthy, both deceitful and a braggart, too. In a similar vein, *Titanic* director James Cameron, who is white, was considered immodest when he proclaimed on receiving the 1998 Oscar as best director, "I'm king of the world!" At least to my ears, Cameron's boast lacked Ali's playfulness.

Many whites are also sure to take any statement that sounds threatening *absolutely* literally, a problem that surfaced in the 1960s and 1970s. Blacks might talk of "taking over" or "burning down" America, and whites would view it as a literal threat, based on their fear of riots or black anger. Blacks, however, were more likely to recognize these statements as rhetorical devices, not an outright declaration of war, and I've seen black people surprised—or amused—that whites took threatening-sounding statements so seriously.

Still, some whites expect exaggeration, shifty language, or dishonesty from black people—these are persistent stereotypes. Whatever inclination for exaggeration some whites can imagine in black people becomes further evidence for them that blacks are overly emotional beings lacking self-control—they're always exaggerating. Many whites—and some black people, too—are suspicious of black orators and preachers whose rhetorical style is grandiose; their suspicion is that old-fashioned rhetoric is a form of chicanery that will easily fool people. In contrast, many whites believe that whites are more influenced by calm, rational arguments.

Some whites distrust Jesse Jackson's use of alliteration, repetition ("Keep hope alive!"), or parallel construction to make his points memorable. His appeal for youth programs is a classic: "We can either fund Head Start and child care and day care on the front side of life, or welfare and jail care on the back side of life." Yet some whites are sure the statement must be too slick to be insightful or true. How odd! This attitude seems to suggest we should be suspicious of what Jackson says because he says it too well.

Nor do most whites shift the meaning of words from one day to the next or regularly attach meanings to words that change with inflection or context, as occurs in Black English. Black usage frequently turns a word around to mean its opposite, as in the use of *bad* to mean *good* in a sentence like, "That's a *bad* hat you're wearing." In fact, the speaker means it's a great-looking hat. White usage seldom embraces such turnabouts, even if whites regularly practice the use of irony in saying the opposite of what they actually mean. Whites, for example, could say, "That's a *great* idea," trusting that expression and inflection will indicate the speaker means the idea isn't great at all. But the meaning of *great* has not changed in the process.

Writes Smitherman in *Talkin and Testifyin*: "For blacks, English words can have potentially two levels of meanings, one black, one white. Since blacks share in the consensus dialect of the American mainstream, on one level a word's referent is the same for blacks and whites. But since blacks also share a linguistic subculture outside the mainstream . . . the same word has multiple meanings and associations."

As a result, many white Americans are discombobulated when black people use the word *nigger* (now usually written as *nigga* or *niggaz*). Some current black usage gives the word positive meanings, including connotations of love, friendship, or even admiration shared among black people. But not all blacks practice this usage, and *nigga*, as used by black people, can also mean low class and ignorant, depending on the situation.

So this is a word with all kinds of meanings. But blacks almost universally agree that whites should not use it—ever. And there is some logic to this: since whites rarely engage in wordplay that inverts the meaning of words, making *bad* mean *good*, how can they claim to be using the N-word in anything but the dictionary context, that is, as a racial slur. Furthermore, since you have to be part of the once disparaged group to use the word in all its richness, whites don't qualify there either. Hence, whites cannot call their black friends "my sweet niggaz" and expect it to suggest affection, because it doesn't do that in standard English usage, only in Black English, which most whites don't speak— or don't speak well. Many black Americans, however, also believe that the use of words like *niggaz* by black people contains an element of unhealthy self-disparagement; they wish the practice would stop.

And some whites ran to their dictionary when a white aide of a newly elected Washington, D.C., mayor resigned in January 1999 in a flap over his use of the word *niggardly*. In the aide's defense, they found that, indeed, the word means *stingy* and has no derivation related to race. So the aide who resigned had done nothing wrong, many insisted. And the black workers who misunderstood the proper use of the word were in error and should not be allowed to dictate new linguistic rules for the workplace. Yet those who come from a culture with a strong oral tradition might argue that they put greater importance on how a word *sounds*. Still, many whites I knew, being properly literal, insisted that the dictionary should have the last word on the case.

Similarly, whites often judge black people according to their adherence to standard grammatical rules. As a result, some whites take note when blacks misspeak and often seem eager to conclude that those who don't follow the traditional rules of English are uneducated, lazy, or stupid. Hence, blacks who say "ax" for "ask" or "mens" for "men" end up encouraging some whites to believe that black people can't make simple distinctions. Yet surely not all black people speak this way. And so what if they did. Perhaps those who draw broad conclusions from such little evidence are themselves being lazy and stupid.

Yet the idea of being faithful to the rules of a written text seems to echo elsewhere in white ways. Black Americans frequently point out that in "white" music, the musicians play the notes as written, a literal approach, while blacks improvise and embellish. The difference, then, would be like that between classical music and jazz, the genius of Beethoven compared to the improvisations of Charlie Parker. White cultural traditions, it would seem, gravitate toward the familiar, the traditional, the known, while black cultural traditions place value on the fresh, the new, and the different.

So much in black American culture seems to spring from improvisation, the sense that we are present at the moment of creation. Meanwhile, so much in Western culture seems to follow the artistic precedents set by the ancients. And each tradition has a richness that should be immune from disparagement. But these traditions can seem to cover much in life, even contributing to the impression that whites are dull and stodgy, always saying the same old things in the same old ways.

When blacks meet whites for the first time, they sometimes come away with another odd impression—that whites are trying to pry into their private affairs. White customs on getting to know strangers encourage asking questions, almost as a courtesy that demonstrates interest in others. Whites consider it appropriate, even polite, to ask where others live, where their children go to school, what kind of car they drive, or what clubs they belong to—and to tell others these details about their own lives—because in this way strangers can find their common ground.

To a lot of blacks, however, this approach seems nosy. Thomas Kochman is insightful in *Black and White Styles in Conflict*: "Typically, whites begin conversation with people they are meeting for the first time by asking for information. . . . These inquiries generally reflect the way whites make conversation and specifically denote their pre-occupations with status and social advancement. . . . [But] blacks con-sider the inquisitiveness and probing that whites demonstrate in these contexts improper and intrusive."

Kochman argues that blacks are more "person oriented," looking for evidence of wit, intelligence, and charm—or evidence of hostility, for that matter. Whites, however, consider asking status-related ques-tions a reasonable way to identify like-minded individuals who share similar tastes or circumstances. And while black people discuss how well they are doing, like anyone else, occasionally to the point of exaggeration, status questions posed by whites suggest, at times, that whites are looking for evidence that black people do not measure up to white standards—or some such similar snobbery. Whites' questions are seen as "getting into your business," and some whites ask or give out information that seems too personal, such as details about per-sonal finances.

It sometimes appears that whites are eager to be chummy with people they've just met, which blacks find strange, as in a situation I witnessed recently. A white woman, who was meeting a black next-door neighbor for the first time almost immediately said, "I sure hope you didn't pay what [the previous owner] was asking, because it was way too much."

The black woman found this to be an intrusion into her personal business but shrugged it off as another case of whites assuming they have a right to pry into black people's lives for whatever curiosities they can find. But is this "white" or merely boorish behavior? Kochman notes the white tendency to ask status questions as part of his con-tention that black and white discourse can unfold under different rules and norms. Yet in "The Black Family: Socialization and Sex Roles," a 1975 study, anthropologist Diane K. Lewis found that blacks and whites also had different opinions on such matters as the characteristics deemed appropriately masculine or feminine. In one case, when given a list of eight characteristics—aggressiveness, independence, self-con-fidence, nonconformity, sexual assertiveness, nurturance, emotional expressiveness, and focus on personal relationships—whites consid-ered the first five to be appropriate characteristics for men and the last three appropriate for women.

Hence, in this gender division, whites considered it inappropriate for women to be assertive or independent and inappropriate for men to be emotionally expressive or nurturing. Specifically, then, the whites believed that nurturing, expressing emotions, and focusing on personal relationships were uniquely feminine, while it is uniquely masculine to be aggressive, independent, self-confident, nonconformist, or sexually assertive.

The blacks, however, considered all eight characteristics to be equally masculine and feminine. As a result, personality profiles of black Americans were often misread on psychological tests that assumed white norms. According to a "white" reading of such tests, there would be something wrong with men who believed nurturing, expressing feeling, or focusing on personal relationships were manly things to do and something wrong with women who were sexually assertive and independent. Thus the normal behavior of black men and women, which does not fit the norms of white society, could easily confuse whites or lead them to conclude that, according to their norms, these black people were abnormal.

By the 1990s, however, some fixed notions about what is appropriately male and female may have broadened as gender roles in white society changed. Also in the 1990s, an academic movement called "white studies" sprouted at some U.S. colleges, purporting to be the study of "whiteness," even if critics found this an oddly conceived focus for academic work. But stereotypically, whites are supposed to count, measure, and study everything. So why not whiteness? When I told black friends about the emerging field of white studies, many suggested this might be one boring class to take, but some said it was probably good that whites were trying to see themselves as others see them. But the movement was soon mocked by critics as a perversion of "black studies," "women's studies," or other ethnic "studies" and, in some quarters, pictured as a further attempt to divide American culture into competing interest groups or "victimized" minorities.

An academic conference titled "The Making and Unmaking of Whiteness" was held in 1997 at the University of California at Berkeley and was generally treated by journalists as a curiosity. By and large, reporters asked, "Good grief, what is this?"

Some commentators suspected the event might be an exercise in guilt about white actions against black people or Native Americans, and the conference was advertised thus: "The event reflects a growing interest in understanding whiteness both as a specific race and as a social category, which has played a central role in perpetuating inequality." Papers listed for delivery included, "Loss of Privilege Inside the White Working Class: Masculinity in the 1990s," "The Not-So-Great White Way," and "The Yiddish Are Coming."

Some participants also apparently agreed that whiteness should be studied so it can be torn down as an artifice of privilege. Yet there has been no evident rush of whites to give up whatever advantages they have, even though part of the conference—and its message— was aired on CSPAN.

White studies emerged in an era dominated by claims that whites are being disadvantaged by privileges granted others under programs like affirmative action. Could academic studies "unmake" the forces causing so many whites to believe others were getting a better deal? It doesn't seem to be happening. At outposts like Berkeley, California, or Princeton, New Jersey, white studies programs may have initiated examination of white attitudes and white ways. But what are the results? I am watching carefully around me. So far, I don't see any.

13
BLACK CULTURE
The Ways of Black Folks

T he theory was long advanced that slavery was such a devastating experience, so evil-intentioned, that it was the goal of white slaveholders to obliterate any sense the slaves might have of who they were; where they came from; or what their culture, language, and faith had been before they were seized from Africa. This idea of slavery as an experience that erased the past for black Americans has been common in the black and white worlds.

The Black Muslim movement is still called the Lost-Found Nation of Islam, implying that it represents the rediscovery of the spiritual and cultural roots that had been stricken from the memory of black Americans. Elijah Muhammad, the movement's prophet, taught that evil whites had robbed blacks of their values or their goodness, leaving them in a state of ungodly emptiness he described in *The Fall of America*:

> The dead are we, the Black once-slaves of the white man of America. We are a mentally Dead people. We are dead to the knowledge of self and others. . . . Bringing us up in slavery time—putting us to a mental-death was something that that slavemaster and his children did because of their desire to make us into something that was other than the truth in order to be able to keep our minds enslaved!

237

Taking the name X, as many Muslims did, was ridding oneself of a "slave" name, but it also embodied the idea of regaining the lost culture and values that whites had corrupted and banished. "'X' is for the mystery," said Malcolm X, "the mystery confronting the Negro as to who he was before the white man made him a slave and put a European label on him."

Yet this idea of a lost people disconnected from their cultural origins was not limited to the Muslims. Others saw black Americans as a culturally blank slate, the theory being that the ethnic ways of African slaves and their descendants were eventually totally reshaped by experiences outside of Africa. Therefore, black Americans were to be considered a total cultural creation of America. "There is nothing so indigenous, so 'made in America' as we," W. E. B. DuBois once said.

This issue is critical to the way blacks and whites think about themselves and each other. If slavery was such a devastating experience that little of the slaves' African heritage survived, we are left to assume that black language and black ways—or black American culture—are largely an imitation of the language and ways of white people, forever the ruling majority. Furthermore, it could be assumed that black people have fallen short in this imitation whenever black culture appears to differ from white norms.

At times, whites have concluded there must be something wrong with black people, if they cannot mirror white ways. Accordingly, it has been considered amusing to view black culture as a hapless failure to match the niceties of white behavior and therefore to assume that if blacks were ever put in charge, chaos and confusion would follow.

Then, too, if black people favored bright colors or chose fashions that were too attention grabbing for white tastes or if some blacks drove pink Cadillacs or wore huge Afros, these were signs to some whites that black people just cannot master "normal" ways. Because this "ineptitude" seemed funny to whites, it was the comic premise behind creations like *Amos 'n' Andy*. And the idea that black people are inept never fully leaves us. Even black people, in moments of despair, sometimes wonder if it is so, forgetting that all God's children are inept now and then.

Many whites saw black incompetence in the collapse of the D.C. government under Mayor Marion Barry in 1996, whether or not Barry was the central cause of the problem. D.C. had become its own racial stereotype of ineptitude, violence, and crime. Furthermore, such failures seem more evidence that blacks cannot function or compete side by side with whites in mainstream society. Yet other cities disprove this theory.

But for many whites, another prime example is Black English. Why can't black people use "proper" English like everyone else? I hear that question often. The conclusion that accompanies it is that many black people are incapable of learning standard English for reasons of intelligence or indifference to learning things the right way. So flaws in English usage, even tiny ones, are included among the evidence that black people can't measure up to white standards.

Importantly, however, this conclusion also assumes that black Americans are a cultural blank slate—that the only possibility they face is to imitate white speech. A different view of black culture emerged in the 1930s and 1940s, and it provided a richer and more complex picture of black Americans. The key element in this view was the extent to which African culture survived slavery and remains a presence in black life.

In 1941, Melville Herskovits, the anthropologist who earlier found that the width of black people's noses and lips was connected to their economic success, published a pioneering study, *The Myth of the Negro Past*. The "myth" Herskovits found to be false was that all traces of African culture had disappeared in the lives of black Americans. To the contrary, he found west African cultural influences, and his work was soon followed by other studies, which made the idea "official," as if blacks themselves might not be believed if they made such claims. The studies included compelling evidence that west African languages were an element in black English, which emerged in this understanding as its own hybrid language, not a poorly learned version of standard American English.

In 1949, Lorenzo Turner reported on the multiple Africanisms in the Gullah dialect used on the Georgia Sea Islands and nearby Gullah communities. Turner traced nearly five thousand words to west and central African languages. And building on this work, researchers have documented a host of African influences that contribute to the distinctiveness of African American culture. So Black English was not a failure of intelligence or a failure of black people to master white ways; it was a product of mixing white ways with the African ways that slaves had preserved among themselves in contravention of white wishes.

Whites, however, can be unimpressed by this, because they are not all that impressed by African culture in the first place. They still think of Africa as a "dark" or "primitive" continent where "natives" go about half clothed. And some whites are disturbed, too, that black people might claim the right to be judged by African rather than American standards, or that black Americans might claim these "black" or "African" standards are just as good as or better than white ones. This "better than" idea becomes strangely worrisome to some whites, as if African ways could infect or cripple America, causing it to tumble into the abyss of history.

Still, many claims about African influences in American life are interesting, though not earthshaking, and they hardly threaten the social order. Molefi Kete Asante, chairman of African American studies at Temple University and author of the book *Afrocentricity,* once told me that the habit of black American men to wear their hats indoors is of African origin. Hence, Asante said, it is to be understood that strictures against wearing your hat indoors are Western in origin and not some worldwide norm or universal truth. In fact, Jewish men wear yarmulkes indoors, too.

Yet I have known whites—and a few blacks, too—to insist that failure of black men to doff their hats indicates absence of social grace. Language, however, stirs many more controversies than hats. In 1997, an Oakland, California, school board proposed that an awareness of "Ebonics," a new term for Black English, be used in teaching standard English to black students. The proposal roused immediate nationwide alarm; the alarmed critics believed that soon Black English would gain such legitimacy that blacks would not be encouraged to learn proper English. Some whites—and a few blacks, too—suspected this could become a first step toward a demand that blacks be given the right to use a black dialect in the workplace or in school. Yet the idea behind the Oakland proposal was actually quite different; the board was saying that knowing how black English works might help in teaching standard English, hardly a linguistic apocalypse.

Once again, however, whites seemed to fear that blacks would get a better deal or get off easy on exams in English 101. Conservatives seemed convinced that blacks were trying to be judged by lesser standards than whites, and whites made so much fun of Ebonics as to suggest they believed black variants in language resulted from stupidity. Here is an "Ebonics" version of the Pledge of Allegiance that appeared on the Internet:

Ah done pledges allegiance
To da Flag

O' da United States
O' America
An' ta da Republic
Fo' which it stands,
One Nation, Beneaf God
Indimuhvisible
Wiff liberty an'
Justice fo' all.

This ridicule, of course, ignores whether Black English results from a unique Anglo-African cultural mix—or whatever. Indeed, claims are made that Black English has its own rules and complexity. And while Black English was *not* being touted as the language America should adopt, linguists noted that certain forms of black speech, including forms that whites denigrate, allow for subtleties missing in standard English.

Linguist Geneva Smitherman refers to the simple sentence "It bees dat way sometime," which was also the title of a 1967 Nina Simone song. Smitherman says the verb *bees*, which whites might ridicule, is not a mere substitute for *is*. Instead, *bees* indicates "a recurring event or habitual condition," not just something now happening. She insists that this linkage in time is an African contribution to black language and that the sentence itself is a particularly African American reflection on life, "a method of adapting to life's realities" that accepts "changes and bad times as a constant, ever-present reality."

And Black English is further enriched by rhetorical devices and a sense of immediate context, including devices such as inversion—giving a word meaning exactly opposite to its standard use—thus facilitating communication among blacks that inevitably whites will not get. This adoption of a special "black" meaning becomes part of the point intended. Use of the word *nigga* as a term of endearment among black people has this effect: it confuses whites, producing consternation and even protests that whites should be allowed to use the word, too. But white usage—standard English—does not include inversion of meanings. Hence, whites cannot use the word as blacks do, because standard English does not operate according to the same rules. To say "bad" in standard English cannot mean good.

An understanding of the origin and complexities of black culture might encourage all Americans to admire the inventiveness of black speech, but surprisingly few whites seem to get this point; they worry instead about grammatical rules and spelling. Whites are more likely to recognize and admire black culture for its musical forms. But certain habits of thought intrude here as well, even as we grant black music its due as a major influence in mainstream American culture.

If you asked white Americans what blacks contributed to the music of America, many might say the "black" contribution is rhythm—the beat. And others might recognize improvisational elements. But if you asked Americans which musical elements—melody, form, or rhythm—is most exalted in terms of intelligence or civilized content, most would say that melody and form are elevated elements, while beat is more primitive. Or many might say that that melody, harmony, and other nonrhythmic aspects of music are cerebral, sophisticated, and complex, while the beat is animalistic or sexual. And assuming such judgments would make the black contribution to American music of a "low" order rather than a "high" order.

Black culture is seen as closer to the sensuality of city nightlife than to the "elevated" standards of concert halls or opera houses. Yet such views embody several errors. They ignore, for example, the intricacy and subtlety of polyrhythmic forms traceable to Africa—rhythmic development in music can be as complex or "intelligent" as any other aspect. And they fail to recognize that improvisational forms can have mind-boggling brilliance, too. However, in recent decades, more Americans have surely accepted black musical contributions as significant art, rather than as rampant eroticism or "the devil's music," as jazz and rock and roll were once considered.

America seems closer to appreciating what it has in its midst.

Questions of culture and language raise the question of what black Americans want to be called. On occasion, whites consider changing vogues—most recently in the emerging use of "African American"—to be capricious and confusing. "Well, which is it—what do they want to be called?" some whites demand. But is this issue of names really so puzzling? As explained in Northwestern University historian Sterling Stuckey's *Slave Culture: Nationalist Theory and the Foundation of Black America* and other sources, changes in usage—*African, Negro, colored, black, Afro-American,* and *African American*—often reflected changing political realities in the country.

Use of the word *African*, as in the name of the African Methodist Episcopal (A.M.E.) Zion Church, founded in 1821, reflected a common preference among people whose connections to Africa were still relatively recent. But shortly thereafter, with the rise of the colonization movement promoting the idea that blacks should emigrate, or be sent, back to Africa, use of the term *African* declined.

One commonly preferred term among black Americans became *colored*, as in the name of the National Association for the Advancement of Colored People, founded in 1909. Also around 1900, the term *Afro-American* gained advocates, but acceptance of the racial designation "negro" eventually rose among those calling for integration. The National Council of Negro Women, founded in 1935, followed this convention. But the word was also the subject of another debate. Should the word be capitalized or not? The *New York Times* opted for capitalization in 1930. But *negro* was still considered a term assigned by whites and also one too closely associated with the notorious racial epithet. After 1966, *black* was embraced as a term denoting people of varied skin color who wished to assert pride in their color, hence the name of the National Association of Black Journalists, founded in 1975.

To some whites, these various names have become another matter about which to be nervous; some whites fear black people will upbraid them for using the wrong term. As a result, some whites say "black" or "African American" haltingly in the presence of black people, praying it will be OK. I've also heard whites fuss that black people cannot make up their minds. But I've heard many black people say that the reality of their circumstances is infinitely more important than what they choose to be called.

In 1989, the suggestion was *African American*, endorsed by Jesse Jackson and others, to reflect a defining of black people based on culture rather than on skin color, much as Hispanics and other ethnic groups have done. Jackson argued that the new term reflected "cultural maturity." *African American* has also quietly emerged as a preferred term, even to the earlier *Afro-American*, in scholarly work on black history, culture, language, and arts. Scholars are concluding that African influences are more central than they'd previously imagined. Stuckey once told me for an article on the question of names, "African institutions and cultural forms have survived here almost intact."

Currently, *black* and *African American* seem interchangeable. But I have not heard anyone refer to a place called "African America," while "black America" still seems a useful concept. Perhaps, some claim, usage of *African American* is more common among the young on college campuses; its use seems especially appropriate when the context is cultural, as in referring to the African American contribution to our culture. Use of *African American* is obviously most popular among those who believe that cultural awareness is important. Still, I might go for days in my neighborhood and not hear *African American* used instead of *black*.

If individual black Americans have a strong preference about what to be called, let them state it. What do whites lose by deferring to their wishes, once their wishes are known? But it would be silly for whites to allow this name issue to add to their unease around black people or for whites to claim that the wishes of black people are mystifying. If *African American* sounds more formal or proper to whites, let them use it—or let them use both, my own choice. To my ear, however, *black* is best used as an adjective, as in "black man" or "black child." To refer to an individual as "a black" doesn't sound quite right, even when "blacks and whites" sounds fine.

The idea that African slaves managed to preserve elements of their heritage and pass it on over generations might rightfully inspire a measure of awe. That African influences have survived at all might cause us to reconsider the role slaves played in the creation of American life. Whatever it is, the *African* element in African America culture was not shipped over on a steamer just in time to produce jazz. Nor did it arrive from Africa on a 747 just in time to produce Michael Jordan. This culture is something African slaves brought with them, savored, nurtured, and preserved. And it is a gift that has been passed on to us from people who got little in return.

Perhaps, assumptions about the superiority of Western civilization have precluded our being able to feel the correct indebtedness toward African slaves as a cultural conduit for much that has enriched American experience. Surely, rock and roll would neither rock nor roll were it not for the influences that came from Africa. Americans are so enriched by the presence of an African heritage that Harvard's Noel Ignatiev can proclaim there is no such thing as white culture but that black culture is an unrecognized part of what white Americans think of as their own. Ignatiev stated the proposition with feeling in a 1996 radio interview on Chicago's WZRD-FM. A transcript of the interview was subsequently circulated on the Internet.

> Culturally, the United States is not a white country. . . . Every American, by virtue of landing on these shores, becomes culturally part Yankee, part American Indian, and part black, with a little pinch of ethnic salt. Just think of the music we listen to, the dances we do, the sports we admire, the dress, the rhythms of speech . . . all of these things indicate a black presence in American life. And Americans by and large enjoy this—although they're not quite willing to admit it. They prefer to deny . . . that the United States is the largest country in the world of people who pass for white. There are a couple hundred million of them who are denying the black presence within their own souls and hearts.

If the One-Drop Rule were applied to U.S. culture, the resulting mix would have to be considered black, much as Ignatiev describes it. Whites have adopted much in black language and music. For all we know, American teens might still be doing the foxtrot or the minuet if African people had not introduced more vigorous ideas. And Elvis would never have been Elvis, either.

Further, much in our misunderstanding of racial differences is also cultural in nature, with issues of economic class as a further subdivide. To some it might seem that Black English and other Africanisms are concentrated among the poor and uneducated who have less contact with the ways of the white mainstream. Yet it is another curse on our understanding to think that "poor" is "black" and "black" is "poor" or that to move upward in the society is to abandon being "black" in any significant way. Black Americans who are economically upscale can speak with black inflections and emphasis and often do so when they get outside of white earshot. And the intellectual life of black America is rich, too, as is its literature and art, and not limited to by-products of slavery and sharecropping.

Yet if even the most essential differences between blacks and whites are cultural, not biological, relations between blacks and whites are still frozen with fear and uneasiness. Notions of biological superiority can easily coincide with claims of cultural preeminence. And many blacks find it dangerous to suggest that they are different, even if the differences are purely cultural, because whites habitually prejudge that anything not white has to be inferior except in basketball.

Whites occasionally meet black Americans who make "being just like us" seem a reasonable, attractive possibility. Another question to consider is what leeway should mainstream culture give to those of African descent so present-day whites are not accused of a cultural tyranny similar to that practiced by slave owners. This issue, like that of Ebonics, puts many white Americans in a tizzy. Some view claims that blacks are culturally different as further demands for special treatment.

In *Two Nations: Black and White, Separate, Hostile, Unequal*, Andrew Hacker, a white author, notes that the claims of some black educators that blacks and whites have different "learning styles" is a "sensitive" subject. Writes Hacker: "Many black educators have proposed that white teachers should be taught to recognize the strengths—and enthusiasms—that black youngsters bring to school. In the early years, for example, black pupils should be given more opportunities for expressive talking, since black culture gives as much attention to style as the substance of speech."

So "expressive talking" and "style" are two elements that a faction of black educators have identified as part of black culture. And while I don't know how to prove this is so or not so, I see much "expressive talking" and an emerging sense of style among the black children in my family. I enjoy it; others find the concepts troubling, including whites who have been raised to believe that "putting style over substance" is wrong, for style is supposed to be subordinate to substance. But then, perhaps, this "style" is misread to mean passing fashions like bell-bottom pants or wide collars, when style in a "black" sense could denote more significant attitudes about life.

Smitherman, for example, sees Black English as "a combination of language and style interwoven with and inextricable from Afro-American culture." Style might involve *not* doing things the way white people do. Or doing things in ways that confuse and perplex white people. Or that defy white people. Style could also mean speaking or behaving in ways whites don't understand. So you might wear your pants sagging down around your knees to be different, and many whites didn't get it when the style began.

It turns out that the sagging pants style was, in part, an inversion—turning a negative into a positive—because it most likely began among people who had spent time in jail, where belts are taken away to prevent prisoners from hanging themselves. So in this way, the wearing of sagging pants became a form of defiance; style became the substance of a message.

Some will surely note that such styles become "team" uniforms, too, just as whites wear "team" uniforms. Yet often, the black styles are importantly *not* like white team uniforms, one point of wearing them. And we often see, too, how a sense of exaggeration can extend beyond language and become a device in fashion. The urge to exaggerate produced the zoot suit of the early 1940s, the outrageous pimp and hustler styles of the 1970s, and the sagging pants of the 1990s. These trends function on the idea that if a little of a fashion detail is good, a lot of it will surely be so much the better. Better than wearing your pants low, wear them absurdly low. But this is not only an exclusively black response to fashion. On occasion some exaggerated styles have been initially popular among members of a lower economic class, yet in other ages, an extreme style was favored by aristocrats, as in the case of 18th-century courtly fashions. The urge to adorn seems to be human at base.

Note, however, that the exaggeration found in black fashion and art is the opposite of the understated styles now favored by whites. Yet curiously, the exaggerations in black style have often been described as *cool* by admirers, and the demeanor that goes with exaggerated dress is *cool*—you act like everything is normal. Let others react, stare, or be surprised; you are the calm at the center of this storm. So you wear something outrageous, but you are *cool* about it. Richard Majors and Janet Mancini Billson, authors of *Cool Pose: The Dilemmas of Black Manhood in America*, describe it this way:

> We might ask why style is so important to cool cats. Styling helps cool cats draw attention to the self and communicates creativity. The African-American man in this country has been "nobody" for generations. The purpose of styling, then, is to paint a self-portrait in colorful, vivid strokes that makes the black male "somebody."
>
> The extravagant, flashy clothes often worn by cool cats, the blaring ghettoblasters playing earsplitting music as they walk or drive down the street, signify their need to be seen and heard. Styling is an antidote to invisibility and silence, a hope in a hopeless world, a defense against multiple attacks on cultural

and personal integrity. . . . The cool cat styles . . . to symbol-
ize the message he wants to portray: "No matter how poor I am
or what has happened to me in the past, this shows that I can
still make it—with class."

Yet the outrageousness of a few pimps and hustlers is itself exaggerated by the tendency of whites to characterize all black people in
terms of the behavior of the few who stand out. To say that every
black person in the United States has a taste for exaggeration is incorrect. Even in music and other art forms, black culture tends to admire
filigree or focus on opportunities to improvise. For example, "soul"
singers don't just hit the desired note but chase up and down and all
around it, too. They don't just sing the melody—they embellish it. But
it should be noted that this urge to improvise and embellish is highly
individualistic. A soloist can do it; an orchestra cannot, because the
result might be cacophonous noise.

Another cultural divide involves movement and dance. It's not that
"blacks can dance" or that whites can't. Often they do it differently in
culturally oriented ways, almost suggesting a different sense of aesthetics can be at work. African-influenced dance encourages different
movements from European-based dance. It has been noted, for example, that African dance allows for bending at the waist, which in most
other cultures is excluded. European dance forms tend to be inflexi-
ble at the waist, an extreme example being the Irish folk dancing featured in *Riverdance*. The posture there is ramrod straight.

Dancing featuring suppleness at the waist also encourages movements of the pelvis, which is suggestively erotic to Western eyes and
seems to fit the familiar stereotype that black people are obsessed
with sex. Such movements are considered primitive or base under
Western aesthetics. Movements in African dance can also seem to focus
on the buttocks, with postures that involve squatting or bent knees
rather than the traditional Western emphasis on straight lines. Again,
this feature of African dance is interpreted as erotic by those trained
to appreciate another set of aesthetic values.

However, flexibility at the waist may be relevant to a phenomenon
we see in sports—the prevalence of black running backs in pro football. Running backs are thought to need flexibility at the waist to make
"moves" or to cut sharply to elude tacklers. Some football experts call
it "hip-snap." So why are so many running backs black? Perhaps, it's
because black culture encourages flexibility at the waist that white

would-be running backs don't develop because white culture encourages stiffness at the waist.

The notion that even hip-snap is learned becomes all the more plausible when you witness black or white children picking up gestures or mannerisms that might be identified as "black" or "white." The youngsters on the black side of my family develop hip-snap, balance, and coordination from the moment they start "dancing" as toddlers. They are encouraged to "dance" almost as soon as they can stand up. When these children "dance"—it starts as little more than bouncing up and down—the whole family reacts with delight. So children learn to "dance" before they can walk.

In watching these scenes, it seems obvious the children are learning to imitate the pelvic flexibility of their elders. And as this "dancing" improves, it is also obvious that these children are practicing skills that increase basic balance and coordination. In his first year, even before he could walk, one of my nephews discovered which button on the stereo turned on music, and soon he started bouncing up and down on his own. He is now one of the most agile, coordinated, and bright second-graders I have ever seen.

My recommendation: if you want well-coordinated kids, teach them to dance as infants.

Meanwhile in our house, my wife is the one who can dance, and it takes no deep investigation to find out why. I grew up in an environment where Mozart was played much more than rhythm and blues hits, and Mozart often still attracts my attention; it pleases me that researchers now claim a "Mozart effect" speeds development of cognitive skills.

But surely there is a salutary rhythm and blues effect, as well. My wife's father died in 1998, and it was recalled at his funeral how he often brought home the latest 45-rpm hits on Friday nights, poured cornmeal on the kitchen floor to make it slick, and the whole family danced. Is it any wonder my wife can dance? What do we need to explain? Such is the origin of so much that we consider "black" or "white."

Many black children grow up in an environment that surrounds them with music and dance. My neighborhood is full of expressive talking, sometimes even at 3:00 A.M. But a problem sometimes arises when black children enter the mainstream in integrated schools; black youngsters are often viewed as unruly, hyperactive, or suffering from attention deficit disorder. Children in my family have been diagnosed with this, yet I wonder if there is really anything "wrong" with them. Some black Americans have come to suspect that white America is plotting to "drug" black children with Ritalin. The issue needs study.

"White" values do not always encourage noise or expressiveness among children. Tradition has been to say children should be seen and not heard, and white culture teaches children that discipline, self-restraint, and silence are important. Yet the separation of blacks and whites for so much of our history has virtually ensured that the two groups will be influenced by distinct cultural experiences.

It seems highly possible that black and white youngsters might each pick up different "learning styles," and I am amazed how my younger black friends can remember large bodies of material merely from a few listenings when I cannot. My friends quickly master entire rap songs, while I can only remember a line or two. In this regard, it appears that I have lost—or never had—the ability that permitted our ancestors to commit the works of Homer to memory. Yet I believe my young black friends could do this.

Would this ability not qualify as a different learning style? Researchers at the Howard University and Johns Hopkins University Center for Research on the Education of Students Placed at Risk say so (in a study written in the lingo of educators): "Recall learning for the African American children was higher when stories were presented in the movement expressiveness/music context as opposed to the context devoid of movement expressiveness/music. In contrast, the European American children's recall learning was higher when stories were presented in the absence of movement expressiveness/music as opposed to the movement expressiveness/music context." It almost sounds like what happened when my friends and I wrestled with rap.

Yet some black educators have carried the idea of cultural difference and learning styles further, claiming that black Americans have inherited broad elements of an African-influenced worldview that embodies such concepts as spirituality, a sense of harmony in the universe, and a special appreciation for communal undertakings. Under the same theory, an African heritage is supposed to encourage black people to embrace feelings, individualism, energetic action, and oral tradition.

In fact, the categories are so broad that others might say they cannot be uniquely African; many whites, for example, also believe in spirituality or that there is harmony in nature. Yet it is even more commonly claimed that an African view of life reflects a sense of wholeness, seeing body and soul or body and mind as one rather than as polar opposites. Writing about the philosophy of the Africans kidnapped into slavery, historian Lerone Bennett, Jr., notes in *The Shaping of Black America*: "The slave was not cursed by the European sin of dichotomizing. For the slave, good and bad, the flesh and the spirit were different sides of the same coin. There was a balance, a wholeness and a complexity to this worldview."

And how threatening can the concept of wholeness be? For those trained to think in dichotomies, it can seem a loss of basic clarity—if good and bad are intertwined, it is harder to tell them apart. While some might agree there is a complex interrelation, others will surely demand a clearer checklist of right and wrong.

On a less dramatic level, some black Americans might sense it is related to a holistic approach to life that many black politicians are also preachers or that many black churches are politically involved. Wouldn't it be "African" to view the moral, spiritual, and political aspects of life as interrelated? In contrast, it might seem "Western" to insist that church and state must be kept separate. Yet separation of church and state is not necessarily *always* the Western view; many European countries do not practice it.

Nor do these broad concepts of "African" and "Western" really help when they encourage us to think of ourselves more narrowly. Must all black children learn through a "movement expressiveness/music" mode? That won't work. Yet if I had practiced that mode, I might better retain what I hear. Cultural conditioning may explain much that is "black" and "white," but it needn't confine us, too. What we can learn, we can unlearn. If whites and blacks can learn to be appropriately "white" and "black," they can also learn healthier reactions to each other, too. Nor are there immutable laws of race that say we cannot learn from each other.

Whites could still insist that theirs is the only plausible or worthwhile way of knowing anything, and they are the majority, therefore right in all things. But that would be foolish. Or whites could realize that other elements in our lives have been traced to Africa—and preserved at great cost. They do not threaten America or its way of life—not at all. They enhance both.

14

WOMEN AND MEN

Does Size Make a Difference?

The relative absence of social and romantic relationships between black and white men and women indicates the degree to which the color line must act as a social and cultural barrier between two different and isolated worlds. Interracial romance appears almost a taboo among a large segment of the U.S. population. Only 6 marriages out of 1,000 in the United States, 0.6 percent, involve black and white spouses, hardly enough to signal a trend in the works, even though pollsters say our attitudes about interracial marriage have undergone major changes.

As a white male married to a black woman, I tend to notice such claims. In 1958, the year I graduated from high school, polls showed that 94 percent of white Americans disapproved of marriages between blacks and whites, and intermarriage was illegal in 16 states. In 1997, however, 61 percent of whites and 77 percent of blacks said they accept intermarriage. Gallup pollsters called this one of the "most substantial" shifts they've found in American opinions on race. But 39 percent of whites and 23 percent of blacks still disapprove of interracial marriage, which adds up to—87 million white Americans and 8 million black Americans, a total of about 95 million Americans who disapprove of marriage between blacks and whites.

As a partner in an interracial marriage, I note that, too. These 95 million Americans could seem a formidable group, whose opinions I do not take lightly. But it is not totally clear what they believe or how hostile they are to interracial marriages. Some in this group probably believe that interracial marriage is ill-advised or that it will place unique pressures on children—that they will be confused about their identity under the One-Drop Rule or possibly rejected by both blacks and whites. These Americans may really be saying they do not believe that our society is ready for interracial marriage.

But if some whites fear that race mixing will lead to the genetic extinction of the white race, who knows how adamant they could become about this prospect? Some black Americans might similarly believe that unchecked intermarriage could lead to cultural assimilation and the extinction of African American culture. Yet the reason for objection to intermarriage could be less important than the result. Any widespread wariness about the contacts that might lead to interracial romance could add unusual stresses to everyday interactions between blacks and whites, making them different from interactions that don't involve the color line.

And whatever the rationale, it appears that 95 million Americans believe that some form of special restraint should govern relations between blacks and whites. Probably, they believe it would be wise for blacks and whites to avoid situations that could lead to romance across the color line. It's OK for black and white guys to talk sports, but men and women should keep their distance. Perhaps, too, they might agree we should thwart the prospect of interracial romance as early as we can, in junior high or thereabouts. Or they might believe that blacks and whites should never get to know each other too well, because it will lower their guard against the flowering of love along the color line.

Scenes of men and women enjoying each other's company might seem troubling to these individuals, if the color line is also involved. Bantering and giggling between black and white men and women might unleash secret furies among those who disapprove. Who knows? And if we are looking for evidence of tormented thinking about race and sex, we need not look far.

It is an American tradition. Indeed, many Americans, both black and white, believe that images from the troubled history of race can rise up to haunt relations between black men and white women or white men and black women. Black Americans who remember the attitudes of white segregationists that produced lynching, are still uneasy when they see black men and white women acting in ways that seem too casual or suggestive of impending intimacies.

And we know that interracial sex or marriage was at the core of segregationists' fears because they said so. "We do not give the Negro civil equality because we are fearful that this will lead in turn to demands for social equality," wrote David Cohn in *Where I Was Born and Raised*. "And social equality will tend toward what we will never grant—the right of equal marriage. As a corollary to these propositions, we enforced racial separation and segregation. . . . It is the sexual factor . . . from which social and physical segregation grows." Cohn was a Mississippi lawyer and writer who later was a speechwriter for Adlai Stevenson, George McGovern, and Lyndon Johnson. "Whenever the Constitution comes between me and the virtue of the white women of the South," a South Carolina politician named Cole J. Blease is said once to have proclaimed, "I say to hell with the Constitution."

This "sexual factor" is a bitter subject to recollect, because it led to so many shameful atrocities against black men. But liberties taken by white men with black women could still stir their own lingering resentments, especially in relations between black men and black women. "It is probable," black historian Leone Bennett, Jr., noted in 1962 in *Beyond the Mayflower*, "that the Negro male's resentment of past intimacies between Negro women and white males persists today."

Race and sex can be a minefield of sorry ideas. Whites have long believed that black people are uninhibited or more direct in their approach to sex—and so did David Cohn, who also wrote in *Where I Was Born and Raised*, "The Negro . . . is sexually completely free and untrammeled . . . to him the expressions and manifestations of sex are as simple and as natural as the manifestations of nature in the wind and the sun and the rain." Some whites imagine that blacks are obsessed with sex, having it all the time, while white people are more reserved and responsible. Or it may seem in some fanciful views that blacks are out of control, having babies right and left, while whites take their social responsibilities more to heart.

But attitudes about sex are also supposed to have changed since World War II in ways that encourage more freedom and openness on the subject. Since the late 1950s, popular culture has insisted that a good sex life is a key to happiness. Women have been encouraged to demand their due as equal partners; this attitude is no longer new. Yet it might seem under these changed rules, that black people are happier and healthier, free from Puritan guilt or hangups about sex. Or perhaps they would be objects of jealousy, imagined to be getting more and better sex. And black people seem to agree that this is so, because blacks have stereotypes about sex, too. Many believe that whites are stiff, inhibited, and generally have less fun.

Still, for whatever reasons, romance that crosses the color line has often been viewed as an unseemly mismatch, with whites frequently accused of viewing black people as representatives of forbidden thoughts and pleasures. Blacks live on the naughty side of town, so to speak, and whites, the inhibited group, are forever drawn to the world where inhibition is allegedly tossed aside. "The white man's unadmitted—and apparently, to him, unspeakable—private fears and longings are projected onto the Negro," James Baldwin wrote in *The Fire Next Time*.

Others in the 1960s agreed that whites project their fantasies about base instincts, "dark" urges, and immorality onto black people. "The culture seems to require that white people find sexual contact with blacks too horrible to contemplate—and white people comply with that requirement in their public behavior," wrote psychiatrists William H. Grier and Price M. Cobb in their 1968 book *Black Rage*:

> Their private attitudes are another matter. They find black people attractive sexually and subscribe to the almost universal myth of their sexual superiority. Here again the impress of the culture is important in determining the quality and quantity of the individual response. The culture designates Negroes as sexually superior and uninhibited in their behavior. It further requires that whites view them with contempt and sexual congress with them with horror.

Many people—both whites and blacks—might think it best to leave such troubled and turbid psychological waters alone, stay with their own kind, and avoid being seduced by longings that others might view as strange or unwholesome. But if both blacks and whites still believe that black Americans are more sexual in nature or that blacks can outperform whites in actual sex acts, these ideas by themselves might have major impact on the prospects for interracial romance. For example, why would black people be drawn to romances with people who are supposed to be cold, physically awkward, and less able at the basic sex acts?

Why indeed?

The number and nature of interracial marriages also raise questions that could be related to the issue of sexual performance. While the number of marriages between whites and blacks has doubled since 1960, they are still a rarity. Yet among the 328,000 black-and-white married couples, almost two-thirds involve marriages between black men and white women, while slightly more than one-third involve white men and black women. Although the numbers are slowly changing, with the number of white male–black female couples rising, the phenomenon remains a puzzle. Why is this happening?

	Total U.S. marriages	Black–white marriages	Percent of all marriages	Black husband/ white wife	White husband/ black wife
Trends in Black–White Marriages, 1960–1995					
1960	40.5 million	51,000	0.12	49%	51%
1985	51.1 million	164,000	0.35	71%	29%
1995	54.9 million	328,000	0.59	62%	38%

Old-time segregationists might claim their fears about black men and white women were warranted. But it also seems clear from what you see in everyday life that an overwhelming majority of black men do not desire or prefer white women. And, maybe too, black women desire white men even less. But beyond that, we need not search too far into the labyrinth of the human psyche to find why blacks and whites don't get married. The most obvious barrier to black and white romance is the simple absence of social contacts across the color line. They don't meet, so they can't fall in love. Our social lives are overwhelmingly segregated, even when they could be otherwise: look at the groups who pass on any big-city street. They are likely to be segregated. And when romance occurs—when "different worlds" meet, as we are wont to say—strange attitudes and curiosities may also surface. We still stare at interracial couples or put their relationship under special scrutiny, wondering: what does she see in him, or what does he see in her?

One idea—or pattern of thoughts—is common. If a white woman chooses a black man, for example, she is considered to have rejected or been rejected by all white men. Or if a black man chooses a white woman, he is considered to have rejected or been rejected by all black women. And this attitude is strange. With couples of the same race, no one is likely to consider all the partners they did *not* choose. Instead, we applaud the couple's good fortune in finding each other. But we are less likely to think this way about interracial couples.

Still, there is a serious practical reason why black women might interpret a black man's choice of a white woman as a rejection. Across black America, there is a major shortage of available black men. And it is a real social problem, a disaster for the future of the black family. The lament that all the black men are taken, gay, in prison, on drugs, dead, or chasing white women is all too common. On college campuses, for example, only about 40 percent of the black students are men. Hence, theoretically, one third of the women would be forced to go without a black male partner. Studies also indicate women outnumber men in the black middle class. For every 1,000 middle-class black women, there are only 772 middle-class black men.

Elsewhere, in many city neighborhoods, the supply of black men has been so limited by violence and incarceration that it represents a disaster for black women looking for male companions and is an obvious factor in out-of-wedlock births. Across America, two-thirds of black children are born to single mothers. That the man shortage is a factor is obvious in my own neighborhood. D.C. has not only been the murder capital of the nation during the 1990s—about four thousand black men have been killed in the past dozen years—it was also found that in 1996, half the black males between ages 15 and 35 in the city were caught up in the criminal justice system, that is, they were being sought under warrants, awaiting trial, on probation, or serving time in prison.

Faced with the shortage of black men, black women might—it would seem logical—seek relationships with men of other races. But according to the statistics on marriage, they don't, even if the number of such pairings is rising slightly. One reason is also obvious in my neighborhood: young black women almost never encounter white males their age. Instead, the shortage of men has produced a variant on polygamy, or man sharing, among an isolated subculture in my neighborhood. Many young men have children by various mothers, and young mothers I know have children by various fathers. Permanent relationships in this subculture are far too rare; marriages are rarer still; and few children have their fathers living in the home. Sadly, funerals for young men are more common than weddings.

Generally, the man shortage in black America has not been widely noted or seen as the cause of other problems. Calls for sexual abstinence or for postponing sex until after marriage are all well and good.

But they won't be as attractive an option in a world where men are in short supply. Abstinence in that circumstance would condemn many women to a childless life, a choice many black women have obviously rejected. Similarly, the disintegration of the black family is not a problem of too much sex but too few men. There are too few husbands and family providers. The man shortage leaves an excess of women for the men there are. As a result, going from woman to woman becomes a lifestyle, because there will always be more women waiting.

All the same, next to the large number of black men killed, imprisoned, crippled by violence, or pursuing dead-end lifestyles, encroachments by white women on the short supply of black men are relatively insignificant, even if they stand out. Other resentments about interracial pairings can easily arise, too. White men might sense their virility challenged when they see a white woman with a black man. Black men might sense their virility challenged when they see a black woman with a white man. Et cetera. But interracial couples also get very positive reactions as well. Blacks, for example, often assume that the white partner in an interracial couple does not have standard white hang-ups and uneasiness about race. You can talk to him or her more openly. And whites may assume that the black partner in an interracial couple does not harbor the anger that whites are conditioned to expect from blacks.

However, with sex being so much the homeland of troubled notions about race, we almost forget that blacks and whites tend to agree on the essential themes in the typical sexual stereotypes. Whites may believe that blacks are more libidinous or animalistic, but many blacks also believe that blacks are more open, honest, and direct about sex. The ideas are similar in their way. And whites may fancy themselves more in control of their sexual urges, but many black people suspect that whites cannot possibly have much fun.

Also both blacks and whites apparently respect one of the oldest and best-known racial archetypes in the folklore of sex: black men are supposed to have bigger penises. We dare not forget that. Even if "serious" discussions about race do not focus on penis size, maybe they should. Few other ideas about race are quite so common.

References to the alleged differences in penis size show up almost everywhere except in serious discussions about race or sex. Some blacks I have encountered believe that blacks are endowed to perform sex acts the way God intended, but whites, being less endowed, have tended to specialize in more devious practices like oral sex.

Yet surprisingly, too, most standard guides on sexuality that address "myths" about sex do not expound on the matter of race and penis size. Does this mean it is *not* a myth? Or that it is pure myth? The guides don't say either. All the guides I found left the subject alone. But they do discuss a psychological problem called "microphallneurosis," the fear of having a penis that is too small. Apparently, men are affected by this fear often enough to suggest that men and women generally believe that bigger is better, and there is no mention of a fear of having a penis that is too large. Most sex manuals try to be reassuring on this issue, promising that size does not generally matter. Some books even say specifically that an erect penis of two inches is enough to produce a happy sex life and satisfy most women's needs.

Still, the absence of any mention about race and penis size, coupled with this insistence that size doesn't matter, could suggest to suspicious readers that the experts do not wish to stir a microphallneurosis epidemic among white men by saying that black men have bigger penises. Or something like that. Here is another instance in which whites could be troubled by feelings of inferiority. Is it possible that blacks get a better deal on sex? Whites might do well to examine their souls to see if they secretly fear this is so.

Author Terry McMillan, who is black, suggests blacks may not always get a better deal. "Of course all black men think they can fuck because they all have at least ten-inch dicks," she writes in her bestseller *Waiting to Exhale*. "I wish I could tell some of them that they should start by checking the dictionary under *F* for 'foreplay,' *G* for 'gentle,' and *T* for 'tender' or 'take your time.' I've wanted to tell some of them that acrobatics and banging the hell out of me is not the same as making love."

But hold everything. What is the truth on the matter of penises? If sex manuals do not say, who does? Well, remember that Canadian fellow, J. Philippe Rushton? In *Race, Evolution and Behavior*, he claims to have scoured the "ethnographic data" on the subject in his search for racial differences. Rushton claims to have averaged out the available data on erect penis size with the result that blacks are largest, Asians the smallest, with whites in the middle.

He also notes there have been claims that "the angle and texture of erection" differs among the three racial groups: Asian erections are "parallel to the body and stiff." Black erections are "at right angles to the body and flexible. And white erections are again between these two extremes. Similarly, he notes that it is sometimes claimed that the female genitalia are placed higher in Asian women, lower in black women, with whites in the middle, which would presumably be nature's manner of fitting the varying angles and textures of male erections to the appropriate female genitalia.

Furthermore, Rushton says, the vaginas of Asian women are smaller; the vaginas of black women are larger; and the vaginas of white women fall in the middle. All this, if true, would suggest that men and women of the same race are made for each other. But wait a minute. More data awaits. The findings of "The Definitive Penis Size Survey," which appeared on the Internet in 1997, shows much less difference between blacks and whites, but this survey had the obvious weakness of being self-reported. Some men might lie about the size of their penises or measure them inaccurately. And it could really only claim to be definitive about the penis size of Internet users. Black men with larger penises, for example, might find other activities more interesting than Internet browsing.

In an early version of the survey, involving 2,111 men, the average penis length reported by black men was 6.4 inches, and the average size reported by white men was—get this—also 6.4 inches. In both cases, this figure is slightly higher than the average of 6.16 inches for men studied by the Alfred C. Kinsey Institute for Sex Research. Meanwhile, Hispanic men reported an average length of 5.7 inches in the "definitive" survey, and Asian men 5.5 inches.

Then in a later tally, with the survey pool expanded to 2,545 men, the average length of a white erection increased to 6.5 inches and the average length of a black erection decreased to 6.1 inches. What gives? All we can say is that some black men apparently do not have penises that are larger than the white average.

The survey data also revealed that penises that are smaller when flaccid expand more in erections than penises that are larger in a flaccid state, so there is less variation between races in the length of erect penises than in the length of flaccid ones. The average length of a flaccid white penis was 3.4 inches; the average length of a flaccid black penis was 3.7 inches. This suggests there could be some validity to the theory that in cold climates, evolution favored penises that were smaller or more protected in the flaccid state, hence less likely to freeze.

Whatever. The actual size of human genitalia may not be as important in race relations as what we *think* the size is and what we think that size signifies. If we agree with the sex experts that size makes no difference, it may have little effect. But if we secretly surmise that size is all-important, it will be more of an issue in race relations. And "The Definitive Penis Size Survey" provides one critical insight about how blacks and whites see things: 80 percent of black men classified themselves as "well endowed," while about 80 percent of the white men classified themselves as "average." This raises the possibility that white and black men have different views about their sexual adequacy. Black men are likely to be very confident about themselves; white men likely less so.

This ratio even seems to play out in reality. Still, outside of X-rated videos or locker rooms, genital size is largely a matter of intimate contact between sexual partners. Everything else is more a function of imagination. But I would be hard-pressed to find anyone in my acquaintance who has not heard that black men are supposed to be bigger and even harder-pressed to find anyone who believes that *smaller* is better.

It is likely the conviction that black men are "bigger" will continue to haunt relations along the color line, whether it is true or not. And the results are almost predictable:

- **White men.** If white men fear that their penises are smaller or that they are only "average" performers in bed, they could feel wary or threatened when black men show interest in white women or vice versa. If white men believe black men are "bigger," they could worry that white women will be drawn to "bigger" men or intrigued by the possibility of having sex with them, and white men will lose out. Some white men might try to keep black men away from white women, one way or another. But white men could also suspect that black women are used to "bigger" men, and they may conclude that black women are *too much woman* to handle, because black women's expectations are based on "bigger" men. The result is white men are wary of black men and intimidated by black women.

- **White women.** Sensing white men are wary and threatened by black men, white women protest that the idea of a "bigger" man with a large black penis is grotesque and frightening. But some white women might be curious and even wonder if they are woman enough to handle such a "bigger" man. Others might consider themselves better off with "smaller" men. Yet in their doubts about satisfying "bigger" men, some white women might envy black women who seem so confident.

They might even sense that black women flaunt the fact that they are getting good sex from "bigger" men, while white women make do with something less. The result is white women are intrigued by black men, envious of black women, but feel safer with white men.

- **Black men.** Convinced they are "bigger" and better, black men believe they are the envy of white men and the object of any reasonable woman's desires. But they also suspect that envious white men are doing all in their power to thwart black men and keep them away from white women. That's why American society, which is ruled by white males, appears designed to estrange, isolate, and emasculate black men—or lock them up. The result is black men are angry and frustrated. But there is an excess of attractive black women that attracts their attention.
- **Black women.** Black women suspect white women believe they are God's gift to mankind. But they also wonder what the allure of white women could possibly be. They suspect white women would like to try "bigger" men or steal them away, but black women wonder how most white women could handle a "bigger" man if they had one. Meanwhile, having heard that white men are "smaller," black women are less interested for obvious reasons, and white men seem intimidated, anyway. The result is black women see the shortage of black men as a major disaster.

But enough of all that. It is discouraging to think that many of these ideas may actually be functioning in American life. Perhaps, more discussion about the role of penis size in our thoughts would be productive, but it is not likely to be. Whites will talk about IQ and race, a subject that favors white egos, but not penis size and race, a subject that might suggest white inferiority. Instead, whites are likely to say that the whole subject is ridiculous—too absurd to dwell on. And thereafter, the mathematics of race goes to work: Whites get to pick the topic under discussion because they are the bigger group. And size matters.

But if penis size doesn't occupy our minds—and that is possible, too— what does? What else contributes to the common belief that black

people are such sexual beings and whites are, well, more civilized? Perhaps it is enough that we have the notion that black people are more "primitive." This contention has been with us for centuries, ever since the discovery of naked "savages" suggested to Europeans that sex was rampant in societies that wore fewer clothes.

A Mythical Divide on the Subject of Sex	
Black	**White**
hot	cold
uninhibited	inhibited
wild	tame
big-assed	flat-assed
abandoned	restrained
direct	indirect
flaunting	hiding
loose	stiff
agile	awkward
natural	kinky

Such ideas were common in the reaction of Parisian audiences to entertainer Josephine Baker in the 1920s and 1930s. Ernest Hemingway called her "the most sensational woman anybody ever saw—or ever will." Others lauded her topless dancing as "instinctive eroticism" or "the return to the morals of primal times."

The notion that sex is the underlying animus in black culture could still be common. Whites have long been sure they can see it in black popular music and dance or the raucous humor of black comedians. From these limited glimpses, some whites might conclude that all black people must have on their minds is sex. Yet this hardly explains the presence of a church on every corner in my neighborhood or the essential conservatism—the concern about *propriety*—that also pervades in black America. Black America, at times, can almost seem too proper.

Whites, however, thought early jazz was sexy and dirty, and these same impressions resurfaced in the 1950s when white parents and ministers were convinced that black-influenced rock and roll was the devil's music. White musicians based profitable careers on cleaned-up "cover" versions of black songs; the results were usually more restrained in their suggestiveness, even if top white performers—Elvis Presley is the obvious example—emphasized and exaggerated the eroticism to great effect, fame, and fortune.

Still, white thinking is shadowed by the idea that the color line separates two worlds, one naughty and one nice. The black side is the wild side, where anything goes, while on the white side, life is civilized and safe. On which side of town do we expect to find prostitutes? Just as we associate criminals, drug gangs, and welfare mothers with black people, the most common idea of a street prostitute is likely to be a black woman flaunting herself to passing cars. Our idea of a white prostitute might be more like Julia Roberts in *Pretty Woman*: you might even marry the woman because she's good at heart.

It is similarly tempting to draw naughty implications from the seeming openness with which sexual suggestion arises in casual encounters among black people on the street. As many sources note, the mores of black culture tend to allow sexual interest to be addressed more openly than in white culture. This openness shows in remarks like, "Hey, baby, can I get some fries with that shake?" This saying, directed at an attractive woman, even became a song by George Clinton. The "shake," of course, refers to that part of the anatomy that Josephine Baker shook with authority. The shake is also what Ray Charles sang about when he said, "she can shake that thing." And the "fries"—well, that refers to McDonald's or Burger King, where milk shakes are also available.

Meanwhile, it has long been considered that white mores demand that sexual propositions be more disguised as something else. An enthusiasm for Mozart will do fine to bring men and women together, alone even, but blacks sometime infer from extreme forms of beating-around-the-bush behavior that whites are incapable of approaching life or sex directly. "The verbal approach of white men," Thomas Kochman writes in the ever-engaging *Black and White Styles in Conflict*, "correspond[ed] to the general cultural norms that women are expected to deny or conceal their sexual interest and that any approach that would force a woman to acknowledge such an interest would be rejected, along with the man making it. . . . In black culture, it is customary for black men to approach black women in a manner that openly expresses a sexual interest, while in white culture it is equally customary for 'respectable' women to be offended by an approach that presumes sexual interest and availability."

Anyone who concludes from banter on the streets that black people are oversexed doesn't know half the story. Black women may get more propositions, but they also *reject* more propositions. In fact, though their approach is more direct, black men assume they will get rejections. Bravado aside, their repeated approaches assume a share of failures. Failure, it might seem, is less a disgrace than not trying at all. In fact, some young black men I know collect phone numbers of attractive women they meet—and call very few of them. Noting this kind of behavior, some black women complain that black men are all talk, no action.

But, as Kochman and others note, when black men make their aggressive-seeming advances toward white women, serious misunderstandings often follow. Even after the sexual revolution, white women are unaccustomed to such directness on the street, except, perhaps, in the case of big-city construction workers. In some cases, white women have characterized the verbal style of a black man as an "attack" or "assault," when it was hardly out of the ordinary for a black environment. Also, white women are likely to be afraid of black men, if only because whites so often are afraid of black men.

So a black man says, "Damn, baby. You with all them curves . . . and me with no brakes."

Or he says, "Nice dress, baby—can I talk you out of it?"

And a white woman becomes frightened. She walks on, trying to ignore the commentator. Whites in general have less experience with the give-and-take of street encounters common in Southern cultures, not just those between men and women. Whites can sense themselves ill-equipped to participate in exchanges of wit or sexual innuendo. And, yes, it is another issue on which they might feel inferior, but whites are also worried about saying the wrong thing around black people, too. So for all these reasons, they believe that guarded silence is the best course, because responding to individuals who make comments only encourages them to do more of it.

However, if this is the conventional wisdom, I beg to differ. Any response, even an insipid one, "Hey, what's up?" might be better than silence. When a white person ignores a comment made by a black person, it too easily suggests that whites, as is often claimed, treat black people as if they were invisible. And according to custom, when his comments are ignored, the individual is likely to press his case in louder tones, a phenomenon known as "loud talking."

Loud talkers often say those who ignore them think they're too good for such encounters, another suspicion some blacks still have about white people: "So you think you're too good for the likes of me. . . ."

Kochman reports a classic response by a loud talker to a woman who ignored his commentary: "What's the matter? You don't recognize me with my clothes on?"

If a white woman is accused of ignoring black people or of acting superior and this accusation is announced in a loud voice, she's likely to sense this situation has turned ugly or even threatening. And the uneasy subject of race could seem to have come up, too, even though any self-respecting loud talker would say much the same to a black woman who ignored him. But white women have less experience with loud talkers; they don't know this.

In fact, fears of experiences like this contribute to whites' wariness about entering black neighborhoods. They expect black people to "say things" that make them feel uncomfortable. However, it is often white uneasiness, itself, not sex, that loud talkers focus on. Black people are sick of white uneasiness, in the same sense anyone would become sick of being surrounded by suspicions that seem to arise for no other reason than one's skin color.

I suggest that whites on the receiving end of such comments do anything but what their instincts tell them: don't ignore it. Smile, and say, "Thanks for the compliment," or make a witty retort, if you can. And if you cannot say anything, proceed on with your business. This is a common conflict between Northern and Southern cultural ways that arises around the world.

Given all this craziness and the tortured history of gender relations across the color line, is it any wonder whites and blacks aren't falling in love willy-nilly? Because they're not falling in love. Don't get that idea. It may be that they just think of each other as too strange—too odd-thinking—to contemplate real closeness. And surely they are not around each other enough for propinquity to work its wiles.

Maybe we look too odd to each other when we get up close and personal. Whites should examine their own "color" now and then—the veins, freckles, and whatever—or their hairiness and imagine how someone with smooth brown skin—and no body hair—might view this allegedly wonderful whiteness. Who said this is *white*? It must be reported that white people can even seem too skinny for some tastes, particularly in the areas of the anatomy that black men usually find most eye-catching.

On occasion, black Americans will quietly note with puzzlement—or amusement—that white people's buttocks are peculiarly flat; this is another case in which it is apparently believed that bigger is better. I've even heard black women, upon catching sight of some white movie star or model, exclaim almost in shock, "She ain't got no ass!" The accompanying suggestion is that she must not be such hot stuff. And white people are occasionally referred to almost generically as "flat-assed white folks."

So what's to fall in love with?

Meanwhile, it is surprisingly common for some whites to find the shapeliness of black people almost disconcerting. A few whites seem to conclude this shapeliness, particularly in the buttocks, is evidence black people are oversexed. Assuming that the shape of one's rear end is an indicator of character or behavior is highly illogical; still, such things happen along the color line.

But what if blacks and whites do overcome all the obstacles to romance? What if they get married? Are such relationships condemned to be a meeting of stereotypes? There are two general theories that attempt to explain what is happening in interracial marriages—or what they mean is happening in the society. One theory is that interracial marriages are a sign of assimilation and evidence that two groups are viewed in the society as social equals. Hence, the relative shortage of black-white marriages in America would indicate the opposite is true: blacks are not assimilating into the mainstream in significant numbers and blacks have not yet reached full equality with whites in all corners of our thinking.

Roadblocks to Romance
Common white suspicions about black people:

- Blacks are hard to understand.
- Blacks come from a more erotic culture.
- Blacks are too "big."
- Blacks have more erotic experiences.
- Blacks can dance, and have better moves.
- Deep down, blacks don't like whites.
- Eventually, blacks will want black partners.

The other theory, however, is that whatever unequal status the two racial races have in society will very likely be reflected, perhaps unconsciously, in the workings of interracial marriages. Hence, the white partner will gravitate toward the superior position, the black partner toward inferior status in the partnership. I do not see this happening in my own life, but the argument might be that it happens subconsciously and I might not see it.

One 1994 study of the division of housework among interracial couples found that men of color married to white women do one-third more housework than white men married to women of color. But these white men still do the same amount of housework as men in same-race marriages. Get it? White women who marry black men are likely to get more help, because according to the latter theory on interracial couples, whites have more status in the recesses of our thinking.

But old ideas about race and status can creep into allegedly loving relationships, and other suspicions could then seem reasonable as well. A black person, for example, might have cause to fear that a white partner would treat him or her as stupid. Or a white person might fear that a black partner would find him or her sexually inept. Or a black partner would expect a white partner to be cold and unresponsive. Yet the most common fear black Americans mention about interracial romance is that in a moment of anger the white partner will call the black partner a "nigger" and mean it.

Roadblocks to Romance
Common black suspicions about white people:

- Deep down, whites think blacks are inferior.
- Whites are awkward, and not "big" enough.
- Whites are cold lovers.
- Whites don't let loose and have fun.
- Whites will use racial epithets in arguments.
- Whites see you as a walk on the wild side.
- Whites always go back where they came from.

This expectation indicates black people still assume this epithet is close to the surface of white thinking. Whites might also reasonably wonder what they have done—or not done—to leave blacks believing they still have the word on the tip of their tongues. Whites might insist it is not so, too, but they have apparently failed to convince black people. So there are big hurdles to falling in love.

Finally, our attitudes about interracial romance may be governed by the degree to which we believe closeness in relationships is a result of sameness—same background, same religion, same education, same race. Many Americans are fond of the notion that similarity is the glue that holds our nation together, and the idea surfaces in debates over our language—English only versus a polyglot of choices. The defenders of English appear to feel threatened, as if English were not the first language of the United States, or soon might not be. And here is a cousin of the fears about a darkening America. Yet how great a threat are these foreign tongues?

Many Americans are quietly wedded to conventional wisdom that marrying someone just like you will produce the best results. Baptists are better off marrying Baptists or Jews marrying Jews. A common background will work best; anything else is risky. A doctrine of sameness is also essential to the survival of many religions and sects. The Amish, for example, might soon disappear were it not for self-imposed segregation and a prohibition on intermarriage. But the inbreeding among the Amish produces a higher rate of certain diseases and birth defects, too.

Nature sometimes favors difference. So, it appears, do other groups that are believed to be clannish in nature. A majority of Jews in America now marry outside the faith, a fact that causes some Jewish Americans to fear for the future of their community and culture. And many parents on both sides of the color line would be shaken if their children made choices that seem to reject their upbringing, although bringing home a partner of another color is hardly such a rejection. Yet that idea may be out there, too.

Those who revere sameness or find variety scary have every right to their preferences. Yet it strikes me that in our concern about the racial divide, one idea is still off-limits. You very rarely hear anyone say it would be a great idea if more men and women fell in love along the color line. So I'm going to say it: more interracial marriage would be good for all of us. Then the issue of race might truly begin to recede in significance.

In a genetically more integrated population, many disparities that now exist between blacks and whites might likely disappear. If there were an IQ gap, as the authors of *The Bell Curve* claim, it might largely vanish in a few generations. (But the U.S. average should remain the same.) The skin cancer epidemic might abate if more melanin were introduced into the overall mix. And the day is surely coming—maybe in about 2099—when interracial couples will not get a second glance, when family scenes will contain a more lively mix. Who is to say it will not be our most wonderful time? But, maybe, many Americans sense themselves still unready for such leaps across the color line, and for the time being, mainstream culture will remain shy and skittish about it.

But interracial couples will eventually become more common in TV sitcoms or Hollywood movies. An interracial chic will arrive, and people will be extolling the virtues of expanding our horizons. Then we will have started to reach some sense on this issue.

Still for now, we can note that if children of mixed marriages face a problem, that problem is us, white and black Americans. We are the ones making it tough on them, and we can stop that. Yet lately, the children of interracial unions are starring in Hollywood movies, making hit records, and winning Olympic gold medals. They are becoming heroic and glamorous figures. So it can't be all bad.

As readers might suspect, I have misgivings and suspicions about those 95 million or so Americans who say they oppose marriage between whites and blacks. As a group, they are similar in number to the 90 million or so white Americans who say they don't have contact with a black person during their average day. And they are also similar in number to that group of whites who say they don't have a black friend.

Perhaps these people are restricted by their own isolation. About a third of the population has the clearest symptoms of our problems about race: they don't have contacts along the color line; they don't want contacts; and they even object if someone else has too much contact. Yet let's not be too hard on them. Some of them surely don't want to be the way they are—they don't want to be ignorant or incomplete—and it would be wrong to write off such a large group. If white attitudes about race have so greatly changed in recent decades, as is claimed, these Americans can change, too. Give them a bit more time. A bit.

15

HEROES AND VILLAINS

What's Sports Got to Do with It?

For years, I accepted conventional wisdom that sports have done good in the cause of relations between blacks and whites. Indeed, some of the greatest triumphs in sports history have involved leaps forward in our attitudes about race. No sports victories—and no sports stories—will ever be more compelling than those of Jesse Owens, Jackie Robinson, or Joe Louis. Their triumphs, their heroism transcended sports, representing our values at the most precious level. In such moments, sports seem to have provided the clearest examples of the good that can transpire along the color line. In these moments, sports can be the model of the way we should act.

These days, sports would seem to provide daily examples of the best in black-white relations. We do not look twice—as we still might at an interracial couple—at the teamwork, camaraderie, and mutual respect among athletes across the color line. We expect to encounter such relations in sports. And in a multitude of ways, sports demonstrate that valor, leadership, and intelligence transcend color. Sports also reveal how the loyalties of fans, too, can transcend race. Whites cheer for blacks; blacks cheer for whites.

But isn't it curious that we turn to the example of millionaires playing games on TV as evidence that race is no longer a problem? Most of these athletes are distant from the rest of us. Their lives are not much like ours. Their lives do not touch ours in any real, everyday sense. These athletes are creatures of television and sports marketing; their world is almost unreal next to ours. Yet we believe it demonstrates how well the issues along the color line are being resolved.

In 1993, I followed the return to baseball of the celebrated Bo Jackson after he had sustained a crippling and possibly career-ending hip injury playing football for the Los Angeles Raiders. *USA Today* sent me to the South where Jackson was going to test his fragile hip in minor league games at Sarasota, Florida, and Birmingham, Alabama, prior to joining the Chicago White Sox. His sojourn in the minors was big sports news. Could he still run? Could he still hit prodigious home runs? And besides being star on the field, Jackson was the protagonist in the well-known series of "Bo knows . . ." TV ads for Nike, which had elevated his celebrity even more than his feats on the playing field. The results were evident each night as the stadiums filled with youngsters pleading for his autograph on baseball cards or other Bo Jackson products.

The sociology of these scenes was intriguing. We were in the old South, yet virtually all the youngsters pleading for Jackson's attention were white. Four decades after Robinson broke baseball's color barrier, white youngsters were embracing black sports heroes like Jackson and Michael Jordan as if segregation had never existed. It also seemed that sports had achieved goals that eluded government, churches, and other well-intentioned institutions. Major corporations now venture millions of dollars on sports marketing with apparent faith that our thinking on race has changed, that there is no color line shadowing sports. Black athletes are prominently featured in advertising and, with few exceptions, are the most heralded athletes of the age. It might even seem that white superstars and heroes are in short supply.

Indeed, we could sometimes wonder where the white sports figures were to match the stature of Michael Jordan? He was a man who could virtually defy gravity. And except, maybe, for Mark McGwire's amazing home-run feats in 1998, repeatedly it was black American athletes who most often captured the world's imagination. In short order—in a matter of weeks, almost—the popularity of golf rose on the shoulders of young Tiger Woods. It was truly amazing how his skills and his charismatic style suddenly opened new interest in a game that had been so pervasively white though most of its history.

Once again, sports seemed the quickest route to mainstream success for black Americans. It was often assumed, too, that the success of black athletes must also have favorable impact on the well-being of black people in general. The presence of so many black athletes in America's most watched games seemed proof that integration was a success. Just look at football or basketball: there were black players everywhere, and many of them were amassing almost unimaginable riches.

How could these examples represent anything but good news for black people? It seemed, too, that we could surely do worse than form opinions about race from what we saw in sports. Yet all was not perfect in the sports world. In the 1990s, fans often spoke bitterly about the huge amounts of money involved in the games they loved. Ticket prices soared, and so did players' salaries. One needed only to listen to callers on radio talk shows to sense the undercurrents of alienation flowing between fans and athletes. Many fans said the money athletes were making was ridiculous. Others noted that sports heroes didn't seem to care about the fans, their teams, or, reportedly in the case of a few NBA players, the children they fathered.

Still other fans were clearly basing opinions about race on the misadventures of a few black athletes. Former heavyweight champion Mike Tyson presents himself regularly as a prime example. He could seem brutish and confused. After serving a prison term for raping a beauty queen, he bit Evander Holyfield's ear in a pivotal fight when it became clear he could not beat Holyfield fair and square. Meanwhile, the antics of the sometimes crazy-seeming basketball star Dennis Rodman, who wore multicolored hair during his years with the Chicago Bulls, were regularly reported. Then basketball player Latrell Sprewell, of the Golden State Warriors, tried to strangle his coach. That was big news for weeks. Of course, a pattern had been set by O. J. Simpson, who represented the ultimate cautionary tale about accepting black athletes into the white mainstream, no matter how nice they seem to be.

Still, on balance, the good that sports represented in matters involving race seemed to outweigh the bad. Many black athletes turned from sports to careers as business executives or sports commentators. And sports itself are special in human endeavors. Often we are convinced we are witnessing some unadulterated truth because sports competition takes place under rules that are fair and equal for all participants.

We even cite images from sports—"the level playing field"—as examples that define fairness, and we wish other aspects of life could be as clear-cut and fair as sports.

Still, a few of the "truths" that sports reveal should cause us to question some of the lessons we are learning. Some of these lessons fall in the category of the all-too-obvious: if black athletes win all the gold medals in Olympic running events, finishing first, second, and third in most instances, the lesson seems to be that blacks run faster than whites or members of other races. Indeed, sports have convinced many people, including both blacks and whites, that blacks must have an innate biological advantage at running and jumping. And even if the scientific nature of this advantage is yet to be determined, the results in sporting events suggest there is a division of labor in the human family that can be clearly recognized according to skin color. We can expect blacks will perform some tasks well, and whites will perform other tasks well. And the evidence this is so will be on display almost every time we turn on the TV.

Furthermore, we tend to see in sports that black people often excel at physical activities, especially running and jumping or activities requiring quick reflexes. And whites often bring other qualities to sports like leadership or intelligence. So, if we believe the lessons of sports, we will expect that the blacks we meet will excel at physical pursuits, while the whites we meet will excel at the more cerebral ones.

This idea about a division of labor is pervasive in the sports culture. For example, as wonderful as he is, Michael Jordan is a stereotype, because he is most noted for his ability at jumping. Of course, with Jordan we can see more dimensions to the man: he is a leader, a business professional, a movie actor, a figure of such wide-ranging talents that it's an insult to say he is a simple stereotype. So why then, with all these possibilities, was jumping the first idea about Jordan that sports marketers focused on? *Air Jordan*—it all began with the leaping, flying man. Did our ideas about race have something to do with it? Did we respond to the marketing of Jordan because he was doing the "right" thing for a black athlete to do? Or was it something else? We'll never know, will we?

Of course, the jumping stereotype that worked so well in the marketing of Jordan does not explain the millions of black people who cannot jump well at all. What's wrong with them? Nor does it explain the feats of Jonathan Edwards of Great Britain, who in 1995 set the world record in the triple jump, which is an Olympic event that rewards leaping. Edwards, the first man to triple jump more than 60 feet, is white.

Still, those who would argue with the claim that blacks are faster or can jump farther would find little evidence to the contrary in the sports shown on TV, because examples that conform to conventional wisdom about the division of labor predominate. Football and basketball repeatedly demonstrate that black athletes have one set of athletic gifts and whites another. In football, black players are grouped in the positions of running back, wide receiver, and defensive back, where fast running and quick reflexes are important. In basketball, the lesson seems clear that blacks excel at jumping, because so much of the game is now played above the rim.

Even Tiger Woods, it must be noted, hits the ball farther than other players, which suggests another physical advantage could be involved. And this would be ironic, because as recently as 1994, when asked why there were so few black golfers on the pro tour, Jack Nicklaus, one of the all-time greats, said it is because blacks and whites are physically different. "Blacks have different muscles that react in different ways," he said.

Indeed, Nicklaus was faulted for these remarks by *Sports Illustrated*. But hold on. Where did Nicklaus get these notions? It could have been in a 1971 *Sports Illustrated* article that attributed the successes and failures of black athletes to racial differences in physique and temperament. Such ideas have been common since the era of Jesse Owens. Whites have appeared to need an explanation why black people succeed at sports. In fact, we go though predictable cycles in these explanations. First, someone like Nicklaus will say it is *not* the exclusionary policy of country clubs that kept blacks out of golf. They were not good players because they had the wrong muscles. Then, along comes a player like Tiger Woods, and sooner or later, it will be said that blacks—or, maybe, players with Asian mothers as in Woods's case—must have a special physical advantage at playing golf.

Such has been the changeable nature of stereotypes: First, one idea prevails; then the exact opposite is believed to be true. Prior to Jackie Robinson's entry in the major leagues in 1947, those who opposed integrated play claimed that blacks lacked the skills to compete with white players. Even the *New York Daily News* called his chances in the big leagues "a thousand-to-one shot." But does anyone think blacks lack the skill to play baseball today? In fact, now it is more likely to be claimed that blacks' physical abilities put others at a disadvantage.

In another example, as recently as the 1960s, it was claimed that black runners were especially gifted at sprinting or jumping—short bursts of speed—but biologically disadvantaged for longer distances that required conditioning, strong lungs, and a steady pace. Whites were supposed to excel at longer distances. However, when runners from Africa began winning major marathons, the stereotype had to be altered. It was then said there must be two types of black people, those with innate ability for sprinting and those with innate ability for running long distances. But even then, it was said that blacks lacked the mental or leadership skills to succeed in such key positions as quarterback.

Doubts about black quarterbacks persisted well into the 1980s. Can black quarterbacks lead winning teams? Can black quarterbacks win the big game? These doubts were often expressed. But you don't hear them anymore, because black quarterbacks were eventually given a chance, and they erased the doubts, which had been nonsense all along.

It might even seem that inexorable trends in sports are moving in another direction: whites are the ones whose ability to compete is now in doubt. Some whites surely see sports as evidence that whites will be edged from prominence in America's future in sports or else-where. But if this idea is coming from sports, the fact is being ignored that the presence of black athletes hardly extends beyond three sports: football, basketball, and Olympic track and field events. Yet blacks' success in those areas has been sufficient to alter the way white males view themselves.

"Today, white fatalism about athletic aptitude marks the end of a certain kind of racial prestige that was originally vested in the colonial male," writes John Hoberman in a book titled *Darwin's Athletes: How Sport Has Damaged Black America and Preserved the Myth of Race.* "In the United States, the slogan 'white men can't jump' . . . exemplifies a gallows humor that acknowledges the twilight of white athleticism and whatever this portends for the supposedly beleaguered Caucasian male. The scenario for white decline can have a seductive appeal for those of liberal temperament, because it seems to present at least a min-imal redistribution of status amounting to compensation for centuries of racial oppression."

Is this what sports are doing to white male egos? It's a wonder those males watch sports at all. And maybe, just maybe, they don't watch as much as they used to, because it is periodically noted that TV viewership is down in major sports, that people are watching cable or pursuing other activities. And the real boom in sports in the 1990s, it should be noted, has been in the all-white contests like stock car racing, which has virtually no black participants or fans. It grew faster than any other major sport in the 1990s. Attendance at NASCAR Winston Cup events more than doubled in the decade, with new superspeedways opening in Florida, Texas, Nevada, and California, while corporations plunged millions of dollars into racing sponsorships.

Meanwhile, figure skating and gymnastics, sports said to appeal to women, were getting major coverage on TV. There were few blacks to be seen in these sports, either. Then, snowboarding and women's ice hockey were added to the Winter Olympics in 1998; black participation in these sports also was minimal. Suddenly, sports like beach volleyball were all over TV, and even though jumping is obviously an important element in beach volleyball, most of the participants were white, suggesting that whites can jump very well in the right situations. And given all these developments, it might even be claimed that the overall picture of sports in America was not darkening at all. White Americans were just taking up new sports, while blacks athletes were remaining focused on the relatively few sports in which they had a history of successes.

It seemed that whites were, consciously or unconsciously, scouting the horizon for white heroes. Not only were ice skaters and gymnasts becoming stars in their own right, whites were buying cycles, skates, boards, and other new contraptions; the sports universe was expanding. Eventually, in May 1998, a front-page cover story in *USA Today* announced: "The world's greatest athlete doesn't dribble a basketball, swing a bat, or score touchdowns. . . . The best athletes no longer gravitate to just traditional stick-and-ball sports."

Indeed, *USA Today* was referring to the proliferation of new sports that also just happen to be overwhelmingly white. *USA Today*'s contender for the title of "worlds greatest athlete" was also white. He was Shaun Palmer, a world champion snowboarder and mountain biker who had success in motorcycle racing, as well. He was hardly well known outside the sports in which he had success. And surely, Palmer was a good athlete. But was he "the greatest athlete in the world"? Who knows?

Most of the comparisons *USA Today* made to establish Palmer's credentials, however, happened to be to black athletes. The newspaper said Palmer was like or better than Tiger Woods, Deion Sanders, and Bo Jackson, that last two stars in more than one sport. Some of my black friends found all this amusing; they believed *USA Today* was projecting this relative unknown as "the world's greatest athlete" in an attempt to resurrect white egos that had been battered by the pre-eminence of black athletes. So, their theory went, if whites cannot be the big stars in football or basketball, they will proclaim themselves number one on snowboards, mountain bikes, and motorcycles. A funny idea, eh?

It is too easy to imagine these developments—this segregation of sports—are part of an old pattern. Whites cannot compete against blacks in traditional sports, so they invent new ones at which they can be the stars. In effect, they run away. Many black Americans would also not be surprised to hear that whites were fleeing from sports that involve direct competition with black athletes and abandoning sports at which blacks are thought to have advantages. In fact, if the conventional wisdom in sports is that blacks have special advantages, it would be logical for whites to look for opportunities elsewhere. And this turn can seem to be the old pattern of white flight: blacks show up; whites leave.

In a 1991 *USA Today* series on race and sports, we found that sports has its own forms of white flight: "Blacks are not just dominating certain team positions and in track and field events; whites are abandoning them." An ongoing example of white flight in the 1990s was the 800-meter run, an Olympic event dominated by white runners in the 1970s and by black runners 20 years later. And as more black runners focused on 800 meters, a curious phenomenon unfolded among the best of the white runners: their times got *slower*, despite improvements in tracks and training techniques and growing financial incentives. And it didn't make sense that whites could run faster in the 1970s than they could in the 1990s. So what happened? "It's implausible that whites have gotten slower," we concluded. "Whites with talent must have taken it elsewhere."

Dr. Frances Cress Welsing, the Washington, D.C., psychiatrist, sees this pattern in sports as evidence that whites fear—as did Senator Bilbo—the genetic power of blackness, which is particularly evident in the competition between males in sports. Here's what she once told me in an interview: "The whole of white cultures is designed to say that whites have certain qualities. Everything possible is done to demonstrate this. First, you have only white players; then blacks come in, but a white has to be quarterback. Western culture has to project white supremacy. . . . A white child is brought up to believe a white has to be superior. Then, as adolescents, they get out on the track and confront the reality that black athletes are performing well. The child can't discuss this with parents . . . so he leaves the sport."

Whites, however, might not see it exactly this way—that they are fleeing football and basketball. They might argue that these trends are not shaped by a fear of competing against blacks. Instead, it is the intrinsic appeal of gliding down a mountain on a snowboard, or the pure joy of skateboarding, mountain biking, rock climbing, sky diving, Frisbee-throwing, playing beach volleyball, or jumping out of an airplane—as it happens, activities with very little black participation. Meanwhile, the National Basketball Association is 80 percent black; the National Football League is 68 percent black; and both figures indicate a continuing trend toward fewer white players. These days, the "whitest" activity in football is kicking extra points, and many games pass without a white player ever scoring a touchdown.

But basketball and football seem to be black-influenced in other regards. At times, they are clearly, for better or worse, becoming expressions of black culture. It started with little details. Beginning in the 1960s, a few black players celebrated their touchdowns by "spiking" the ball or by dancing in the end zone. It was something very new; players had never done anything like that. They usually handed the ball to the referee and returned to the bench, without expressing outward emotion—that was the white way.

In basketball, the high-flying, slam-dunking style that black players developed on city playgrounds soon became a basic appeal of a game that hit its own boom times in the 1980s. Basketball, some noted, became one of the few activities in America where the prevailing prejudice worked against whites, not for them, because black players were presumed to be better. And the very "style" of the game had changed. It was much more a high-flying show, which led some observers to view basketball as a new black art form. "When you see Michael Jordan going to the hoop, you're seeing the African American approach to things," Kariamu Asante, a professor of African American studies at Temple, once told me. "Some may say it's a phenomenon of 'nature.' But it's really a cultural phenomenon based in rhythm. It's what these athletes grow up with. From the moment they're carried into the room as babies, they're immersed in an environment of rhythm that's rooted in traditional African culture." This idea is, of course, no more unusual than the theory that listening to classical music as an infant can boost your spatial IQ or your creativity, as is claimed by proponents of the "Mozart effect."

Even Jackie Robinson had seemed to bring a new cultural dimension, a new mind-set, to previously all-white baseball by being more aggressive in running the base paths, as had been the style in the old Negro Leagues. And Muhammad Ali was surely another landmark figure who brought new elements of the black American conversational style into the sports mainstream. For all his unique athletic skills—and "dancing" in the ring was among them—Ali established a cultural independence from the way white athletes had previously behaved as only a uniquely talented heavyweight champion can. Ali was loquacious and outspoken—he boasted, exaggerated, jested, recited poems, and belittled opponents. No white athlete had ever done anything quite like this. Ali seemed to turn the rules upside down.

Once again, sports became a classroom about race, the suggestion being that there is a cultural divide between the black and white ways of doing things. The newly discovered "black" way was loud, showy, individualistic. And, maybe, the "white" way involved modesty, reserve, and self-sacrifice for the sake of others or the team. But in a TV age, it also turned out, the showy approach was much easier to sell and more fascinating to watch.

In this new age of sports, modesty and respect for authority came to be regarded as "old-fashioned" values, which seemed to link them to eras when most sports heroes were white. Sportswriters and fans often imagined that in those bygone times, athletes played for the love of the game, not money, sacrificed personal glory for the sake of their teams, and treated others with respect, as if to say that this new era with more black athletes had different values.

Meanwhile, no single act more symbolized the spirit of new age in sports than the slam dunk. It was all artistry and spectacle and a blow to the opponent's psyche, too. Also, it was certainly not the easiest or most efficient way to score two points. The slam dunk represented a triumph of form, style, and spectacle over the simple demands of function, whereas in the old way of doing things, style was a decidedly secondary matter.

In new age values, winning wasn't everything. Looking good was important, too. And as Kariamu Asante saw it, African values were involved, too. When Michael Jordan performed a slam dunk, it expressed "a desire to adorn," she said, and this was another concept promoted by African culture. "There's an understanding that you're looking at a thing of beauty, an elevation of things. It's not just that a player can put the ball in the hoop; there's no aura in that. It's *how* you put it in the basket. It goes beyond sport. It becomes show and ritual."

Certainly, not all of the new age sports heroes were black. Also in the 1960s, New York Jet quarterback Joe Namath and a sequence of "bad-boy" tennis players like Jimmy Conners and John McEnroe demonstrated that whites could be brash and individualistic in their own way. Whites, too, wanted to appeal to the youth market, where black superstars did so well. Eventually, ads featuring white tennis player Andre Agassi proclaimed, "Style is everything," carrying the values of the slam dunk one step further.

Meanwhile, some fans and sportswriters held to old-guard attitudes, and it was possible they were not influenced by the race of athletes at all, even if the color line also seemed to mark the divide between old-guard and new age attitudes. Writers like *USA Today* football columnist Gordon Forbes, an old-guard loyalist, believed the pursuit of style had gone too far. Under a headline, "Showboating has gotten out of hand," he wrote:

> In the beginning, there was the spike. The majestic high-five, followed by the tricky low-five. And then New York Jets defensive end Mark Gastineau's sack dance and Cincinnati running back Ickey Woods' shuffle. But this year, the gyrations have gotten worse. And if it's not show time, it's style time. If it's not the Ickey shuffle, it's a dangling jersey. Or an altered knee pad. Or a nasty finger in your face, baby.

Was race somehow involved here? Only by inference. It could have been noted that high fives, the Ickey Shuffle, and other expressive improvisations in sports had their origins in black culture, as did much of the "in-your-face" behavior, too. But Gastineau was white, as were other follies Forbes denounced.

Surveys of sports broadcasting in the 1970s and 1980s found another variant on the color line: White athletes were still being described as hardworking, determined, sacrificing for their team, or demonstrating leadership and character. Black athletes were consistently described as having spectacular physical ability, God-given moves, and an instinctive sense of showmanship. And another common stereotype also slipped into this mix, the belief that white players are tough, that they will "play hurt," enduring pain so as not to let their teammates down. Meanwhile, black players were often suspected of malingering over minor injuries and of being less willing to sacrifice for their team or risk injury when they didn't feel quite right.

The Mythological Sports Divide	
Blacks	**Whites**
fast	slow
foot speed	brains
fragile	tough
showy	reserved
ornate	functional
high style	low style
talk	action
individualists	team players
slam dunk	layup

These ideas had been around so long, their origin was obscure. But the suggestion that whites are rugged frequently showed up in stories about quarterbacks, still a white-majority position in the 1990s. Numerous quarterbacks suffered concussions, and in several cases, it threatened their careers. But this battering was a weekly fact of NFL play. One by one, quarterbacks were knocked out, and because most were white, it seemed to represent a "white" predicament: tough white quarterbacks, who play with pain, were bravely enduring beatings from huge, physically superior linemen who, as it happened, were often black. Yet it could have been said that race had nothing to do with it, because as the number of black quarterbacks rose, eventually they got knocked out, too.

One concern about race that plagued sports in the 1960s and 1970s proved to be wrong—that white fans would not support black teams.

NBA coaches from the 1960s now recall an "unwritten" rule that teams should put no more than two black players on the court at a time. Then it was three black players. But it turned out white fans would support teams on which the best players or most of the players were black. Not only did whites continue to support their teams as the number of black players rose; the popularity of pro basketball also increased. Sociologists studied the phenomenon, too, finding that whatever preference white fans had for white players, they preferred teams that won even more, and most white fans also believed that black players were better.

White fans also came to expect they would see black players on the college teams they supported. Colleges with relatively few black students frequently fielded football and basketball teams on which a majority of the players were black. It even became the expected thing to do if you wanted to win. Schools recruited athletes out of black neighborhoods in big cities or wherever else they could find them. In many cases, these athletes lived in a world largely apart from other students on campus. It was a simple divide: on some campuses, whites were thought of as students; blacks were assumed to be athletes or less than fully involved as scholars. Once again, sports were teaching a lesson about race—and perhaps not an altogether good one—through the existence of virtually all-black sports teams on virtually all-white campuses. Once again, sports were providing evidence that black people excel at physical activities and whites excel at more cerebral pursuits. Many intercollegiate athletics seem to become contests between "our" blacks against "their" blacks.

Some athletes complained that instructors and others on campus did not view them as intelligent or serious students. The assumption that they had physical skills and little interest in anything else followed them around. They were like gladiators recruited to perform physical feats. And the fact that black athletes were recruited for the sports that produced the most revenue, football and basketball, sometimes also led the athletes to wonder if they were being exploited.

Meanwhile, along the fringes of campus sports, boosters occasionally acted as if black people had different values than the rest of society. Accordingly, it was considered OK to give black athletes under-the-table gifts or help them pass courses without their having done the work, because that was supposed to be the way black people are. They're not real students anyway.

On some campuses, the misadventures of athletes led to suspicions that athletes were being given license to do as they pleased or that football and basketball programs were careening out of control. Many colleges were investigated and sanctioned, including teams that won national championships. But this could seem another "lesson" that sports were teaching about black people: when black athletes are involved, trouble is likely to follow. Newspapers even set aside space on the sports pages under headings like "Jurisprudence" for reports on the misdeeds of athletes, further contributing to the idea that sports in the era of black-majority teams was becoming a cesspool of cheating and lawbreaking.

Sportswriters and fans often complained that these scandals were "distractions" from the purity sports were supposed to represent, or they lamented that youngsters no longer had worthy heroes to admire. And because black athletes were so prominent in big-time sports, some of them were inevitably cited among the negative examples of sports' decline from grace. It could even seem that black athletes brought these negative images with them from big-city ghettos, because it was often noted that they came from tough backgrounds, broken homes, and an environment where violence and criminality are common. But it was also presumed that sports were great gateways for black Americans into the American mainstream and that sports were doing significant social and economic good for a multitude of black people. This was a major illusion sports fostered: black Americans were getting ahead through the sports you could see on TV; it even suggested that black Americans have less right to complain about the inequities of life, when they are obviously doing so well in sports.

This view, of course, overlooked much evidence to the contrary. Opportunities in sports are very limited. There are, for example, only 360 players in the National Basketball Association; the NBA cannot possibly be a significant source of jobs for 35 million black Americans. But black Americans, it seemed, were also prime victims of this illusion that basketball is a viable career path. The odds on a black youngster making the NBA are more than 150,000 to 1, but as the movie *Hoop Dreams* showed, thousands of black youngsters imagine they have the talent for a career in basketball, when almost anything else would be a more realistic and useful ambition. In fact, it is the NBA that makes out well when these illusions are fostered, because the league is ensured there will always be a huge pool of youngsters striving to be the next Michael Jordan, even if only a few will ever make it near the pros.

Often, too, during my years as a sports journalist at *USA Today*, I was surprised how bitter sports fans had become in the 1990s about the games they claimed to love. How could this be? Fans were cynical, suspicious, and angry, and one needed only to turn on the radio to hear it. Sports talk shows were awash in complaints about players' salaries, players' attitudes, players' antics, or players' lack of character. There sometimes seemed to be no limit to the mean-spirited or disdainful comments fans wanted to make about well-paid athletes. And it seemed that most of these bitter fans were white. Yet there was no way of knowing if this bitterness had its roots in race or whether it was a reaction to the economic trends in sports; that some athletes made millions seemed to give fans license to complain about them at will.

Sportswriters, too, complained that players were stupid, greedy, self-centered; but it was also obvious that the culture of the athletes and that of the sportswriters were different, separated, among other things, by the color line. Most journalists were white, while the athletes they covered were often black, and the relationship between the two could be tentative and testy. At the same time, black athletes learned early on that it was unwise to raise race issues or even make the comments that black Americans often say to each other.

Black athletes who spoke out on race might find themselves accused of whining and complaining. Millionaire black athletes who raised the race issue in any way were sometimes treated by white sportswriters as too stupid to see the irony in their well-heeled circumstances. How can millionaire black athletes complain about racial inequities?

As a result, most black athletes remained silent on the subject, much as other black Americans guard their silence in offices and workplaces across the land, fearing they will be labeled angry or dismissed as having an attitude. For athletes, it was considered a relative surety that you wouldn't get any endorsement deals, either, if you raised the issue of race. So the rules were not to speak up and be happy. And in this way, sports again maintained an illusion that most black athletes had few complaints related to race, and that all is going well along the color line.

And then what happened to that generation of white youngsters who wanted Bo Jackson's autograph? They appear to be slightly more open-minded in their attitudes about race than their elders; hints to this effect show up in polls. Young people are more tolerant, for example, of interracial dating. They have also grown up in a world where there is lots of sports equipment to buy. They have gone through love affairs with skateboards, in-line skates, mountain bikes, snowboards, etc., and these activities have sometimes taken on heroic stature among members of their generation.

So it may also be that scoring the winning touchdown or hitting the winning basket in the last second are less a part of their fantasies than in generations past. Instead, maybe they dream of rushing down a mountain, recognizing that scoring winning touchdowns and baskets is more likely to be done by black people.

White fantasies have headed in other directions in one particularly notable case. Millions of fans now play "fantasy league" baseball or other "rotisserie" sports, in which you "draft" real big league players for your team and compete with others in your "league" according to the statistics your players compile during their season. Fantasy sports became the rage in the 1990s, and *USA Today* fed this trend by publishing the mountains of statistics that fantasy league players needed. Still, it must be noted that the central fantasy in these games is not about making stellar plays yourself; it is about *owning* the players who make the stellar plays. But then this fantasy could actually be more appropriate for white fans than dreams of scoring touchdowns, because team ownership is still a role in sports that is almost exclusively played by white people.

It may also be that we still pick our heroes though the prism of race, too. It may be that we see the good guys and the bad guys in these terms, too. Did whites find an extra thrill—or redemption—in Mark McGwire's pursuit of baseball's home-run record because McGwire was white? He seemed more popular with Americans in polls and surveys than the likeable, outgoing Sammy Sosa, McGwire's Dominican homer derby adversary, who is black. For a change, a white athlete was the hero in a major sports quest and beating a black competitor. Was race a factor, too, in the outpouring over Cal Ripkin, Jr.'s, record for playing in the most consecutive games? Indeed, it might have seemed appropriate that a white hero had the toughness—that stereotype again—required to become baseball's iron man. And Ripkin even had a contract to endorse milk. How "white" can you get?

Yet other than Pete Rose, I struggle to think of white villains or other individuals in sports whose misdeeds are as widely published as Mike

Tyson's or whites whose allegedly strange behavior gets as much attention as Dennis Rodman's. But perhaps it is mere coincidence that these athletes happen to be black. Maybe, they are not viewed as "representatives" of their race at all, even if they seem to exemplify common stereotypes about crime, violence, and unfathomable behavior. Hockey superstar Wayne Gretsky and other white stars appear to be such good guys. NASCAR stock car racing has produced a host of wholesome heroes like Rusty Wallace or Jeff Gordon, and even the "bad" guys like Dale Earnhardt, who might knock you off the road if they got the chance, are really good-hearted, too. We are repeatedly told that that they're just tough competitors who live to win. Get the picture?

Sports and the popularity of figures like Michael Jordan had indeed demonstrated that black and white athletes could have crossover appeal just like musicians and entertainers. But society at large eventually produced the most unusual examples of this phenomenon. There was the arresting case of Colin Powell topping President Clinton in a hypothetical 1996 presidential race, with blacks supporting Clinton and whites favoring Powell.

However, the continuation of strong black support for Clinton during the Monica Lewinsky scandal was even more widely noted, to the point that Nobel Prize–winning novelist Toni Morrison even called Clinton "our first black President" in an article in the *New Yorker*.

> African-American men seemed to understand it right away. Years ago, in the middle of the Whitewater investigation, one heard the first murmurs: white skin notwithstanding, this is our first black President. Blacker than any actual black person who could ever be elected in our children's lifetime. After all, Clinton displays almost every trope of blackness: single-parent household, born poor, working-class, saxophone-playing, McDonald's-and-junk-food-loving boy from Arkansas.

Meanwhile, on the fringes of the political right, it was suggested that Clinton had unfortunately adopted the hedonistic sexual values that are stereotypically linked to black culture. Hence, to call Clinton "black" led to the blaming of Clinton's behavior on black people. But why was black support for Clinton so strong, particularly when his policies have often fallen short of the political desires of many black Americans?

This white Southerner consistently gained high approval marks from black Americans, more so than from any other group. When his overall approval rating was 63 percent early in the Monica Lewinsky scandal, Clinton's approval among blacks was at 85 percent. A year earlier, a survey found that Clinton was the most respected figure, black or white, in black America, with an approval rating of 90 percent, surpassing Jesse Jackson (86.6 percent), Colin Powell (69.7 percent), and Louis Farrakhan (40.1 percent). How could this be?

Just as black and white athletes sometimes seem to have an easy rapport that is to be admired, Clinton reached out to black Americans in everyday ways—and black people noted this. He had close relationships with black people and trusted them; he vacationed and played golf with black friends like Vernon Jordan; and he seemed to genuinely enjoy their company. He often attended black churches and got misty-eyed during services. As a result, many black Americans saw Clinton as a caring, compassionate figure, who actually enjoyed having black friends and associates around him, even though his political policies and personal choices were often imperfect. In a sense, style triumphed over substance, but style in this case included the critical detail of wanting black people around. It is also worth noting in Clinton's case that many black Americans responded to gestures—gestures that represented an effort to reach out across the color line.

In other cases, black people have also given importance to simple gestures. For example, some black journalists were surprised how many black Americans—and particularly women—were touched by the death of Princess Diana. "I would never have thought a celebration of that which was white, blond, blue-eyed, thin, rich and royal could capture the hearts of so many women of color," wrote Courtland Milloy, columnist with the *Washington Post*. Yet one gesture the whole world had seen as exemplified Diana's caring nature: she had touched and held black children with AIDS. She had also visited with the victims of land mines in Angola, and she touched them, too, that salient detail. For this, she was surprisingly beloved across black America, standing far apart from other British royalty, who seemed such cold fish and oddly hostile or unresponsive to this beautiful young woman. If anything, Diana seemed a person of feeling, a "black" person, if you will, surrounded by forever stiff and standoffish aristocrats who were indeed, very "white" in their ways.

Therefore, as a rule—and it's a very simple one—many black Americans respond positively to whites who reach out and seem to care about others. But what do whites respond to when the color line is involved? This answer often appears to be disarmingly simple, too. As a rule, white Americans are more comfortable with black people who do not appear to be angry or accusatory—we are all waiting for simple gestures that reassure us of acceptance in each other's worlds.

Outside sports, Clinton was one of the few whites in the public eye who appeared at ease in a black context, and black people picked up on this. Otherwise, the illusion that sports presents of a racially harmonious society does not always carry far from the courts and playing fields. Sometimes, it hardly even carries into the stands. But we would still like to dream we can all operate together like a team—the Bulls, Cowboys, or Yankees—even as some Americans think they see other troubling news in sports. Some think they see black people "taking over" sports—blacks everywhere—and now Hispanics and others are coming. You can see that in sports, too. It's wonderful or disconcerting, depending on your wish.

Indeed, the sports we love keep sending out their messages.

III
CROSSING THE DIVIDE

16
GETTING IT RIGHT
Give a Little, Get a Little

W e citizens must recognize that the basic circumstances of race in America—the mathematics of race—will not soon change. Whites will continue to be a very large population group, blacks a much smaller one. Members of a larger group will still know less about members of a smaller group than vice versa. That pattern will continue. Whites will still find black people puzzling and mysterious; blacks will still tire of being treated as mysterious and strange.

Millions of white Americans will have little contact with black people and even less of an idea about what black experience is like. That's a given. A cultural divide will continue, perhaps even grow wider with whites seeing things one way and blacks seeing them another. On occasion, whites will express self-serving, ignorant opinions, but so will blacks. Blacks will sometimes suspect that whites are up to no good, and whites will have the same concern about black people—a given, too.

With whites as the overwhelming majority, whatever they think or worry about will always get more play in American life. White fears and fancies will dominate the American agenda. Soon, blacks will find themselves outnumbered by Hispanics, new cause to sense themselves ignored. But they may also find comfort in having white anxieties focused somewhere else. That could be a relief.

This is a big picture but it will also have impact on little pictures of life along the color line. Whites will still worry about saying the "wrong" thing when black people are around. And an incident on December 1, 1997, may haunt white thinking. On that day, multimillionaire Golden State Warriors basketball player Latrell Sprewell became upset about something his coach, P. J. Carlesimo, said. And Sprewell, who is black, tried to choke Carlesimo, who is white. Or so it was repeatedly reported.

This was not a good example for race relations. Thereafter, it became harder to tell whites not to be wary of the verve and vitality of black people. Whites became all the more nervous when black people were around, especially when blacks seemed excited or raised their voices. Sprewell's actions, which persisted in the news for weeks, exactly highlighted what whites have long feared: they will say the "wrong" thing—and all hell will break loose.

Over the years, numerous whites have admitted to me that they are uneasy around black people. They say they believe that an innocent remark, truly no harm intended, will offend blacks. And *ka-boom*. Call it a Sprewell syndrome or a Mike Tyson syndrome—these guys are archetypes in white nightmares. So it is inevitable that black Americans in the 21st century will still find themselves confronted by uneasy, jittery, cautious white people, who will pick their words carefully or say nothing at all. And black people will be left to wonder, as they long have, about the motivation behind such behavior. Is it an aversion to black people? Is it hatred or a wish that black people would go away? How can you tell? Therefore, it is inevitable that the uneasiness of white people will sometimes be mistaken for racism, even though it may not be that at all.

Unfortunately, race relations work that way. Ideas get planted and then you can't get rid of them. First, whites are fearful, and then whites act strangely; the result is that black people interpret what they see negatively. Sometimes you wish you could grab people and shout, "Stop it!" If whites weren't so edgy, maybe it could stop the cycle; if blacks weren't so convinced that edginess stands for something worse, maybe it could stop the cycle.

Yet there are numerous provocations that whites cannot stop slipping into, and although these promptings might seem trivial, their effect is devastating. Whites still have difficulty treating black people as a normal part of the everyday scene. Whites are surprised when they encounter black people at the theater, opera, or symphony; or on the ski slopes; or any other place where whites normally expect to be alone among other whites. And it shows. Some aspect of white demeanor—a gaping mouth or wide eyes—seems to ask, "What are *they* doing here?"

Can whites stop such conduct? You would think so. It sounds easy, but it must be harder than it seems. For example, it is almost inevitable that a few white people will assume any black person in a fancy hotel lobby or a posh restaurant is a porter or parking attendant. In fact, white Americans make this "little" mistake often enough that it is etched on black people's minds as an example of "white" thinking and behavior. A few whites will actually hand their car keys to a black lawyer, business professional, or professor, expecting that he or she will park the vehicle.

Does this conduct sound bizarre? Unbelievable? To black Americans, particularly upscale black Americans who visit fancy hotels and posh restaurants, this blunder is shockingly common. It even happened to the venerable John Hope Franklin, who is a Harvard Ph.D., a professor of history emeritus at Duke University, and the chair of President Clinton's advisory panel on race. As Franklin recounted in news interviews, when he was in Washington, D.C., to receive the Medal of Freedom in 1995, he stayed at Cosmos Club, where he had been a member since 1962. While there, a white woman in the lobby asked Franklin to fetch her coat from the cloakroom. A few months later, at New York's St. Moritz Hotel, a white woman thrust some trash in Franklin's direction and told him to throw it out. And a few weeks after that, a white man at the Waterford Hotel in Oklahoma City offered Franklin his car keys and said, "Here, boy, go and get my car."

And, incidentally—get this—Franklin was 80 years old at the time.

Incidents like this, of course, make one wonder what white people could possibly be thinking. What fog or time warp are they in? Are white people that *out of it?* And still it happens, even though you would think whites would eventually stop. But apparently some can't. Is it any surprise, then, that black people treat these "mistakes" or "slips of the tongue" as if they are windows on the white soul? Many blacks believe this behavior reveals the *truth* about what white people think: that all black people should be porters and parking attendants.

And it's strange, too, that these black people who are handed the car keys or bits of trash, do not explode like Latrell Sprewell. (Nor do they drive off with the car in any case I've heard of.) Instead, they hold the anger within, where it only takes its toll on the selves of those who are treated thus. And this frequent, admirable restraint in the face of attacks on one's dignity goes unrecognized. So when I am suggesting to people that they should give a little, sometimes I think about John Hope Franklin. Franklin has already given plenty, I'd say. Now it's someone else's turn.

Even in these odd cases, our problems often have at least partial foundation in the isolation that the mathematics of race produces. Isolation, mixed with massively retarded thinking, produces whites who haven't yet heard that black people are lawyers, professors, and doctors. Yet less virulent cases of the isolation malady are much more common; the mathematics of race dictates that millions of white Americans will be uneasy and unsure of what to say. And how should we deal with this—ask black people to be endlessly forgiving? Ask black people not to draw negative conclusions from things whites still do? Ask white people to be more aware and awake? The most immediate remedy might be to know how this basic black-white predicament works. Maybe whites can curb some of the obvious signs of their jitters, and blacks can try to draw a few less negative conclusions.

And just what can whites do about being nervous and awkward when black people are around? One guideline could be simple: how would you behave if the person before you was white? Try that. Don't search for something to say that is "black," because that is likely to sound foolish and condescending. Also, try to curb urges to approximate your idea of "black" dialect. Talk the way you normally do. And do not bombard black people you've just met with personal questions that might seem prying and too personal. How do you know if a question is prying? Would you ask this same question of your boss? Talk about the weather, if you must. It's better than saying nothing.

Some whites may find making such efforts unnerving; it may seem they are being forced into the heartland of their fears. Do it anyway. And what does this concept of giving a little really signify for white Americans? How about approaching life with a generosity of spirit? Millions of white Americans have every comfort the times have to offer: they are well fed, well housed, and well entertained; they have VCRs, dishwashers, computers, and cars; they can fly anywhere they want or cruise the Caribbean. Plenty of reasons to be generous of spirit.

How black Americans respond to white Americans' efforts to be more giving is another matter. The generosity of black Americans toward the white majority—the amount of forgiveness they have shown, in particular—often goes unappreciated. Millions of black Americans are not "angry" at all in their dealings with whites. Sensing that whites suffer from their own isolation—or whatever—black Americans often give white people a generous break. They don't point out whites' awkwardness; they don't blame whites for slavery. In fact, kindness has been the strategy of black people for centuries: blacks must adjust to the whims and ways of the white majority, not vice versa.

Yet black Americans have every right to feel that being treated as frightening and strange is insulting. If some black Americans seem brusque and unforgiving to whites, especially whites who hand them the car keys, we should understand they've had enough. But don't expect whites to respond well to "angry" blacks; that's just not in their nature.

Whites, however, should also recognize that acting in ways that manifest worry and fear only invites disrespect or retaliation from those who take offense at such behavior. Some of the young men in my neighborhood do this: they see nervous whites approaching on the street and they glare menacingly. The whites do not speak; the young men do not speak. And who's really to blame in this standoff: whites for being nervous or blacks for being angry about whites being nervous? I wish it could stop.

But let's not get dreamy-eyed. Whites can protest—and often do—that they harbor no ill will, but do they expect black people to read their minds? There's a rub. Whites could have the warmest thoughts imaginable toward others, but others won't know unless whites express themselves better. And what are blacks *and* whites to do when they encounter negative responses? Take umbrage, if you must, but *don't generalize*. Some people don't want to get along, but that doesn't mean all people don't want to get along. Some whites and blacks are mean-spirited, foul-tempered, and self-obsessed. But that doesn't mean all whites and blacks are that way. No one would expect me to change my opinion of my wife because I met a black sorehead during the day. So don't draw similar conclusions.

Ideas most often considered insulting are witless generalizations—claims that everyone in a population group is alike. Hence, it is witless generalization to say that all Germans, all Poles, all Jews, all whites, or all blacks are alike. Furthermore, the most fatuous generalizations are those that characterize everyone in a group by the worst example: that all blacks have murder in their hearts because O. J. Simpson allegedly did or all whites want to kill blacks because three white men in Jasper, Texas, killed a black man.

What do we give up if we decide to avoid making silly generalizations? Generalizing from specific instances is a primary logical fallacy. Many strictures of political correctness probably began as well-meant attempts to avoid unwarranted generalizations. Don't say all Mexicans like beans, all blacks like fried chicken, or all whites have tiny sex organs. Is that unreasonable? But given the ire that political correctness rouses, it must be that many Americans feel so compelled to generalize that they will cite their constitutional right to do so.

Whites might hope, for example, that others would stop saying that whites are selfish, coldhearted, awkward, and scheming. But these are not majority opinions in America; whites do not imagine themselves being viewed in these terms when they walk down the street. As yet they do not complain too often about the vicious things being said about them. Black people, however, suffer from generalizations that they are unintelligent, lazy, volatile, and sexually uninhibited; they know these things are said.

Here, for example, are 20 generalizations about black people that we would all be better off without. But are they going to disappear? Not likely.

1.   All black people are alike.
2.   Black people are stupid.
3.   Black people are unfathomable.
4.   Black people live in ghettos.
5.   Black people are good athletes.
6.   Black people love to sing and dance.
7.   All black people love fried chicken and collard greens.
8.   Black people have criminal tendencies.
9.   Most black people are poor.
10. Black people are violent.

11. Black people are lazy.
12. Black people are oversexed.
13. Black people have too many children.
14. Most people on welfare are black.
15. All black people want handouts.
16. Black people use race as an excuse.
17. Black people are noisy.
18. Black people are too excitable.
19. All black people know individuals in drug gangs.
20. Black people should just try to be more like whites.

All these generalizations are wrong. Avoiding them might seem easy, and the payoff for whites might be worthwhile, too. Whites would not need to worry half so much about saying the "wrong" thing. Unfortunately, however, some black people will hear generalizations even when whites swear they have not intended them, or that they said the exact opposite.

Here's how that works. Some stereotypes like those about intelligence are so pervasive and have black people so on guard that the negative idea jumps out unbeknownst to others. Hence, to say, "You've got to meet my black friend, Kiesha; she's so intelligent," can trigger the thought that you are really saying, "You've got to meet my black friend, Kiesha. *Unlike other blacks*, she's so intelligent."

Suddenly, a complimentary remark can seem to reveal a hidden truth about a negative white mind-set—or "where they're coming from." Whites who insist that their black friends are "articulate," "smart," or "educated" can seem to be saying that this runs contrary to what you might normally expect from black people. But "articulate" is a special category, a favorite term that whites use to describe black people, who—truth be told—are articulate in many cases. Being articulate—skilled in orating—is an area of human endeavor that whites are willing to cede to blacks, whose oral presentations will often be described as "emotional" and "passionate," even when they are hardly so. In this thought pattern, white presentations are more likely to be "reasoned," and black presentations that are "reasoned" will often be viewed as a turnabout on normal expectations as in this *USA Today* description from the Simpson trial:

> LOS ANGELES—Most analysts said Johnnie Cochran would rely on emotion for his closing argument, waving red flags about police corruption, igniting racial anger and painting O. J. Simpson as the tragic victim of a "rush to judgment."

That's not how it turned out Wednesday. Although Simpson's lead lawyer sprinkled his delivery with emotion, experts were more riveted by the precision of his factual arguments—starting with a crushing attack on the prosecution's murder timeline so successful some suggested he may have reasonable doubt in his grasp.

At times, comments representing generalizations about black people can seem a plague. For example, when White House lawyer Cheryl Mills, who is black, finished her presentation in defense of President Clinton in his Senate impeachment trial, the first comment by MSNBC anchor Brian Williams was that her performance was "like Johnnie Cochran," even though the only possible connection between the two is that both lawyers are black. Theoretically, it appears that all black lawyers will "be "like Johnnie Cochran" to some whites.

Nor, however, will it be considered a compliment if you tell black acquaintances, "You're not like *them*," meaning not like other black people. Quite simply, it is not flattering to be told you are an exceptional member of an otherwise inferior group. And by the way, "them" is a generalization—it lumps together all blacks or all whites, whoever "them" is, as essentially the same, as do "you people" or "your people." Would whites recognize themselves as "your people"? Why should blacks? But generalizations sneak into our behavior as insidious reflections of the way we think. When a black friend wore her hair in braids to a Washington dinner party hosted by whites, the hairdo was widely noted and complimented. And what's wrong with that? The white hosts even announced that their cook, another black woman, was also wearing braids and asked the cook to come into the dining room to display her hairdo, which quietly irritated my friend.

Was she being too sensitive? Was she wrong to mind being compared to the cook? The hosts were clearly trying to be open-minded about black hairstyles, and this has not always been the case among whites. So shouldn't that be a plus? Yes, but there was an unfortunate generalization being made, too, that said in effect: "Look, everybody, isn't it wonderful how all these black people do their hair alike?" Or "Look everybody, my guest and my servant do their hair alike." Consider how whites would have responded if the host summoned a white cook to demonstrate that she came to work with the same hairdo as the white guests? Wouldn't that have seemed odd?

So it isn't easy. Whites think they are giving a little, and they discover they are being annoying. More often, they don't know what they've done. Black people say nothing, accepting that there will always be bumps on the road to black-white comity. Generosity of spirit seems most meaningful when the rewards to be gained are not clear or when we do not let one setback deter us.

The 1999 flap over the use of the word *niggardly* by a white aide to Washington Mayor Anthony Williams was a classic example of the need to give a little—or practice a greater generosity of spirit. The situation cried out for both blacks and whites to be more accommodating, yet initially that did not seem to be in the offing. The aide, David Howard, said he used the word in this way in an office discussion: "I will have to be *niggardly* with this fund because it's not going to be a lot of money."

He meant *grudging* or *miserly*, as the word is defined, but one of his staff members, Marshall Brown, thought he heard the racial epithet and told others Howard was a racist. And word, so to speak, spread. Faced with accusations of racism, Howard quickly submitted his resignation, which the mayor accepted, saying that Howard had been insensitive; the mayor indicated that using *niggardly* around black people is dangerous, like smoking in a refinery. (And, it should be noted, this was a case of a black person, the mayor, describing black people as potentially volatile, which fits an image whites are already likely to have.) But, for the record, Williams also likened use of *niggardly* to saying "chink in your armor" in Chinatown, according to news reports.

Williams was criticized by both blacks and whites for being too hasty in accepting Howard's resignation. Howard's attitude was this: "I resigned not because I used bad judgment in using the term *niggardly*, but because of the rumors that spiraled out of that."

The story was soon in the national news, and it summoned up many fixed ideas that blacks and whites have about each other. Blacks think whites are insensitive; whites think blacks are overly sensitive. In D.C., some whites noted that Brown, who mistook *niggardly* for something else, was a supporter of former Mayor Marion Barry, and they saw his protest as an attempt to run whites out of city government. Howard's most adamant supporters also said it was unfair to think that he should have known better than to use *niggardly* when he used the word correctly. How could he know it would be misinterpreted? Are we handing over the country to people who don't know the meaning of words?

To some blacks, however, it seemed disingenuous for whites to insist that blacks should not hear "nigger" in the word *niggardly*, even if the origins of the words are unrelated. Many black friends insisted they can't help but hear the epithet—and they know the meaning and derivation of the word. And a *New York Times* essay by Steven Pinker, a scientist at Massachusetts Institute of Technology and author of *The Language Instinct* and *How the Mind Works*, agreed. Pinker said that making a connection between the two words is unavoidable because of the way the brain works. The brain instantaneously sorts through the sounds of words and parts of words for all possible meanings before eliminating those that don't fit the context. "Thus it is impossible for anyone to hear 'niggardly' without thinking, if only for a moment, of the ethnic slur," he said.

Still, some whites were suspicious that race was being used against them even though many black media commentators sided with Howard, urging that he be kept in his position. And it must be noted that Brown's reaction to *niggardly* exemplified negative stereotypes many whites have—that blacks are unintelligent or uneducated and they use race to gain unfair advantages. Among those whites, Brown could be cited as an example why whites should oppose affirmative action or programs that give blacks an advantage: this is what you will get.

In this mess over *niggardly*, both blacks and whites had reasons to think badly of each other, if that was their wont. But in the end, Washington's new mayor recognized that *everybody* was losing: Howard, black people, the city, and Brown, too. So the mayor offered Howard his old job; Howard said he didn't want it; and the mayor gave him another one.

Case closed? Not quite. The mayor said he had learned not to be so hasty in his decisions on such matters—accepting Howard's resignation and, one presumes, talking about black people as refineries. And Howard told the *Washington Post* he had learned, too: "I just feel very pleased that this whole thing has a silver lining," he said. "The silver lining is that this has led to a discussion that can help everyone understand each other better. . . . I used to think it would be great if we could all be color-blind. That's naive, especially for a white person, because a white person [can] afford to be color-blind. They don't have to think about race every day. An African American does."

I learned something, too. Among whites I spoke to, most of those who supported Howard's absolute "right" to use the word *niggardly* were individuals who have few personal contacts with black people and no close friendships. And whites who believed Howard should have known better than to use the word tended to be individuals who have closer relations with black friends and associates. These perceptions raised questions. Does refusing to give a little in race relations mean you end up with no friends across the color line? Or does having no friends across the color line increase the odds you will resist giving ground on racial matters? Both ideas seem plausible. And it could be an indicator of whites' potential for functioning along the color line. Those who insist on an absolute right to say *niggardly* probably won't do too well. And those who are willing to give a little will have more possibilities.

Yet unfortunately these issues are, relatively speaking, social niceties. They are important—sometimes very important—and we should work on them. But they are not as deeply tormenting to relations along the color line as the issue of crime. Crime is killing race relations—sometimes literally but more often figuratively. Crime is widening the divide between blacks and whites more than any other factor, yet neither group is eager to address the problem candidly.

Even if there are multiple misunderstandings about crime—about who commits most crimes or how many crimes committed by blacks involve white victims—too many Americans are too terrified about crime to make much sense about it. Millions identify crime with black men, which in itself is having a disastrous impact on our society. At every educational and economic level, it appears that black men are the outsiders, doing much worse than black women. More black women attend college than black men; black women are paid more closely to white norms than are black men. And so it goes.

Yet whites will often insist they are afraid of crime, not skin color, as if to suggest that if black men stopped committing crimes, all fear of black men will go away, too. I'm not so sure. A society that is afraid of black men is likely to marginalize them. And as long as black men sense there is no place for them in the mainstream, there will be some who turn to outlaw lifestyles.

As things stand, Americans have chosen a "get tough" approach, which has resulted in black men being incarcerated in record numbers, even as we also note that too many black families are headed by single women. Got that? According to figures in 1996, we lock up 526,200 black men, or 8.3 percent of black males, between 25 and 29 years old. And then we wonder why so many black women are raising children alone. And then we predict that this breakdown of the black family will produce more maginalized black men and lead to more social disorder. And where will they end up—in jail? When will this cycle stop?

Quixotic as it might be, we might wonder at some point what would happen if white Americans would stop being so afraid of black men and stop trying to keep their distance from them. Would fewer black men end up marginalized or drawn to criminal lifestyles? Would fewer be imprisoned? Would fewer children be raised by single mothers?

Whites need to search their consciences about all this. Are they afraid of black men? Are they ostracizing black men in any way? I sense whites are keeping their distance, maybe because it seems wise. But white Americans will have to gauge the degree to which they avoid black men or do not welcome them into mainstream society.

Nevertheless, a continuing drumbeat of evidence about black men is rousing white fears: notices of street robberies and other mayhem, for example, regularly appear on a Capitol Hill E-mail network that goes to hundreds of homes in my neighborhood. Should whites be advised to ignore this information or pretend such events are not happening? That would be crazy, too.

Following is a typical E-mail sent by this network:

15th and Independence SE, 6/3, 11:20 P.M.

Two people were walking to a takeout shop when two suspects approached. One said, "Where's your money?" and the other went thru pants pockets of one victim and took cash. Both fled. Descriptions are the usual: black males, one 30 years, old the other in his 20s, both about 6 ft. tall, etc. One did have facial hair, including a mustache.

Since no weapon is mentioned, this kind of incident is sometimes classified as "robbery fear," where the victims give over their money without seeing a weapon. And this notice is like dozens of others, except for the reference, "Descriptions are *the usual*: black males . . ." a slip of the tongue, so to speak, for which the editor of the E-mail, a white woman, soon apologized. But her faux pas was also an accurate statement; black males are the "usual" suspects in Capitol Hill robberies. So the apology was the nicety of a community that imagines it cares about the sensitivities of others. But it is a small gesture toward amity next to the dagger that crime plunges into the heart of race relations.

Some black Americans believe crime rises in relation to the lack of economic opportunities for black people. In this way, they also see crime as a result of how whites have treated black people over the centuries. But crime does not balance the scales of economic justice, at least not in my neighborhood; most crime occurs in connection with the endless hungers of drug addiction. Nor is there overpowering evidence that a fear of crime motivates whites to act better; usually it encourages them to support building more prisons.

At the same time, as in the Simpson case, many whites suspect that black Americans are sympathetic toward black criminals. Whites, in their isolation, do not hear black people speaking out against crime. They hear stories, generated in locales like my neighborhood, about blacks who do not cooperate with police, which also becomes a standard police excuse for not making arrests. So the idea of blacks supporting criminals spreads farther.

Nor do whites note that black Americans are leaving crime-infested cities for the suburbs—evidence, it seems, that they want crime-free neighborhoods, too. But we should also be aware that if whites have bad impressions of black people, it is not always Hollywood's fault. Reality contributes its share, and the drumbeat of examples is almost a daily affair in communities like Capitol Hill.

More samples:

110 7th St. SE, 6/5, 9:45 A.M.
Victim approached from rear, suspect placed knife to throat. Suspect grabbed purse, victim screamed. Suspect put hand over mouth and said, "Shut up." Witness yelled at suspect and he fled without obtaining purse. Description: black male, 20s, 6 ft., 1 in. to 6 ft. 2 in., med. weight, blue slacks, white shirt.

320 15th SE, 1/7, 12:25 P.M.
Victim reported that suspect punched him in the face and took $13 and a watch. Description: black male, 25 years, 6 ft., 160 pounds, light complexion.

15th & D SE, 11/23, 7:55 P.M.
Two suspects approached from rear, struck victim on head knocking him down. Suspect #2 held victim at knifepoint while #1 went through his pockets. Stole pager and $100. Descriptions: #1 black male, 28 years, 5'9" tall, medium weight,

medium complexion; #2 black female, 25 years, 5'5" tall, thin, dark complexion.

Occasionally, these robberies turn deadly. On February 27, 1997, a 32-year-old white resident, David Johnson, was attacked on his way home on Capitol Hill. "Units responding to the location," the police report said, "found the decedent lying on the sidewalk suffering from multiple stab wounds to the chest and neck." Maybe, it was a random act, like being hit by lightning, but if whites seem, at times, to view black people as dangerous, menacing, predatory enemies, we must also recognize where these ideas come from.

There was no evidence Johnson was doing anything; he was not buying drugs or trying to rob people. Within a block of my house, there have been two dozen killings in the 1990s. Most of the victims in these cases were black. But should that make whites ignore 24 murders in which only 4 victims were white?

Unfortunately, few individuals in the neighborhood were as memorable as Henry "Little Man" James, a teenager who lived a few blocks away. In 1991, James told passengers in the car they were riding in on a D.C. expressway that he "felt like killing somebody." So he pulled his gun and randomly shot a 36-year-old woman riding in a passing car. At trial, James claimed he was out "maintaining [his] composure" that night.

In 1993, the violence in D.C. was so bad that children, including several from my street, told the *Washington Post* how they wanted to be dressed at their own funerals and what songs they wanted played. The story quickly got national exposure.

"What will white folks think?" my wife sometimes wondered. Yet the real unknown that tortures her and other mothers of black sons is that the killing—and the destruction—of black men seems without end. Hollywood didn't create "Little Man" James; my neighborhood did. And how can we get that right? I may be personally motivated to have friendships—or at least be as straight dealing as I can—with black youngsters and young black men and women. But it's hard to demand this effort from others who are unlikely to encounter young black men or women.

There is pathetically little traffic across the color line at the points where the marginalization of black men begins. Where can the teenage boys in my neighborhood find enriching contacts with white people? Where can these youngsters learn that whites do not necessarily look down their noses at them? Where can they learn that a white manager might give them a job if they applied? Where would they learn that some whites don't see them as criminals?

I am challenged to think of many occasions when the positives of race-relating are affirmed for many of these youngsters. But I also wonder how many whites even care about questions like these? Not many, I'll bet.

I admire the approach to the divide of crime that one black neighbor took when she suspected that her nephew, a drug addict, was responsible for a series of house burglaries. It was merely a gesture, but she reached out all the same. Bless her.

When she heard that a white woman's house had been burglarized, she went to the house even though she did not know the woman. And she knocked on the door, apologized, and explained that she was trying to get the police to arrest her nephew and get him help, which was in fact the case. The white neighbor was surprised and impressed, and maybe even felt better about the neighborhood, too.

Such gestures are rare. Obviously, this black woman, who is also active in community affairs, could have chosen not to face the shame her nephew represented. She could have shrugged off his crimes as the inevitable result of being a black in America. Or as often happens, she could have assumed that whites have insurance to pay for their losses. But she did none of these. I later asked her what had motivated her when it might have been so much easier not to do anything. "I prayed on it," she said. "And that's what came to mind."

I noted, too, that the town of Jasper, Texas, population 7,500, was trying to get it right after the 1998 murder of James Byrd, Jr. Maybe, some will dismiss such gestures as naïve, sentimental, and way too late. But city leaders and clergy formed a task force to bridge racial divides. Six months after the murder, 75 blacks and whites tore down an iron fence that had separated the black and white sections in the local cemetery since 1836.

Again, it was only gestures, but I am challenged to think of a better way to start. According to news reports, Father Ron Forsage of Jasper prayed that this move would have significance for the town: "For many of us, this fence has been a symbol of segregation in our com-

munity. Give us the power and strength through this rotten and broken fence to repair the fences in our own lives."

Often, I encounter white people who have sincere desires to get it
right. But their approach can be confused—discombobulated, really—
as in the case of one white woman who was flustered about her dealings with black employees in her new job as an office manager.

Sometimes, I have a hard time telling these stories about whites
being upset by the subject of race without my black friends saying, with
irony, "What's with your people?"

This woman was sure she would be seen as a racist—absolutely
sure. She recognized the office had problems and few resources to
resolve them, which somehow made her assume that racism would
inevitably be blamed. "Do you think I am a racist?" the woman asked
me. "Maybe I am. But if I am, why did I just choose to live in a neighborhood where there are so many black people?" She was in a tizzy.
And this behavior might seem odd unless you considered she had little previous experience with black people. She was entering what to
her was strange territory, and she was bringing common, unsettling
expectations to the situation. "I'm sure I'll never figure black people out,"
she said. "Why do they get so worked up about everything? Why can't
they discuss problems calmly?" So she was sure blacks and whites must
come into conflict, which is one stereotype. And she was sure that
blacks are mysterious and unfathomable, another stereotype, or that they
easily get worked up and overwrought, a third.

Yet for all her fears, all hell did not break loose. Eventually, she
discovered the black employees were individuals, not members of a
frightening group. Some were excellent workers; some were less so,
as is true of workers from any group. And race was not the issue she
feared it would be.

Meanwhile, many of my black friends find this dithering and worrying about black people silly or, worse still, insulting. "What's wrong
with white people?" they want to know.

"This behavior starts off from isolation and inexperience," I say.

"But how come there's so much of it?"

"Because there's an inexhaustible supply of isolated and inexperienced white people—millions and millions of them."

"Lord, have mercy."

Yet it may be a hidden—and unappreciated—factor in race relations that many whites wish to do the right thing. They just can't figure out what the right thing is. One white couple who recently moved to a black-majority neighborhood in Chicago was looking for ways to reach out across the color line. They were new in town; as yet they had no black friends, but they had hired a black nanny, with whom they had what seemed a friendly rapport. They wondered if they should raise racial issues with the nanny, if only to broaden their own understanding.

Realize, of course, that this dilemma of finding black people to talk to is not unusual. It is typically "white." Meanwhile, to black Americans the "problem" seems evidence that whites must be isolating themselves deliberately. How can they have such difficulty finding black people? Typical black experience in the American mainstream puts blacks in contact with whites all the time; they're surrounded by whites.

So this idea of whites asking, "How can we get to know black people better?" can seem mystifying. Or in this case, "Should we discuss race with the nanny?" seemed an odd query to my black friends who immediately wondered, "Don't they know anyone else?" Their consensus on forcing discussions with the nanny was, "Goodness no." They insisted it would be unfair to expect a black employee to reveal opinions about race to a white employer, who, in turn, might not like what she had to say. Furthermore, the situation is more likely to force the nanny to "tell white people what they want to hear." So what's the point?

And I might have agreed, except that much happens along the color line that cries out not to be ignored. What kind of race relations do we have that we might ignore an atrocity like the killing of James Byrd, Jr., and say nothing? If blacks and whites are not mentioning such events among people they know, what are they saying? Surely, we should recognize that awful events happen and—importantly—say we are profoundly horrified by them. Anything less would be odd.

So it seems I *might* speak to a nanny about race. And if I wanted to talk about issues without forcing her to take a personal stand, I might ask, "What are your friends saying?"

"But that's you," my black friends said.

These friends do not anticipate as a happy prospect having whites asking willy-nilly about their feelings on race. They also tend to believe that whites are always looking for easy answers—like hoping a magic bridge will show up to carry them painlessly across the divide of color. There's no such bridge, my friends insist.

Before whites can talk to black people in depth about anything, whites must have *relationships* with black people. And before they can talk about race with black people with whom they have relationships, whites will need to have demonstrated that they want to hear what black people have to say. And then it must be clear that whites do not just want to talk things over to browbeat blacks into agreement with whatever they think at the moment. Whites must demonstrate not only that they can listen and learn, but also that they are willing to accept disagreement from blacks with the same equanimity they might display with other whites. And whites must show, too, that they are willing to change their minds now and then.

Otherwise what's the point of having the discussion?

And then sometimes we do the right things, and we fail nonetheless. Sometimes we reach out across the color line to let people know we want to hear them out, and they don't feel like talking.

Many times we will need to weigh our choices—to give a little or not to give a little—trying for the greater good. My friend Karen DeWitt, an expert at pinpointing dilemmas of color, tells of attending Catholic mass while she was a visiting professor at Kansas State in Manhattan, Kansas. Right off, she noted she was the only black person at the church. But so did the white parishioners, who were eager to express their welcome—smiling, nodding, and holding out their hands in friendly greeting. This friendliness continued after the service, as well. Everyone, it seemed, wanted to say hello.

In other words, the white parishioners made their welcome abundantly clear, which is what we should do more often along the color line. So what could be wrong with what the parishioners did? Karen says the issue for her was in never being able to escape from the shadows of skin color. She did not go to mass intending to open an initiative in racial healing, and she does not want to be reminded that she is a black person in a white world during every single moment of the day. Can we follow that? But, of course, this was not exactly possible with white parishioners so intent on doing the right thing.

Karen and I have revisited this incident several times. I say it is difficult to ask the congregation to do the right thing—be welcoming—
and expect them to gauge exactly when not to be too intrusive. But
other black friends know exactly what Karen means. Can we ever get
it right? Maybe not as long as we live in a world that recognizes differences and worries about them so. Maybe, in an epoch after that. Yet
surely these parishioners did nothing wrong. In fact, they were as right
as we can be now. For the time being, Karen will have to endure an
excess of welcoming, because it beats not being welcomed at all.

17
THE GOLDEN RULE
What About the Self-Evident?

The best advice is sometimes the most obvious. And the most obvious advice is often the least appreciated. We sneer at suggestions we could solve the problems related to race merely by acting better toward each other. Yet it is excellent advice, if we would only follow it. The solution is obvious, but apparently acting well toward others is sometimes against our nature. That's the catch.

Examples of this flaw in our character keep arising. And race is one of the most likely flames that attract this moth. We make bad jokes and stupid statements; we commit brainless acts or undertake truly evil endeavors. To do otherwise often seems outside our nature. Like teenagers who mindlessly vandalize cemeteries and tip over tombstones, we cannot explain why we act so—defying sense—but all the same we do.

Whatever origin our irrational urges have, our worst selves will occasionally overwhelm our better instincts. The simplest way to solve all our problems—especially regarding race—would be to practice the Golden Rule: "Do unto others as you would have others do unto you." What a great idea! But the shadowy forces in our nature often get the better of us.

The Golden Rule is particularly appropriate when race is involved, because it assumes a common humanity. To understand others, it says, search your own desires. But that's another catch—our sense of common humanity most often fails when race is involved. Yet the Golden Rule has been cited in cultures around the globe. If nothing else, we are all alike in our discovery of its wisdom.

- The Bible says, "Therefore all things whatsoever ye would that men should do to you, do ye even so to them: for this is the law and the prophets."
- Islam says, "Not one of you is a believer until he loves for his brother what he loves for himself."
- Judaism says, "What is hateful to you, do not do to your neighbor."
- Hinduism says, "One should not behave toward others in a way which is disagreeable to oneself. This is the essence of morality. All other activities are due to selfish desire."
- And in Africa, a Yoruban proverb advises, "One who is going to take a pointed stick to pinch a baby bird should first try it on himself to feel how it hurts."

Arrayed against this good advice are the mindless forces in the shadows of our nature. These forces need not be logical; they are powerful enough to drive us to acts against our own self-interests, for which we will be deeply ashamed—or suffer deeply. And we know that race can trigger our worst selves to appear. We are forewarned, yet it is predictable that men and women will act badly when race is involved.

Knowing this, we expect the worst will happen at the color line. Our negative expectations are part of the problem. We expect mindless forces to prevail, not the Golden Rule. The Golden Rule could neatly resolve many issues. For example, whites may find themselves uneasy around black people; they worry about what to say, fearful they will say the wrong thing—a classic "white" dilemma. And what would the Golden Rule advise? It suggests that whites should ask themselves what they would want said at such a moment—a perfect solution: say to others what you would want said to you.

Need we ponder this issue further? That is all you need to know; better advice is not available. Yet it is our nature to assume that the simple and obvious can't work in the real world or that dealings along the color line must be tortured and shadowy. Meanwhile, millions of Americans may not see the issue of race as all that pressing; they don't do much race-relating; that is a normal situation in America. Do onto others . . . what others? And if white or black Americans want to distance themselves from each other, they still can. In the vastness of Montana, the ratio of whites to blacks is about 311 to 1; in Teton County, Montana, it is 2,051 to 1. And there are neighborhoods and housing projects in big cities that are just as isolated; blacks can escape, too.

But for how long will this option be available? If our world is truly shrinking, as is so often claimed, the inability to treat others fairly and squarely should eventually become a serious liability. It might even be wise to consider dealings along the color line as job training for the future. With all the talk about a global economy, has no one thought of this eventuality? Residents of the United States are only 4.5 percent of the world population—or about 1 out of every 23 people—which suggests that those who can deal with the other 95.5 percent are likely to have an advantage when the world comes calling.

Doesn't that sound plausible?

And if truth be told—and the color line is a training ground for success—black Americans will have a big advantage, because they get more practice crossing the color line.

Haven't whites thought of that, either? No—white experience is more happily isolated; many whites still believe it is best to stay away from color lines. They believe that the less attention you pay to race, the better off you will be. And if you ignore race long enough, you will not have to deal with it.

Meanwhile, even as we are supposed to be ignoring race—and being color-blind—we remain expert at seeing the worst in each other in quick glances. It can seem to whites that all homeless alcoholics and addicts are black; it can seem to blacks that all white women are clutching their purses protectively. Such scenes produce much of the information that's traded along the color line—a commerce in bad ideas.

Suppose blacks and whites are waiting in a line. And suppose the whites are annoyed; they look about impatiently in ways that announce, "I've got more important things to do." Indeed, blacks in the line could have the exact same feeling, but the whites, in their manner or body language, might suggest that *theirs* is the real problem, causing blacks to wonder, "What makes them think they're the only ones with something important to do?"

Quickly, this little situation has—correctly or not—reaffirmed one stereotype blacks note about white people: they think they're more important than everybody else.

Whites might protest this claim, saying it's ridiculous. We didn't say anything of the sort. Yet the unfortunate perception remains.

Having been raised to believe it is impolite to stare, many whites try to avoid eye contact with strangers. Some will avert their eyes quickly.

But what are black people to think when they catch this move? Is it additional evidence that whites don't want to see black people?

Next, we are in a store, where the simple act of handing money to a clerk can contain hidden signals. Suppose a white customer lays the money on the counter, perhaps merely intending to see that it is the correct amount. But what if a black clerk instead suspects that the white customer is using this ploy to avoid touching a black person? Just such an idea turned into a culture clash between blacks and Korean merchants in Washington, D.C.—all because Korean shopkeepers seemed reserved in their manner. And some customers assumed it meant that the Koreans did not want to touch black people.

Yet as unfortunate as it was, the misunderstanding was also instructive: the response of the black customers was hardly unfathomable; whether warranted or not, customers took offense at behavior that they interpreted as disdain. And conversely, in many situations black people respond to friendly or easygoing behavior in friendly and easygoing ways.

The lesson seems obvious: which do you prefer—friendly or hostile treatment? Too often whites expect blacks to be hostile, and expecting this, they are guarded in their manner. And blacks are guarded in return. Instead, expect your encounters with black people to be pleasant—and that's what you'll get. I expect encounters with black people to be enjoyable. And that's what I usually get. It's that simple.

Furthermore, it is easy to anticipate the behavior blacks will find most irritating, because we have a long history of bad relations. Blacks if asked could suggest these don'ts:

- Don't act superior, like you know it all and are above talking to others.
- Don't act afraid like something is worrisome about others.
- Don't be sour, as if being pleasant is not worth your time.
- Don't be impatient, as if others are in your way.
- Don't be too full of yourself, as if you are the center of the universe.
- Don't blatantly ignore everyone else.

Understand that the color line magnifies troublesome behavior, escalating it to a daily disaster along the color line.

Of course whites will surely object to a suggestion that they modify their behavior. Human nature always fuels the cry, "What about them?" So let's agree that race relations will improve only when everybody—black and white—becomes more accommodating. And let's agree that neither side has a monopoly on virtue.

One of the first efforts blacks and whites could undertake *together* would be to make a regular effort to greet each other warmly—smile, say something nice: "Hi," or "How are you?" Why is such a simple gesture helpful? Because blacks think whites don't want them around, and whites think blacks don't want whites around. The question of who's welcome where is very real in America.

Warm greetings are not a pointless exercise. Black Americans, who do most crossing of the color line, frequently suspect they are unwelcome in their everyday encounters with whites in schools and offices, and once again, it is little details of behavior that—often unintentionally—send the "wrong" messages.

And if these impressions were always wrong, we could merely advise black people to adjust their expectations—don't draw negative conclusions. But these impressions are not always wrong. Some whites want blacks around and some—a few maybe—don't. But the messages they both are sending look very similar at times.

So here are few suggestions whites could consider:

- **Try being more pleasant.** Recognize that you are being judged on the way you act toward others. Try saying "hello" to black people or smiling in elevators or on the street. Say "please" and "thank you" whenever it is appropriate. How can it hurt? I try to treat others as though they are important to me—just a gesture. I try to be more outgoing; I start idle conversations; often such a move makes the day more enjoyable.

- **Look for opportunities to interact with black people.** Although most whites have little contact with blacks, you can try to change that. Take the initiative in crossing the color line, if it means walking across the room or driving across town. Try to be sincerely welcoming to black people in professional and social settings.

- **Don't always leave the effort to others.** Some whites might choose volunteer activities that help the poor, the sick, or those less fortunate. But do not view interacting with black people as charity. Wouldn't it be more appropriate, perhaps, to consider blacks as the generous ones in welcoming whites who are "poor" in experiences outside their own world?

- **Show genuine interest in other views.** Many black Americans claim that whites do not care what blacks have to say. So include black friends and colleagues in what's going on. Ask for their views and listen to what they say. Each day, in varied settings across the land, blacks sense they are being ignored. But this problem could easily be solved.

- **Try not to overreact.** Black Americans feel whites are quick to dismiss black opinions as irrational or angry. Blacks often expect whites to respond: "That doesn't make any sense"; or "Please calm down. Let's talk about this rationally"; or "That can't possibly be so." So try not to conclude that blacks must be angry, that they "have an attitude," that they hate whites, or that they must be "playing the race card." These clichés are not helpful. Also, do not assume you must defend white people or the "white" position at all times. No great calamity will befall white people if you don't.

- **Avoid being a bully.** Some whites exaggerate possible threats to their well-being—the sky is often falling. Frequently, these alleged threats are used to gang up on black people.

Take the example of Senator Orrin Hatch, who often speaks somberly against affirmative action, "racial preferences," and "racial quotas." Hatch's concern appears so deep that it might be good reason to wonder what threat whites face in Utah, his home state. Indeed, the situation in Utah is startling, but actually because whites are so *unthreatened*. Black residents are 0.7 percent of the population, and the ratio of whites to blacks is about 140 to 1. Here's what the situation looks like:

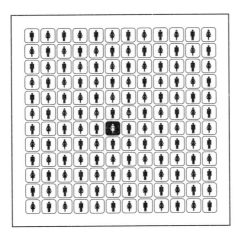

What threat can 1 black person represent to 140 white people? Actually it would appear that whites could relax more about black people in Utah. But like an elephant that's upset about the activities of a mouse, Hatch has stomped and bellowed about preferences and quotas until . . . well, you would think whites in Utah would be embarrassed.

Meanwhile, as a nation we are becoming less straightforward about the racial segregation around us. While many whites worry that blacks will get unfair advantages, others seem to live in a dream world that America is an integrated country . . . and that there are no color barriers . . . and that it's against the law to discriminate . . . and that there's little else to say. Yet the segregation that stares us in the face at every turn doesn't bother us half enough.

Do we notice it at all?

I live across from an all-black elementary school, and it seems perfectly acceptable to all concerned that these 400 black youngsters have no white schoolmates. But should white Americans be concerned? To a white American, the issue is removed and abstract—these 400 black children are unavailable to interact with white children; they have been removed from the equation of integration. And that means that white children *somewhere* are correspondingly more isolated.

In the absence of contact with black youngsters, some of these white youngsters might grow up to be uneasy about black people; they might be the ones who will still wonder what to say if black people come around. Or they might have stranger ideas. And they will be a little less prepared for a future that might include people other than whites.

But currently whites, I guess, are not worried about these unfortunate possibilities.

To black America, the situation at the school means that 400 additional black children have no contact with white youngsters. Hence, they are growing up in an environment where it is easy to hear it said that white people are strange or hateful. But that doesn't seem to bother anybody, either.

Is this good training for adult life in the so-called real world? I would guess that these 400 children are being better trained for life in an all-black world. This situation might also increase the hesitancy these youngsters will have about crossing the color line, where, unfortunately, it looks like most of the jobs and opportunities are going to be. But this prospect does not seem to trouble anyone greatly.

These days, we hear surprisingly few complaints about the effects of isolation and segregation. Do whites sense something amiss in all-white gatherings? Hardly. Do blacks see something wrong in all-black gatherings? Even less so. Many whites are willing to embrace a segregated society if the alternative contains any suggestions that blacks get a better deal, and many whites seem eager to imagine this is so. Many whites in effect chose segregation in California in 1996 by voting for Proposition 209 that ended affirmative action programs in the state. The results were predictable: fewer black and Hispanic students would attend schools like the University of California at Berkeley or UCLA, so white students and Asians, whose admissions rose slightly, would have less contact with black and Hispanic students.

Did that bother anybody? Obviously, a majority of voters believed white students don't need contact with black and Hispanic students. Whites also apparently see no need to improve their skills—or their children's skills—at relating along the color line. But black Americans are not crying for integration either. Blacks demand opportunities and justice—not opportunities to rub elbows with whites.

Most black Americans I know would be insulted if you suggested they need whites around to have full lives. Are you kidding? From the pages of *Essence* and *Ebony* to scenes in the streets, nightspots, and eateries of our cities, we see blacks and whites going their separate ways. We don't enjoy enough the pleasure of each other's company.

On summer weekends, we also have humongous gatherings of white people that are at least as "white" as the Million Man March was "black." But nobody considers it alarming—nobody questions stock car racing, the fastest growing major sport in America. Stock car racing fans are white; the drivers and pit crews are white; the team owners and corporate representatives are white. These white multitudes gather at sacred spots such as Daytona, Florida; Talladega, Alabama; or Darlington, South Carolina, where some in the crowd occasionally wave Confederate flags, a detail guaranteed to make blacks wary about stock car racing. In fact, today's sport began in the 1940s as a pastime among rural whites in the segregated South.

But even as this sport spread into the North and coast to coast, it remained sociologically insular. Foreign cars are not allowed. All those brightly painted racecars are patterned on "stock" U.S. models with big V-8 engines, creating the illusion that Fords, Chevys, and Pontiacs still rule the planet. Stock car racing thrives on the idea that big, American cars are the ideal—and the fastest drivers on earth are white males, many of whom happen to live in North Carolina.

In the 1990s, NASCAR, the sport's ownership group, filled seats with white fans as fast as new seats could be built, so when NASCAR President William C. France was asked about attracting black fans, he was taken aback. "There probably hasn't been much looking into that, in all honesty, because the seats have all been full," he said. "We're encouraging all Americans to come. African Americans are a part of America just like anyone else, and we certainly want to reach a cross section of Americans."

But stock car racing has no affirmative action program. And that, plus the Confederate flags, ensures that stock car racing will remain overwhelmingly "white" for the foreseeable future. But NASCAR did ask Supreme Court Justice Clarence Thomas to be grand marshal of the 1999 Daytona 500, a duty that involves saying, "Gentlemen, start your engines." And Thomas said it sonorously.

But what's my point? I enjoy stock car races, although I do not believe there is anything intrinsically "white" in enjoying the competition or in the skills required to drive fast cars. I have taken black friends to stock car races, and they enjoyed themselves, too; nothing untoward happened. So I've done my part to integrate stock car racing. My brother-in-law also loves the sport. He is one of the sport's few black fans and roots for Dale Earnhardt, who is white and comes from North Carolina, too.

Right now, stock car racing is riding high. Few fans would entertain the possibility that it misses something important in its lack of black participants, but I believe it does. Yes, stock car racing can be exciting, but all the drivers seem to be the same guy. They're named Jeff or Dale; they come from the same place; and they say the same things in the same accents. What stock car racing could use is someone different—maybe a few black drivers. Even one good one would do.

Mark my words: if a black driver ever wins the Daytona 500, it will not portend that stock car racing has become less significant or less interesting. It will mean the sport has taken on a new dimension. Maybe, NASCAR and its fans can't imagine it, but the example of Tiger Woods in golf is awfully tempting to cite. Golf got bigger and better when Woods appeared on the scene. Does anyone claim that golf has been diminished? And baseball changed for the better, too, when Jackie Robinson joined the Dodgers. Football and basketball are better off with black and white stars. Does anyone claim otherwise?

The world is always richer and more interesting when the competition is joined from as many directions as possible. Too bad we can't adopt this as another rule to live by.

As things stand, black Americans and white Americans obviously face different predicaments in the world. There is no mystery to this. The Golden Rule aside, what might be wise counsel for one group is not necessarily relevant advice for the other. Whites are the larger, dominant group. Blacks are a smaller group that still needs to watch what the dominant group is up to.

Most of my earlier suggestions for whites centered on the idea that whites are less aware of the impressions others have of them—and sometimes they don't seem to care at all what others say, what blacks think of them. But blacks need much less warning about how others see them; they already know, because it is intrinsic to black experience that whites' reactions will be a concern. Blacks are always dealing with white reactions, one way or another.

Even today, one of the biggest obstacles black Americans face is white fear of black people. Whites might wish that blacks could do something about this—stop being so scary. But as we know, whites sometimes are afraid when there isn't anything to be afraid about; much in such fears is in the eye of the beholder. And blacks are well aware that whites are scared; they've devised many strategies to deal with this fear.

Some blacks believe they can disarm white fears with charm or by laughing and joking. Whites like that approach, and some blacks are good at it. Yet not every black American is a natural-born comedian, and many consider it demeaning that whites are looking for comic performances. It means whites don't want to treat blacks seriously. Other black Americans say you need to "tell whites what they want to hear," which is apparently easy to do. You just find out what worries whites and agree with them. Still other blacks warn, "Never let whites know how smart you are."

And sad as it may be, all these strategies must work at times. Or why else would black people recommend them? Apparently, some whites are content being told "what whites want to hear." And they prefer to think they are smarter than black people, too. But the problem with such falsehoods is that you have to keep telling them, and the strategy advances no larger cause: whites make no progress toward being more understanding. And blacks make no progress toward being better understood.

My black friends, however, insist that being honest with white people is risky, especially if it involves being forthright with your boss or anyone else who has power over you. Interestingly, too, I hear this most from black friends with the most experience—and apparent success—dealing with whites. They insist that whites act strangely when black people challenge them or point out errors that whites have made. Whites become very flustered, defensive, or angry. A few almost seem to froth at the mouth, my black friends say.

I also fear that many whites will insist it is preposterous to claim blacks cannot speak freely to whites. They will maintain that blacks are as free to speak as anybody. And besides, sometimes whites cannot speak freely with their bosses, either—whites, too, must say whatever the boss wants to hear. So speaking up poses a much more universal problem.

But my black friends also insist that whites have difficulty with basic understandings about black people—particularly the ones that require a belief in common humanity. Whites tend to assume blacks are different or that their minds work in different ways. Therefore, the Golden Rule doesn't really apply; whites cannot use their own desires as a reference to understanding black people.

And how long will this go on, my black friends ask.

Since the basic mathematics of blacks and whites will continue into the 21st century, which seems to mean that blacks will continue to encounter whites who need to be educated and reassured. My black friends find this prospect *truly* discouraging. They wish they could escape from having to deal with whites and focus their attention on solving black problems instead. In the process, they say, black people could develop their own economic base and political power and become as independent from white people as possible. And then if they wanted to, they could say the heck with white people.

This is a highly pessimistic view of whites that assumes whites cannot change or that whites are virtually helpless when it comes to understanding anyone else. But, then, I note that 78 percent of blacks say they have white friends, while 73 percent of whites say they have black friends. We're back to that slim ray of hope on an otherwise shadowy scene—the polls on interracial friendships.

Right off, we might ask ourselves how "close" these friendships actually are. Have these friends ever been to our house? Have we ever been to theirs? Possibly, there is more relating to be done here—and we could do that. In the vastness of all the unrelating that is going on along the color line, we could try to make these friendships stand for something more valuable than an excuse to claim everything is fine.

That is one hope. If 73 percent of whites claim a black friend, it also suggests that having a black friend has become desirable among whites. And if this is the case, whites will not want to lose a black friend over something a black friend said—what with black friends in such short supply. So maybe black friends can speak up a bit more.

I'm almost sure they can.

Blacks should also understand that whites use their black friends in ways that give what blacks say extra gravity. Whites consider their black friends to be designated spokespersons, interpreters, and cryptoanalysts for all black people and all black culture; whites cannot stop believing that all black people are essentially alike. As a result, many whites consider black politicians, "leaders," and advocates to have less credibility, because their own black friends don't express the same ideas or make the same charges.

See the problem here? If Jesse Jackson or Louis Farrakhan says one thing and the black friends that whites count on say something else or nothing at all, who are whites most likely to believe?

Being a designated spokesperson, interpreter, and cryptoanalyst for black people becomes an important responsibility. But if black friends are wary about being honest around whites, or if blacks feel too embarrassed or angry to talk about the demeaning treatment they've faced—or the suspicions they have—whites will never hear about such realities from the sources they most rely on—the black people with whom they have actual contact.

I would suggest it is time to change that. And perhaps the following suggestions for blacks could help in some small way:

- **Don't let whites mystify you.** Most whites are products of isolation, which does not necessarily mean they are vicious bigots. Most whites don't want to be bigots. Maybe, instead, everything they know about black people comes from TV sitcoms.

Many whites, however, do act oddly—I've seen it. But some of those who act oddly actually want to know black people better; they just can't figure out how. This is what isolation does—it stupefies you. So try to be forgiving. What else can I say?

- **Whenever possible, tell the truth.** If whites believe race is no longer an issue, it is in part because black people have not corrected them. Many whites would be glad to hear more of what their black friends think, but they're afraid to ask. I'm also sure that many whites would be flattered if black friends chose to share their feelings about race or told them of incidents and situations they have faced. Please consider that possibility.
- **Have confidence.** Whites are nervous and full of doubts about race. And maybe you frighten them, too. But odds are that you have more experience dealing with whites than they have dealing with blacks. So you have an advantage. Don't forget it.

Alas, we must still remember that people can be evil, too, and there are so many whites in the United States that even if a tiny percentage are bigots, that's millions of bigots on the loose. The thought can be scary. Any recommendation that black people should be less wary of whites asks for a huge leap of faith. Millions of whites may still believe they are members of a superior race, culture, or social stratum. Why should they want to listen to black people or take blacks seriously?

Considering how isolated whites are, I have wondered, too, why well-known black Americans don't speak out more—especially those to whom whites might listen to or give extra credence. But this is an unfair question that always surrounds successful black Americans—why don't they speak out about injustice or whatever?

Still, I've wondered why Bill Cosby has not been more outspoken about race, because I inferred from a telephone conversation I had with him in 1990 that he might have something interesting to say. At that time, he and his wife, Camille, were helping a black racecar driver, Willy T. Ribbs, cross the color frontier into the previously all-white world of Indianapolis 500 auto racing. Ribbs eventually made the race in 1991, and for those who don't know, the Indy 500 is a different kind of racing from stock car racing. The cars are much faster. Still, before Ribbs, Indy car racing was just as "white" as NASCAR.

At the time of my conversation with Cosby, Ribbs was having difficulty gaining corporate sponsorship, which is virtually required in big-time racing, and Cosby was not optimistic that corporate America was eager to back Ribbs's entry into an all-white sport. I was optimistic for Ribbs; Cosby wasn't. Cosby said that you can never underestimate the power of "the stuff in the shadows." I well remember that phrase.

Some might assume, of course, that Cosby has climbed far above "the stuff in the shadows." But if he were to say something on the subject, I always assumed that whites would take him seriously. Yet to my knowledge, Cosby never talked about "the stuff in the shadows," and perhaps I was naïve in wondering why not.

My black friends say Cosby had no choice, because if you go around talking about the "the stuff in the shadows" in America, you cannot make TV commercials for Jell-O, too. White Americans might decide that Dr. Huxtable is too angry for their tastes, so talking about "the stuff in the shadows" can have a self-destructive aspect. And Cosby seemed to stay away from it, even after his son was murdered in 1997.

The next year, however, Mrs Cosby wrote a surprising essay in *USA Today*, where she said: "I believe America taught our son's killer to hate African Americans. After Mikail Markhasev killed Ennis William Cosby on January 16, 1997, he said to his friends, 'I shot a nigger. It's all over the news.'"

Was this "the stuff in the shadows" that her husband referred to?

She continued: "Yes, racism and prejudice are omnipresent and eternalized in America's institutions, media and myriad entities," and she even noted that pictures of slave owners still adorn most of our paper money. And our dictionaries "define 'black' as 'harmful; hostile; disgrace; unpleasant aspects of life,' while 'white' is described as 'decent; honorable; auspicious; without malice.'"

Of course, the essay, which echoed ideas often heard in black America, roused its share of controversy. Writer David Horowitz, who is white, asked in *Salon* magazine, "What can be said about a mother who exploits the tragic death of her own son to deliver a racist diatribe against a nation that has showered her with privilege, making her family wealthy and famous beyond the wildest dreams of almost anyone alive, including the very objects of her hate?"

Horowitz accused Mrs. Cosby of "irrational hatred of America in general and white America in particular" and concluded: "On what planet is Camille Cosby living?"

Los Angeles radio talk show host Tammy Bruce, who also is white, characterized Mrs. Cosby as "incredibly unstable, crazy, paranoid, delusional, just nuts," according to her station's subsequent apology. The station further apologized for Bruce's additional comments that Bill Cosby had "multiple illegitimate children as a result of multiple extra-marital affairs with white women," and that he "secretly funded the criminal defense of O. J. Simpson." Really now—what was on *her* mind?

Allegedly all this response was inspired by Mrs. Cosby's essay, but Bruce was suspended, then replaced—which became its own controversy. Yet it was, at least, curious to note how closely these attacks echoed the common stereotypical claims about black people: blacks are irrational, blacks are angry, blacks hate whites. And the charge that black men are overly interested in having sex with white women got thrown in, too.

Did the essay constitute clear evidence that blacks are irrational, angry, and hateful? Or that black men lust for white women? Or are these ideas that whites are carrying around ready to let loose when the opportunity strikes? And do I need to hunt for any further explanation why Bill Cosby stayed away from talking about "the stuff in the shadows"?

Apparently not.

Some might claim it's because there is less "stuff in the shadows" than meets the eye. And that's always possible. But it seems more likely that my black friends are right about what it's like to be in the minority. When there's something still lurking in the shadows, it's always wise to hold your tongue.

18

WHAT TO KEEP/ WHAT TO TOSS AWAY

Giving Good and Bad Ideas Their Due

The vagaries of race relations seem like a runaway train. We shout "Stop!" but the train plows forward on the inertia of bad ideas and habits too weighty for its brakes. Sometimes, mere trivialities get us going, like white women "flipping" their long hair and black women perceiving this as white women believing they are superior. The train barrels on. Yet consider that white women might protest this view of hair flipping is all wrong, and then they might try not to flip their hair in black women's faces in crowds and cramped elevators. That would be progress.

And black women might try to understand that this unconscious habit indicates no claim of racial superiority, and that white women flip their hair also when no black people are present. So if each side could give a little, one bad idea could be tossed off the train.

But then some black women ask, "What about the crying thing?"

Curiously, this "crying thing" is a common impression black women have. They believe that when the going gets rough on the job or wherever, white women will burst into tears. And black women interpret this outburst as a ploy for sympathy, especially from white men. Black women, who have heard about this ploy, are resentful, believing that they do not have the option of using hurt feelings to get sympathy from whites, especially white men. And some black women ask, "When have whites ever shown sympathy for the feelings of black people?" Some black women say they consider it undignified to show hurt feelings in front of white people. "I'd slap them in the face," says one friend, "before I'd let them see me cry." What is going on here?

Successful black women are often described as "no nonsense": "Ms. Barrett, a spunky, no-nonsense black woman, holds the distinguished post of Fulton County Sheriff." "Prior to her election to the U.S. House of Representatives in 1990, Congresswoman Maxine Waters already had attracted national attention for her no-nonsense, no-holds-barred style of politics." And it would seem that "no nonsense" is intended to suggest toughness or a hardened exterior. Do some people imagine that one becomes "no nonsense" by growing up in poverty (as if all black people come from poor families)? Then, it must follow that whites are more into frills and other "nonsense," because they come from a privileged environment where you can get your way with a few tears.

How deeply are these ideas embedded in our thinking? What can we do to get rid of them? How can we slow the train? The government can't intervene. The Supreme Court can't make a definitive ruling. It's going to be up to us.

Some ideas are so bad we should just toss them out. We should trash the One-Drop Rule, for example. This misbegotten notion has warped white thinking for hundreds of years. Whites have believed their "whiteness" would be compromised if they mated with a black person. The insidious dictate that *black* + *white* = *black* defies biological sense, but it has left some whites fearful that they are genetically vulnerable. And this formula would be merely a silly folktale were it not that this marker of racial identity is embedded in our political and social mores.

Mississippi Senator Bilbo worried about "mongrelization" in the 1930s and 1940s; some in the Council of Conservative Citizens worry that the white race is endangered today. And we are still tempted to consider that the child of one white parent and one black parent is black, which further suggests that whiteness has a "purity" that is destroyed when anything black is added. From that evil premise comes the notion that white is good and black is bad, and that's no good either.

Another distinction is troublesome. For whites, the One-Drop Rule becomes an exclusionary dogma, defining who cannot be white, excluding anyone with a black person in their ancestry, however remote. Yet for blacks, the One-Drop Rule is an inclusive concept that increases the number of people who can be considered black. As a result, the One-Drop Rule produces a varied "black" population, which, in turn, produces more "black" voters, more "black" influence.

Inevitably, many whites and blacks have accepted as a social reality that blackness has a genetic power whiteness cannot match. Whites have accepted the idea that blacks produce blacks in matings with other races, but whites produce more whites only by mating with their own kind. Hence, it would seem that black is strong, white is weak; or black is dangerous, white is vulnerable. Although these ideas lack logic, they give whites an excuse to worry about threats from a minority that they vastly outnumber, because black people have genetic might.

Yet a retreat from the One-Drop Rule would make the "black" population shrink, on paper at least. Eliminating this rule from our thoughts might do wonders for the white psyche. It would also allow individuals who were previously "black" to slip away and define themselves as "biracial," "multiracial," or something else. And this redefinition could make the "black" population seem less of a social and political force.

So here *everybody* is worrying about being diminished. How curious! White people know they will lose to blacks when they mate with darker people. But what could possibly cause this result other than the desire to mate with darker people? Whites who fear whites will disappear are worried about choices whites might make of their own free will.

Black Americans, meanwhile, worry about their cultural survival—that whiteness will engulf them—because if fewer people choose to consider themselves "black," then maybe some will start acting "white" or otherwise reject "blackness." But once again, we are talking about a choice people will make. Even recognizing that the majority culture has awesome power, blacks will not choose "white" ways or whatever unless they want to. Again, the worry is about what individuals will do of their own free will.

And is what individual people choose to do in these matters any of our business?

In fact, African American culture remains one of the most enduring threads in the American fabric; pervasive racial segregation across centuries has assured that result. Black people remain one of the least assimilated major cultural groups, hardly having disappeared into the white American mainstream as white ethnic groups have. Hence, the uniqueness of other ethnic groups is much more at risk.

The 15 million Americans who say they are of Italian ancestry must recognize that Italian American culture has been greatly assimilated in recent decades. The old Italian enclaves in many cities—Little Italys— are disappearing, as is the use of the Italian language. Yet Italian Americans don't seem to be complaining. Enough of their cultural heritage survives, and they find increasing success in the mainstream, too.

American Jews, a group blacks often envy for their apparent togetherness, face a more perplexing dilemma. Jewish Americans are a much less cohesive group than generally imagined. The Jewish population is currently about 5.9 million and that figure is not rising, in large part due to a rise in intermarriage with non-Jews. In 1960, only 9 percent of Jews married non-Jews. Three decades later, the figure topped 60 percent, leaving many Jews concerned: "Will our grandchildren be Jewish?" Meanwhile, in the 1990s, only about 6.5 percent of married black Americans had a white spouse, so there is correspondingly less concern in black households that one's grandchildren will be "white."

What is needed is a reality check about these changes, real and imaginary. Neither black Americans nor white Americans will disappear as a group. Contact with extraterrestrial beings will probably happen before blacks or whites amalgamate. In the meantime, whites in particular should wean themselves off the One-Drop Rule and the notions that accompany it. Enough of this nonsense—please.

Slavery promoted other ideas we should toss out. Yet it is curious how commonly we resurrect slave owners' complaints about slaves as a form of truth about race. Slave owners grumbled that slaves wouldn't work, that slaves ran away, and that slaves were dim-witted. Why should we agree? In fact, most Americans would now declare that working as little as possible and running away were sensible, smart, and wholly justified responses to being forced into slave labor.

Slave owners, of course, thought otherwise. In 1851, Samuel A. Cartwright, a Louisiana physician, wrote in an article published in the

New Orleans Medical and Surgical Journal, that running away was a slave's disease—he called it "drapetomania"—for which, in all seriousness, he prescribed harsh medicine, "whipping the devil out of them."

Cartwright "discovered" another slave disease, "dysaethesia aethiopis," or lethargy of the mind, and prescribed a cure: "Put the patient to some hard kind of work in the open air and sunshine. . . . Making the slothful Negro take active exercise, puts into active play the lungs, through whose agency the vitalized blood is sent to the brain to give liberty to the mind."

Yet it is also widely understood that slaves adopted a shiftless approach to their dealings with whites as a form of resistance, thus diminishing the expectations slave masters had for their slaves. And eventually whites generally came to assume that blacks were shiftless and stupid. Behavior in that vein became an essential element in farcical portrayals of black people, such as those by black vaudeville comedian Stepin Fetchit, who billed himself as "The Laziest Man Alive." In the 1930s, Fetchit took his slothful routine to Hollywood, made dozens of movies, and became a millionaire.

But it is noted that Fetchit's routine was based on an act concocted to fool white people, who couldn't have been all that smart themselves, because they believed it. "Fetchit's shuffling, apparently inept and inarticulate character had clearly defined folk roots," writes Mel Watkins in *On the Real Side*, his history of black humor. "Slaves had used these tactics to avoid barbarous work regimens and, while assuring masters that they were indeed superior, to achieve their own ends. Fetchit, like others before him, had adapted this slavery ruse, amplified its comic overtones to reveal the underlying deceit, and brought it to the stage."

Over the years, blacks have played out this act in various guises. Pretending not to know anything became a common strategy for dealing with whites. "Ah ain't seed nobody," one clever character tells a cop in a Chester Himes's crime novel set in Harlem. "Ah just setting here minding my own business and ain't seed nobody." And, of course, the white cop believes that this inept-seeming fellow is incapable of seeing anything. And that's how a clever fellow fools the cops.

But this strategy of playing stupid—or of never letting whites know how smart you are—has taken its toll, because too many whites took the act for the real thing. Watkins writes, "This caricature [playing the shiftless fool in front of whites] was more intricately connected to the behavior of ordinary blacks than many are prone to admit." And it has gone far enough. So, no more feigning ignorance around white people; no more hiding how smart you are; and no more telling white people what they want to hear.

And white people should wise up, too: quit believing everything you hear.

Speaking of bad ideas to toss, *The Bell Curve* contained more than a few. If the authors, Charles Murray and the late Richard Herrnstein, intended deliberate harm against black people, they succeeded. But *The Bell Curve* was also a pessimistic and hopeless work from any point of view. Why would we embrace a notion that little can be done to change the destiny in our genes? And these authors predict other horrors, too, for our gene-dictated future: "Racism will reemerge in a new and more virulent form," they write.

The authors are also uncomfortable about the values upon which the United States was founded. The idea of equality really bothers them. "In everyday life," they write, "the ideology of equality censors and straitjackets everything from pedagogy to humor. The ideology of equality has stunted the range of moral dialogue to triviality. In daily life . . . the moral ascendancy of equality has made it difficult to use concepts such as virtue, excellence, beauty and—above all—truth."

Having found an enemy in backers of equality, the authors have more in common with the losing sides in the American Revolution, the Civil War, and World War II, three conflicts in which equality was an underlying issue. Yet to claim that an "ideology" of equality suppresses discussion of truth and beauty seems wild; what they really object to is that those who believe in equality keep challenging their ideas about truth and beauty, which is legitimate in a free society.

As a nation and as individuals, we cannot be casual or cavalier about equality and the protections it affords. We have faced the ideological conflict over inequality before. Now we need a faith in equality, if only because the other possibilities are so horrible. Belief in equality takes us down one road and appeals to our better selves, while a belief in inequality sends us in another direction, where the results can be troubling. Down that road, slavery and Nazi terror flourished.

Meanwhile, our best American ideas, including the concept of equal protection under the law, depend on agreement that we are all of equal worth, even when this supposition does not register in IQ tests,

Olympic footraces, or other so-called objective measures. Yes, evidence persists that human beings are not equal in many ways. Some are smarter, some are faster, and some are better looking according to vogues of the moment. The evidence for inequality is plentiful, while the evidence for equality defies counting and measuring.

Yet our belief in equality is deep, arising from our own sense of self-worth; we refuse to believe that we are of less account than those around us. And the logic is similar to that of the Golden Rule: grant unto others the same worth that you would wish others to grant unto you. My father, Henry A. Myers, a professor at Cornell University, taught this message and wrote of it—this individualized discovery of equality—in a 1945 book called *Are Men Equal? An Inquiry into the Meaning of American Democracy.* I cite this passage, too, as evidence our sensitivities about equality can change—and some would say progress. How interesting that half a century a ago a man could, in a book about equality, use *man* to stand for both men and women without getting into trouble.

> Probably no man has ever lived who has not at some time or other discovered meaning in the idea of equality. This likelihood is not so much at odds with the other facts of experience as it may seem at first to be. The shortcoming of measurement is that it never settles the question of ultimate worth. It is hard to put a man in his place with a tape measure. Weigh him and find him wanting: He will insist that others are no better than he. Bigger, stronger, cleverer, more determined they may be; better they are not. Our fellow, by measurement small in one way or another, simply rejects the standards used against him. Without knowledge of philosophical terms, he denies their validity, as easily as a baby breathes or cries without words to describe its actions.

We need to recognize that belief in equality benefits us in our daily lives, especially when race is involved. And those who have no faith in equality maybe can force or buy the loyalty of others, but those who believe in equality can gain allegiances on the basis of trust, free of charge.

Next, we must rethink the matter of racial pride.

Should blacks be proud of being black? Should whites be proud of being white? We are confused about this issue. These days, custom allows black Americans to say they are proud to be black. Yet calls for white pride set off alarms. What gives? Some whites sense this is a paradox and suspect their rights are being denied.

Actually, the ethnic or racial pride we most fear is the type that took hold in Nazi Germany. When racial pride becomes a claim of racial superiority, it is dangerous to all those on the list of inferiors, especially when the proud group is large and the alleged inferiors are a minority. Yet some whites insist on posing the question about pride in these terms: if blacks can be proud, why can't whites be proud?

Other questions, however, are far more pertinent: Why should anybody be proud? What good does it do? Until recently, having pride was not considered virtuous. Pride was traditionally listed number one among the Seven Deadly Sins, and the Bible warns, "Pride goeth before destruction, and a haughty spirit before a fall." Philosophers throughout the ages have been suspicious of pride.

Still, our attitudes about pride appear to be in flux. In 1982, the primary definition in *Webster's New World Dictionary of the American Language* was "an overhigh opinion of oneself; exaggerated self-esteem; conceit." A decade later, the top definition in *The American Heritage Dictionary of the English Language, Third Edition*, was "a sense of one's own proper dignity or value; self-respect," while "an excessively high opinion of oneself; conceit" was fifth on the list. What has happened?

Apparently, the change has been promoted by the human potential movement, which insists that to function well we must feel good about ourselves. Therefore, pride, self-respect, or "positive self-esteem" has been advanced as especially necessary for members of any group that ever languished in the shadows of others' disdain. So we accept pride—even applaud it—if it serves this remedial function: as long as members of a group might be plagued by feelings of inferiority or shame, they are free to say they are proud.

Hence, whites in the 1940s proclaimed Joe Louis "the pride of his race"—and blacks were proud of Louis, too—but at the time many whites couldn't imagine much else that black people had to be proud about. Then came the more self-assertive Black Pride movement in the 1960s; it scared many whites. Still, it represented an understandable effort to readjust black consciousness after generations of second-class status.

Since then, black children have been encouraged to believe they are descended from early African kings or Egyptian pharaohs, even if as egalitarians we do not believe in the merit of aristocracies. Still, the primary intention of telling black youngsters about the wonders of

Egypt seemed positive—to establish self-esteem by telling black young-sters that dark-skinned people have played important roles in history.

Who would fuss about that?

Well, a few white people did, that's who. Conservative critics of the Afrocentric movement noted that Egypt, so often central to these dis-cussions about "black" history, is in the northeastern corner of Africa, while slaves came from West Africa, thousands of miles away. And Egyptians and West Africans were two different population groups. Furthermore, some whites worried that black Americans young and old might get glorious illusions about themselves or end up oversupplied with self-esteem.

But what does pride really get you? That is the crux of the matter. If white pride came into vogue, what would whites gain? Maybe, some would sense themselves uplifted through a link to the collective genius of the Wright Brothers, Mozart, and other white visionaries. But does this mean that all whites can invent airplanes or compose symphonies? Obviously not. If we are vessels into which has been poured the col-lected genius of our race, then it's likely that all the foolishness of our racial forebears has been dumped in there, too. And racial pride ignores half the story.

Such efforts at pride attempt to bolster our sense of self-worth by allowing us to believe we are connected to the accomplishments of oth-ers, when we are not. Whites who have a need for pride should ask themselves what sense of inferiority they are trying to overcome, or hark to the words of a black man who addressed the subject of race pride, both black and white, succinctly. "The only excuse for pride in individuals," said Frederick Douglass, "is in the fact of their own achievements."

Here's hoping, too, that whites can stop whining about black people getting a better deal. Claiming that black people have more fun, live off the efforts of others, or use race to get unfair advantage sounds like envy, number six on the list of Seven Deadly Sins. Whites are much better off according to virtually every indicator; the claim that blacks have an unfair advantage is ridiculous and embarrassing.

So let's have an end to such contentions. What good do they do?

Whites, for example, who complain—and I've heard it—that it is unfair that blacks enter the Miss America contest and have a Miss Black

America pageant, too, are not making a significant point about justice. Why, they should be asked, do they want to enter the Miss Black America contest? And if they don't want to enter, why are they fussing?

Whites must also be careful about congratulating themselves for the advances blacks have made or for how well blacks are now supposed to be doing. The logic is problematic. If white actions are the reason blacks are doing better, white actions could be the reason blacks are still not doing well enough. The economic disparities between blacks and whites are clear, even as it is noted that aspects of the economic gap between blacks and whites are closing. Thus, it is said we should be pleased that the average annual income of black women has reached 89 percent of the average of white women and the average of black men is climbing to 67 percent of what white men make.

Given this "good" news, whites often expect patience from black people, and blacks wonder why they should not be frustrated and angry when there is much bad news still to see. Blacks wonder why whites can't appreciate this. Suppose you bought an air ticket from New York to Los Angeles, but the airline dropped you off in Phoenix. Would you be satisfied? The airline says be patient—you're much closer to L.A. than you once were. But you say you're still far from your destination.

Longevity: Unequal Expectations			
	Whites	Blacks	Difference
1940	64.2	53.1	11.1 years
1950	69.1	60.8	8.3
1960	70.6	63.6	7.0
1970	71.7	64.1	7.6
1980	74.4	68.1	6.3
1990	76.1	69.1	7.0
1995	77.0	70.3	6.7
2000	77.6	70.2	7.4
2010	78.8	71.3	7.5

Other disparities between blacks and whites are stark. A white child born today can expect to live seven years longer than a black child born today. A seven-year-gap in life expectancy has persisted since 1960; before that it was even wider. Whites in 1995 had a life expectancy of 77 years; blacks had a life expectancy of 70.3 years— and the gap is projected to continue.

Yet we hear very little about the longevity gap. Since most Americans are white, they're not the ones dying before their time—so they aren't focused on this problem. And this longevity gap is similar to the one between women and men, so maybe some accept it as "normal." Then again, it could be that many whites believe that black Americans cause their own shortened lives through bad lifestyle choices or an alleged predilection for violence.

However, many factors of longevity are in part controllable through efforts against infant mortality, dangerous lifestyles, or epidemics such as AIDS. Some research also links the prevalence of hypertension among black people to the stress of being black in America—and whose fault is that? Blacks are also more likely to die of infectious diseases in general and are twice as likely to die of kidney disease or diabetes. Surely better health care would help. And black American men have the highest rate of prostate cancer in the world.

It is no surprise, then, that many black Americans are fatalistic about the amount of concern white America has about the health and well-being of black Americans. Harvard Law Professor Lani Guinier says blacks are the sacrificial canaries in the American coal mine—a highly fatalistic image. "The canaries were the first to feel the presence of gas in the mines," she says, "and we serve that purpose in society in many respects." This idea is, of course, that if whites paid more attention to what was happening to black people, whites could benefit.

The suggestion of premonitory link between black and white America also rings true in recent decades for drug use, gun violence, and the disintegration of families. When these problems rose in black America, it preceded a parallel rise in white America. Hence, it is argued that addressing problems in black America might hasten understandings that should apply to white America, too. But whites don't see events in black America this way. They don't expect black experience to teach them anything, because they expect black experience to be inalterably different.

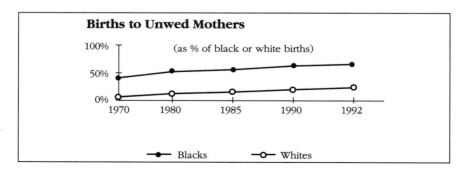

Yet the trend in births to unwed mothers demonstrates otherwise. While births out of wedlock were rising to epidemic proportions in black America, the same trend was at work in white America, if to a lesser degree. Births to unwed mothers rose in both worlds almost in parallel. So are whites all that different from blacks? Not in this example, and similarities might easily be recognized elsewhere—that is if whites were willing to hear the echoes of their own predicament in what black people say. But this leap many whites find difficult to make. Whites too often assume that if blacks complain or find fault, they must necessarily be criticizing white people; how could blacks and whites be complaining about the same thing?

This comparison suggests that whites will get defensive when blacks cite universal aspects of the human condition, which is odd. However, to the degree that blacks blame whites for everything, whites are likely to be wary and sometimes justifiably so. But whites also puzzle, for example, over complaints about race from seemingly successful black Americans. Whites ask how come the complaints, if these people are well paid and have all the material trappings of success. What more could they want? Here is how Ellis Cose described black discontent in *The Rage of a Privileged Class:*

> Again and again, as I spoke with people who had every accouterment of success, I heard the same plaintive declaration—always followed by various versions of an unchanging and urgently put question: "I have done everything I was supposed to do. I have stayed out of trouble with the law, gone to the right schools, and worked myself nearly to death. *What more do they want?* Why in God's name won't they accept me as a full human being?"

The complaint is against white people—right? Yet maybe it is not totally so. Something here could echo—or at least be recognizable—to whites who also feel they have done everything right, attended the right schools, and worked themselves nearly to death. Many whites, too, do not feel their jobs are the full measure of their worth. Could it be that blacks and whites suffer from a similar malaise? Blacks can blame white people, because it seems to make sense to blame those who are most in control. Blacks can also dream that a black-run world would be better, much as women can believe that the world would be better if women were in charge. It is more difficult for disadvantaged whites, however, since whom can they blame if they find themselves downsized after years of loyal service?

And blacks may have another perspective. Having been excluded for so long, blacks have every right to wonder if the struggle is worthwhile. Is the American dream everything it's cracked up to be? Having hunger for *freedom*, black Americans can justifiably wonder if a shiny car and a big screen TV are enough. Or is something missing—something more important?

Often it seems that my wife and many of my black friends dream of a world in which black people are in charge, and they don't have to explain themselves to doubting whites all the time. But would this all-black world—or an Afrikan world order—be a better one? Of course, they say it will be, but we can argue this one. In my experience, anything humankind devises produces winners and losers, the satisfied and the dissatisfied. And this would probably be so in a black world, too. But who can say?

It is white folly to sense criticism of white people in everything black people say; it is black folly to believe that whites are the cause of everything wrong. And whites have not found the answers to life's questions either. I'm sure of that. Often, they seem lost, restless, and rootless in their own right. Today, they put their hopes in pills that will produce more hair or firmer erections; tomorrow they want surgery to rid themselves of wrinkles; and the day following that it will be something else. In 1997, *Time* reported that white Americans were "fleeing to small towns." But no sooner did they arrive in small towns than white teenagers opened fire with guns on their schoolmates and teachers in small-town schools. Suddenly, big cities, led by New York, were reported to be making an amazing comeback. They were the new place to be.

You follow all this? Who has it figured out? If I listened to journalists, I would think we are all rushing about this way and that, sometimes fighting wars this week in places we'd never heard of the week before. White people periodically worry about blacks, then about Hispanics, then about the Japanese or the Chinese or the Yugoslavs. Or they worry about themselves. They will complain that blacks are too emotional, too carried away. But the next moment, they're paying for seminars on how to get in touch with their feelings. So which is it to be? We don't know.

"And what about affirmative action?" whites ask. "What do you say about that?"

Many whites saw affirmative action as the most important race issue in the 1990s. They believed the darker population of America was growing, or would soon be the majority. And if all these darker people were given the extra advantage of affirmative action, no opportunities would be left for whites. So, many whites were against affirmative action.

See the problem?

Many whites were operating on the erroneous premise that darker people were taking over, and that made affirmative action scary.

Darker people are not taking over. They will remain a minority, so affirmative action should not be so scary. And the next question is whether you want integration or segregation. If you want integration, then you must explain how eliminating affirmative action will promote integration. And if eliminating affirmative action promotes segregation, then why do you want to eliminate it? And if you really want to promote segregation—well, what kind of person are you anyway?

I favor integration. I am an integrationist.

Meanwhile, my wife insists that black Americans have only been full citizens with access to the American mainstream for about 35 years—since the Voting Rights Act of 1965. And look how far they have come—a long way. But she wonders why whites seem to expect such miracles from others—how can anyone say that things are fair when whites have a running start of centuries and black people got to the starting line in 1965?

She has a point. Why do whites insist that fairness has been achieved when blacks still seem so far behind? "Maybe whites are worried because they believe blacks are fast runners," I tell her.

But affirmative action could be considered part of a compact between blacks and whites who agreed that America would be a cooperative venture after 1965. At the time, white America agreed to give black Americans full citizenship rights—never mind previous half-measures—and, in effect, white America said to black people: "You come with us—don't go your own way—and we will set a place for you at the American table. We will ensure that you get a fair share of the jobs, educational opportunities, and whatever else the American dream has to offer."

That was the promise whites made. And why did whites want this deal? Yes, whites wanted something—they needed to bring black people into the mainstream to escape the shame they would face in the eyes of the world if they didn't. The threat of international communism forced whites to demonstrate that democracy works and that American values apply to all people. So white Americans gained greatly from the promise of integration, because their very credibility was at stake.

Meanwhile, it may not have seemed that black Americans, coming out of segregation, could be giving up anything of value in return for the promise of integration. Whites believed that blacks wanted integration and had marched for it; they never even contemplated the possibility that blacks might be making sacrifices, too. But that is what happened. Blacks gained new access to mainstream life—no doubt. A costly downside appeared as the cohesion of black communities suffered when talented and upwardly mobile black Americans left black enclaves for the suburbs of the integrated world.

Big-city ghettos became more isolated and poor; many black businesses foundered as black customers headed for mainstream malls. Many black people made it across the color line—and did well—but some sectors of black America have been devastated. And looking at the overall picture of how well black Americans fared, the nation must recognize that the black family disintegrated more precipitously, black crime skyrocketed, drug use became epidemic, and our prisons filled with black men as never before in our history.

Is there any doubt about these trends? In preintegration 1950, about 30 percent of the U.S. prison inmates were black; today more than half are—and that's a huge leap. In 1950, about 17 percent of black births were out of wedlock; today it's more than two-thirds, another giant leap. So it seems that in the very decades when whites thought they were doing right by black people—even giving them advantages that seemed unfair to whites—the social fabric of black America was coming apart.

These facts need to be remembered in the discussion about affirmative action. For whatever reason, many black Americans did not find their promised place at the American table—that's still a real issue. Millions of black people are isolated from the American mainstream; many are mired in skepticism and fatalism or, worse, in bitter outlaw lifestyles. In my neighborhood, an appalling number of youngsters will grow up assuming that there is no place at the table for them. Many will grow up also hardly knowing what a traditional family is like, so rarely do they see one.

And what it to be done about it? What are white Americans doing to convince skeptical black Americans that there will be a place for them at the table? Right now, many white Americans say ending unfairness to whites is the most important issue. But surely, too, many of these whites overestimate the harm that affirmative action does and barely recognize the alienating effect that ending affirmative action will have on a black population that's already skeptical about white intentions.

So which will it be? Will the nation address the problem of whites who think they are being treated unfairly or the problem of blacks who expect the worst from whites? If it comes to a vote—majority rules—unfairness to whites will be addressed and the alienation of blacks will not. Whites will go their happy way; blacks will go theirs less joyfully; and the divide between whites and blacks will have widened, despite all the interracial friendships we claim to have.

I am frequently asked if I am optimistic. If you are writing about race, you will be asked that. And how could I be optimistic as an integrationist, when I see impasses along the color line like the one over affirmative action? Yet how can I *not* be optimistic when my relationships along the color line are so rich and engaging? Or when I hear that young people seem ever so less disposed to make old racial distinctions?

When I leave my house, I see much to be pessimistic about. I have had friends killed in the violence that has overtaken sections of our cities, and a few blocks from my house I can visit outposts of isolation in time and space that are hard to believe. This cannot be in 21st-century America. Where are we? Yet I can find these same lost souls wandering in almost every American city. And what can possibly reconcile these scenes with the rest of the land?

My reactions are a paradoxical mix. I am optimistic about the potential we have as individuals along the color line. I am optimistic when I talk, laugh, and learn new insights or when I encounter the fullness of my own family life. I am optimistic, too, when I sense that race is truly understandable, not a mystery.

How do we resolve all this? The questions keep coming, and sometimes I can only think of my own way of doing things. Inevitably, there are "white" and "black" perspectives, mixed reviews on whatever the future holds. Forces are pulling us apart; forces are pushing us together. Who can tell which ones will prevail? And this uncertainty should be a warning. Our future on the color line is not clear. We'll still need to work on it. Too much is unsettled for comfort.

What do I believe? There are no miracles or innovative management strategies, only what works well for individuals. Some whites and blacks interact in ways that nullify the color line as an issue. For them the line does not exist as a wall. Instead, it is the opposite: an engaging, even exciting landscape to explore. It is not that these individuals are color-blind toward each other—not at all. They may even be more aware of the intricacies of color and difference. For them, crossing the color line is adventure, a joy, and a good reason to be alive.

What special attitudes do these individuals bring to the meeting? Certain ones are obvious: these individuals—blacks and whites—are at ease with each other; they are not nervous about what to say; they have achieved a basic trust that allows them to be honest. And they talk about all manner of things, race included, without fear. They can explore with great relish the very topics that others are so eager to avoid.

Truly close relationships between blacks and whites usually reaffirm three basic principles that must be shared for their relationships to flourish:

1. Both parties must believe that if you give a little in human relations, you will get as much or more in return.
2. Both must attempt to live by the Golden Rule: Do unto others as you would have others do unto you.
3. Both must have an abiding faith in human equality that will transcend passing claims to the contrary.

None of these precepts is new or esoteric; they have arisen across time in societies around the globe. Those who can affirm these principles wholeheartedly have the key to good relations. Those who cannot will have difficulties. Indeed, such individuals may be dysfunctional along the color line, and there is no way to hedge this fact. Those who lack generosity of spirit, mistrust the Golden Rule, or preach inequality are ill equipped for integration, because these beliefs cannot be hidden for long.

If practicing the three precepts does not work out well in every instance, it will work out well in most. But these principles require faith—and no trick, ritual diet, or mystical incantation can substitute for faith. Either you have it or you don't. But perhaps we should recognize that some people are not equipped for this trip. Maybe, they cannot assert the faith required to cross the color line in any functional way. And maybe, too, we're better off when they stay by themselves. What could they have to offer us anyway? Similarly, many insist they are not prejudiced in their dealings. But don't take their word for it if they doubt the three principles.

One last note: no matter how well race relations go, racists and psychopaths will always be with us. We must accept as a given that evil is ever present. Therefore, the solutions we seek must succeed— and we must pursue them—despite the awful setbacks that occur.

The good moments will call us together; the bad moments will drive us apart; and faith is the means we have to make the good triumphant.